Critical Literacies in Action: Social Perspectives and Teaching Practices

TRANSGRESSIONS: CULTURAL STUDIES AND EDUCATION
Volume 34

Scope
Cultural studies provides an analytical toolbox for both making sense of educational practice and extending the insights of educational professionals into their labors. In this context *Transgressions: Cultural Studies and Education* provides a collection of books in the domain that specify this assertion. Crafted for an audience of teachers, teacher educators, scholars and students of cultural studies and others interested in cultural studies and pedagogy, the series documents both the possibilities of and the controversies surrounding the intersection of cultural studies and education. The editors and the authors of this series do not assume that the interaction of cultural studies and education devalues other types of knowledge and analytical forms. Rather the intersection of these knowledge disciplines offers a rejuvenating, optimistic, and positive perspective on education and educational institutions. Some might describe its contribution as democratic, emancipatory, and transformative. The editors and authors maintain that cultural studies helps free educators from sterile, monolithic analyses that have for too long undermined efforts to think of educational practices by providing other words, new languages, and fresh metaphors. Operating in an interdisciplinary cosmos, Transgressions: Cultural Studies and Education is dedicated to exploring the ways cultural studies enhances the study and practice of education. With this in mind the series focuses in a non-exclusive way on popular culture as well as other dimensions of cultural studies including social theory, social justice and positionality, cultural dimensions of technological innovation, new media and media literacy, new forms of oppression emerging in an electronic hyperreality, and postcolonial global concerns. With these concerns in mind cultural studies scholars often argue that the realm of popular culture is the most powerful educational force in contemporary culture. Indeed, in the twenty-first century this pedagogical dynamic is sweeping through the entire world. Educators, they believe, must understand these emerging realities in order to gain an important voice in the pedagogical conversation.
Without an understanding of cultural pedagogy's (education that takes place outside of formal schooling) role in the shaping of individual identity–youth identity in particular–the role educators play in the lives of their students will continue to fade. Why do so many of our students feel that life is incomprehensible and devoid of meaning? What does it mean, teachers wonder, when young people are unable to describe their moods, their affective affiliation to the society around them. Meanings provided young people by mainstream institutions often do little to help them deal with their affective complexity, their difficulty negotiating the rift between meaning and affect. School knowledge and educational expectations seem as anachronistic as a ditto machine, not that learning ways of rational thought and making sense of the world are unimportant.
But school knowledge and educational expectations often have little to offer students about making sense of the way they feel, the way their affective lives are shaped. In no way do we argue that analysis of the production of youth in an electronic mediated world demands some "touchy-feely" educational superficiality. What is needed in this context is a rigorous analysis of the interrelationship between pedagogy, popular culture, meaning making, and youth subjectivity. In an era marked by youth depression, violence, and suicide such insights become extremely important, even life saving. Pessimism about the future is the common sense of many contemporary youth with its concomitant feeling that no one can make a difference.
If affective production can be shaped to reflect these perspectives, then it can be reshaped to lay the groundwork for optimism, passionate commitment, and transformative educational and political activity. In these ways cultural studies adds a dimension to the work of education unfilled by any other sub-discipline. This is what Transgressions: Cultural Studies and Education seeks to produce—literature on these issues that makes a difference. It seeks to publish studies that help those who work with young people, those individuals involved in the disciplines that study children and youth, and young people themselves improve their lives in these bizarre times.

Critical Literacies in Action: Social Perspectives and Teaching Practices

Karyn Cooper
University of Toronto, Ontario Institute for Studies in Education, Canada

Robert E. White
St. Francis Xavier University, Canada

SENSE PUBLISHERS
ROTTERDAM / TAIPEI

A C.I.P. record for this book is available from the Library of Congress.

ISBN 978-90-8790-573-6 (paperback)
ISBN 978-90-8790-574-3 (hardback)
ISBN 978-90-8790-575-0 (e-book)

Published by: Sense Publishers,
P.O. Box 21858, 3001 AW
Rotterdam, The Netherlands
http://www.sensepublishers.com

Printed on acid-free paper

TABLE OF CONTENTS

Section I – Critical Literacies in Society

Section II – Critical Literacies in Action

Section III – Critical Literacies in Practice

FOREWORD

The term "literacy" has been around for a very long time. Although in the past one who was considered to be literate was one who was able to read and write, society no longer allows for such a simplistic definition. Literacy today means much more than functionality, particularly in terms of its characterization, its variety and its importance to global citizenry. The very meaning of "literacy" has become increasingly more complex due to a number of factors, including the expanding notion of what constitutes modern literacy as well as the need for greater understanding of the increasingly technological nature of the world within which individuals live and learn. As such, a new horizon in literacy research has appeared, promising to renegotiate traditional meanings of the term "literate" and what is required to be literate in this increasingly complex world.

In essence, this book asks how educators can become more experienced in order to truly support literacy, particularly for children of poverty or for those who have been labeled "at-risk". This is important in current times, especially since a literate person is one who is able to involve him- or herself within a continuum of lifelong learning to achieve personal goals and to participate fully in the wider society.

Definitions of literacy have also evolved along with the evolution of the computer. Currently, the term "literacy" describes a commitment to and participation in a multiplicity of meaning making systems, many of which are exhibiting ever-greater degrees of interdependence with one another. The term "Critical Literacy" has come into use relatively recently and is generally regarded as a sub-category of Critical Pedagogy – Critical because it promotes an agenda for positive social change.

This book is divided into three sections. The first section, entitled "Critical Literacies in Society" establishes Critical Literacy as a driving force within the society at large. Section II, entitled "Critical Literacies in Action", describes how Critical Literacy is being used in schooling today's youth. The third and final section of this book is entitled "Critical Literacies in Practice" and delves into the theory and practice of Critical Literacy.

"Critical Literacies in Society", the first section of this volume describes some of the larger considerations that educators and researchers may wish to consider as they embark on a study of what it is that makes literacy "critical". The first chapter, written by John Willinsky, entitled "Of critical theory and Critical Literacy: Connections to the legacy of Critical Theory", reminds us of the rich connections that Critical Literacy has to the Frankfurt School. This valuable lesson in history takes note of the enormous contributions of Theodor Adorno, as well as those of Herbert Marcuse. Professor Willinsky's work provides an important background to the chapters that follow.

In the second chapter of this work, Robert E. White introduces the connections between Critical Thinking, Critical Pedagogy and Critical Literacy before embarking upon a tour of literacies, which have the potential to be Critical Literacies. In this chapter, entitled "Above and beyond: Critical literacies for the new millennium", Professor White notes that literacies do not become "critical" by default, but depend upon how they are utilized to promote positive social change.

The next chapter, "Critical alternatives: Solutions to ease discrimination, oppression, and youth violence", written by Wendy M. Pullin and Karyn Cooper makes a timely connection between youth violence and the need for greater literacy strategies that can be termed "critical". Professors Pullin and Cooper suggest that in order to meet the needs of disenfranchised youth, society needs to assume the responsibility for determining the causes and providing solutions to this growing epidemic. They claim that it is easier to portray violent youth as "dangerous others" than to accept that society has failed to address conditions of social injustice that such youth endure. One solution is for critical educators to provide adequate opportunities for youth living in socially toxic environments to read, speak, and write their authentic points of view. Critical psychologists can also provide solutions by working more effectively in communities to create more communication and support networks with students, schools, and communities.

The final chapter in this section, written by Kelly and Peter Freebody, entitled "Engaging and critiquing challenge in the process drama classroom: Socio-economic status as topic and resource", follows two groups of students through an improvisational drama class as they discuss their ideas around happiness, sadness and the connections between these states of being to one's economic situation. Not surprisingly, students had varying views on the advantage of being born into an upper socio-economic status household and how this may or may not influence one's choice of future careers.

Section II, entitled "Critical Literacies in action" refocuses the view of the society at large and brings it to bear on the classroom. Chapter 5, written by Kate Pahl and Jennifer Rowsell, entitled "Traveling objects and reconfiguring identities: Meaning-Making and multi-modalities" describes two studies, one in Princeton New Jersey, and the other in a school in South Yorkshire, UK. In both studies, using ethnographic approaches, attention was paid to multimodality and how transformations across modes enhance children's literacy learning. In one study, the researcher observed a grade two teacher implement an environmental box project as part of ongoing action research into her practice. In the second study, Professors Pahl and Rowsell look at how a secondary teacher uses multimodal teaching to foreground identity in literacy work.

In "Uncomfortable positionings: Critical Literacy and identity in a post-apartheid university classroom", Carolyn McKinney presents classroom-based research conducted in a first year English and Cultural Studies course at a South African university in an attempt to answer what it means to take student identity seriously in Critical Literacy practice and how one engages productively with student resistance to critical pedagogy? Professor McKinney considers how students are represented and positioned in and by the local curriculum materials representing the apartheid past that are on offer in the course as well as how they respond to and often resist such positionings. She uses classroom data to illustrate that such resistance does not necessarily prevent productive engagement; on the contrary, it can provide powerful teaching moments. She argues that resistance is a complex, rather than homogenous process and is uneven – that is, students can resist different texts in different ways, and can return to accept texts that they previously resisted. While not part of a linear progression, resistance may be a necessary process for some students and may be the only way that they can engage with particular texts at particular moments. She concludes that Critical Literacy should not be used to overcome resistance, but rather to engage with it.

In "Outside more common spaces for Critical Literacy: Exploring issues of language and power", Chapter 7 in this volume, Vivian Vasquez and Sarah Vander Zanden take readers outside more common spaces to locate Critical Literacy work along Critical Literacy paths less traveled or talked about. The researchers work from the position that classroom are frequently populated by people who have migrated from somewhere else. In their diversity, they bring with them multiple identities and multiple perspectives. In this chapter those diverse perspectives come to life as students and teachers together work to understand how texts, both social and written, work to position them in particular ways as they explore the relationship between language and power. Throughout the chapter, the researchers bring to life classroom conversations and literacy events where students and teachers act as active designers of both print based and technologically based text.

In Chapter 8, entitled "Countering the rhetoric of warfare: A framework for practical media criticism and curriculum on the war in Iraq", Jonathan Arendt discusses how he used a variety of texts and representational material to ensure that his students were able to develop a greater capacity for thinking critically. He attempts to broaden their horizons and, in the process, recognizes that his strategies are not only encouraging students to question biases and the sources of information that they are consuming, he also realizes that this is not necessarily safe terrain. His reflections on the rhetoric of war allow a recognition that the topic of warfare raises serious emotional and ethical issues.

The third section of the book, entitled "Critical Literacies in Practice" combines a theoretical and a practical perspective on the topic of Critical Literacy. The first chapter in this section, Chapter 9, Written by James Paul gee and entitled "'Basic Information Structure' and 'Academic Language': An approach to discourse analysis", attempts to show how an approach to Critical Literacy would apply to a specific piece of research on children. The piece of research focused on is a well-received study of abused children's responses to anger, published in major journal. Professor Gee's analysis has implications for how we think about research and human subjects, the place of research in institutions, and how we read research when we care about children. This chapter ties in to education primarily around the issue of how teachers, researchers, and educators ought to think about the "hard" research data they consume in regard to children, as well as how they ought to think about academic forms of language connected to schooling and research. This chapter reveals how at one level—a fairly deep level of linguistic analysis—there is a sense in which even the researchers know that what they did was unethical. This, of course, raises the question of why they did it and why the paper is widely accepted by people in its field. This issue is particularly important now with the current focus on and interest in the connections between "academic language" and school success.

In Chapter 10, "Critical Literacy: Methods, models and motivation", Hilary Janks puts into practice some of the discourse analysis procedures used by James Gee. Her chapter focuses on three key concepts that underpin a critical approach to language education; dominance, diversity and access. Professor Janks notes that Critical Literacy requires that we simultaneously engage with and distance ourselves from texts; reading with a text and reading against a text. Such a procedure is bound to produce contestation and change. Reconstruction needs deconstruction in order to understand the many relationships that take shape and come into play when such a process is applied as a teaching and learning strategy. Professor Janks tries to show how these concepts can assist in constructing lively classroom activities.

Chapter 11, written by Jackie Marsh, is entitled "'Am I a couch potato?' blog: Blogging as a Critical Literacy practice". Professor Marsh suggests that recent proliferation of social software and the emergence of a range of web products and services that enable user-generated content have given rise to a wide range of internet-based, Critical Literacy practices. Elementary and primary schools, consequently, have adopted some of these practices, but not always in ways which privilege pupils' agency and voice. In this chapter, Professor Marsh draws from recent projects undertaken in primary schools in England in order to explore how teachers can develop productive strategies that create opportunities for critical engagement with new literacy practices and which, at the same time, foster social justice.

The final chapter in this volume is written by Peter Trifonas and Greg O'Leary and is entitled "The difference of Critical Literacy: A diverse discourse dialogue on 'taken-for-granted practices' in English education". Theoretical underpinnings and reflections are interspersed with a study of how subject English has undergone a metamorphosis in Eastern Canada. Official curricula from different periods in subject English's past involve problematizing taken-for-granted categories to show how they have helped to shape discourse in the past. This approach allows for multiplicity, openness, and new ways of thinking about the way we read texts and conduct research. It calls for active analysis of that which has been archived and accepted. A text is also defined by its underlying message and that which has been omitted. Thus, it is within the affirmative ethics of a "community of the question" and multiple sites of literacy that arise from within it that a synthesis of democratic education can occur. This may assist in providing both a philosophical and methodological means through which to rethink educational equity beyond the competing distinctions of dichotomous categories that separate us.

We, the co-editors of this volume hope that you, the reader, will enjoy and gain from these contributions. We hope that you will continue to benefit from these writings as we have benefited and that future studies will owe a debt, at least in part, to the analyses and discussions that occur between the covers of this book.

Karyn Cooper
Robert E. White

SECTION I
CRITICAL LITERACIES IN SOCIETY

JOHN WILLINSKY

CHAPTER 1

Of Critical Theory and Critical Literacy: Connections to the Legacy of Critical Theory

Among the approaches to teaching reading and writing, Critical Literacy offers connections to the larger world of ideas that are among the most impressive and challenging of any program that makes a claim on the school day. Even in its more innocuous forms, Critical Literacy can be said to owe a striking debt to the twentieth-century legacy of Critical Theory. Critical Theory represents a body of work that was produced, in large part, by the Frankfurt School or Frankfurt Circle associated most notably with Max Horkheimer, Theodor Adorno, Walter Benjamin, Eric Fromm, Herbert Marcuse, and Jürgen Habermas (Jay, 1973). Critical Theory amounts to a philosophical take on social theory, informed by Marx and Freud. During the middle decades of last century it offered an unrelenting critique of contemporary sources and cause of oppression and repression. It was given to intellectual acts of resistance that were intended to undermine the increasing regulation of life, in an effort to create a counter-weight to what was seen as the mass deception fostered by political regimes that were sustained by the culture industry.

THE INFLUENCE OF CRITICAL THEORY

The educational influence of Critical Theory is most immediately present, and often openly acknowledged, in the Critical Literacy work associated with Shor (1999), Steinberg (2005a), Davies (1996), Luke (2000), Comber (2002), Knobel and Lankshear (2002), and others, while the larger educational influence of Critical Theory extends to the more broadly directed *critical pedagogy* that informs the work of Joe L. Kincheloe, bell hooks, Henry Giroux, Roger Simon, and others (Kincheloe, 2004). Kincheloe writes of how "critical theory forms the foundation of critical pedagogy" (2004, 45), while his chapter on "the foundations of critical pedagogy" devotes a section on Antonio Gramsci, among the figures most commonly associated with Critical Theory (Kincheloe, 64-66). See Lankshear and Knobel (2002) for distinctions to be made between critical pedagogy (focused on teaching) and Critical Literacy (on language), while acknowledging that Critical Literacy has formed at "the intersection of critical theory and pedagogy with literacy studies". Leonard (1990) also credits critical pedagogy as a political practice of Critical Theory.

Through the 1990s, Critical Literacy emerged as a "coalition of educational interests committed to engaging with the possibilities that technologies of writing

K. Cooper and R. E. White (eds.), Critical Literacies in Action: Social Perspectives and Teaching Practices, 3–20.

and other modes of inscription offer for social change, cultural diversity, economic equity, and political enfranchisement," as Sandy Muspratt, Allan Luke and Peter Freebody put it, following a pair of conferences on Critical Literacy held at Griffith University in 1992 and 1993 (1997, 1)

How Critical Theory, as a thoroughly German philosophical school (think Kant, Hegel, and Marx) that first arose in the 1920s and 30s, came to have such a sustained influence on a number of education scholars who are now reaching their prime could be cast as a story of the 1960s. The more bookish, left-leaning elements of the generation that came of age during that decade found in Marcuse's *One-Dimensional Man* (1964), second perhaps only in back-pack popularity to Kerouac's *On the Road* (1958), a new and invigorating way of making sense of the world. Marcuse opened this book by flatly declaring that "A comfortable, smooth, reasonable, democratic unfreedom prevails in advanced industrial civilization, a token of technical progress" (1964, 1). Compare this to Kerouac's opening line: "I had first met Dean after my wife and I split up" (1957, 1).

Marcuse nailed the bankruptcy of suburban life in a way that *Time* and *Life* magazines managed to miss, giving sacred democracy no leeway (amid the cold war), and throwing in ironic punch-line tokens, at least in the case of this opening sentence. The book provided a relentless critique of the here and now for the industrialized world–"the totalitarian universe of technological rationality is the latest transmutation of Reason" (123) – and sold over 300,000 copies. One testimony to the receptivity of the readership at the time is the general accuracy of Michael Walzer's critique that "Marcuse's prose [in *One-Dimensional Man*] is cumbersome, harsh, repetitive, abstract, only sometimes compelling, never beautiful" (1988, 170). Paperback Marcuse gave the counter-culture a philosophically critical edge, in exchange for beads and flowers, and it cut through the smooth and comfortable lives of our parents' generation like the wail of an over-amplified electric guitar. Marcuse's opening lines at his talk at the Dialectics of Liberation conference in London in 1967 were, "I am very happy to see so many flowers here and that is why I want to remind you that flowers, by themselves, have no power whatsoever, other than the power of men and women who protect them and take care of them against aggression and destruction".

Some 40 years on, it may be tempting to wonder how far this critical sensibility has come since Marcuse first asked, "How can the people who have been the object of effective and productive domination by themselves create the conditions of freedom?" (6). What now of the harsh note on which Marcuse concluded *One-Dimensional Man*? In a final section entitled "The Chance of Alternatives," and on the book's final page, he saw no better path ahead than to give one's life up to what he termed "the Great Refusal" (1964, 257). It was "just say *no*" in the biggest way. And why? Well, as Marcuse saw it, "the critical theory of society possesses no concepts which could bridge the gap between the present and the future; holding no promise and showing no success, it remains negative" (Ibid.).

Today, one has to wonder if traces of the great refusal could possibly be stalking the hallways of "effective and productive" schools of education in the guise of *Critical Literacy*. I would have said *yes* and *no*, too (to stay true to Critical

Theory's negative spirit). That is, Critical Literacy does carry forward this legacy, but not entirely and often for very good reason. This chapter offers a way to reconsider the balance between what is brought forward and what is left behind, just as it considers whether the value of Critical Theory can be so selectivity retained. To pause over just what these difficult, relentlessly critical works demanded of readers and students is to reconsider the origins of what was critical at the root of Critical Literacy, as well as the mix and balance of critical and affirmative elements since the grateful refusal played so well to so many. Revisiting earlier work in Critical Theory, particularly that of Horkheimer, Adorno, and Marcuse, remains a way to root about in the basic principles of Critical Literacy. To do so, you may have already realized, is to risk riding the current wave of 1960s nostalgia that tends to grip my generation at this time in our lives. I am writing this, for example, as the fiftieth anniversary of Kerouac publishing that generation-mobilizing *On the Road* is being celebrated, as are the 40 years that have passed since San Francisco's Summer of Love, where all that mobilization seemed to converge at least for a moment. Less celebrated is the fact that, also 40 years ago, Theodor Adorno's *Prisms* (1967) was published as his first book to be translated into English.

THE FRANKFURT SCHOOL

On the other hand, my intention is not to call anyone on the carpet for a lack of fealty to Adorno's negative dialectic. Such dogmatic gestures are so obviously contrary to what Critical Theory is all about. If it was not always the case or ever enough, it was at least Marcuse's boast that "critical theory is, last but not least, critical of itself and of the social forces that make up its basis" (1968, p. 156). Certainly, the feminist take up of Critical Theory's shortcomings on gender continues to follow in the best tradition of extending its own critical dialectic (Hebeale, 2006; Marcuso, 2006), as are more recent critiques of its Eurocentrism and other ethnocentricities that critical pedagogy seeks to move its critical work beyond (Kincheloe 2007). Marcuso, for example, uses the "emancipatory project of early Critical Theory" as a means of reminding feminists of the degree to which they have more recently "curbed its political aspirations and narrowed its theoretical field" with a goal of being able to "diagnose when and how critique loses its *critical* cast, when and how it reproduces the rationalities of power it purports to resist" (2006, 88–89).

Those who contributed to Critical Theory were attentive to history, even if historical developments promised no relief from the need for critique: "Critical thought... does not abandon its commitment even in the face of progress" (Horkheimer and Adorno, 1972, ix). Marcuse speaks of how "critical theory concerns itself with preventing the loss of the truths which past knowledge labored to attain" (1968, 152). It "must concern itself to a hitherto unknown extent with the past – precisely insofar as it is concerned with the future" (158). Adorno, too, held to this sense of the past's subtle persistence. He wrote toward the end of his life that "whatever was once thought, however, can be suppressed; it can be forgotten and can even vanish," only to affirm that despite this suppression, "it cannot be denied that something of it survives" (1991, 203).

Critical Theory itself bears the marks of its own rough history. The Frankfurt Circle was forged out of the experience of largely Jewish exiles forced to flee their imagined homeland under the threat of initially having their right to teach and then the very right to life denied (itself a great refusal). They then took various paths (tragically aborted in the case of Walter Benjamin in 1940) through Paris, Oxford, New York, California and then back to Frankfurt, with the Frankfurt's homelessness itself becoming the ethical ground on which the critique is built, or as Adorno was to plainly put it: "It is part of morality not to be at home in one's home" (1984, 39). Another aspect of this remaining apart can be seen in the active pursuit of the Institute of Social Research's independence, which gave rise to the Frankfurt School, as that independence was maintained through the philanthropic support of the Weil family and by means of affiliation with the University of Frankfurt (Jay, 1973, 3–9). Max Horkheimer, in his foreword to Martin Jay's history of the Frankfurt School notes that with Weil's support, "a group of men interested in social theory and from different scholarly background, came together with the belief that formulating the negative in the epoch of transition was more meaningful than academic careers" (Jay, 1973, xxv). In the course of this history, members of the Frankfurt School sought, as Habermas was to sum it up, "to think through the political disappointment at the absence of revolution in the West, the development of Stalinism in Soviet Russia, and the victory of fascism in Germany" (1995, 116).

How, then, does Critical Literacy, today, with its Critical Theory roots rarely showing, reveal more than a trace of this earlier history? It is so clearly and comfortably at home in the schools by this point that you can find Critical Literacy listed as one of the reading topics promoted by the International Reading Association (IRA), which represents tens of thousands of teachers in its promotion of professionalism among those involved in literacy instruction. Still, in the IRA's coverage of Critical Literacy, something of a family resemblance can be found with Critical Theory's earnest unmasking of consumer and economic ideologies. The IRA advises teachers that Critical Literacy entails encouraging "active, engaged reading" with students, which "means approaching texts with a critical eye—thinking about what they say about our world, why they say it, and whether the view they promote should be accepted" (Focus on Critical Literacy, 2007). The IRA then goes on to offer teachers a lesson on determining a writer's "point of view" as an instance of Critical Literacy in practice. A closely related and no less popular approach to Critical Literacy is to teach students to "detect bias" with a focus on the news media: "Despite the journalistic ideal of 'objectivity,' every news story is influenced by the attitudes and background of its interviewers, writers, photographers and editors" (Media Awareness Network, 2007).

Identifying *bias* as the issue can make these acts of misrepresentation and distortion appear as no more than a passing prejudice, a slight unconscious tendency, among certain media people who should know better. Yet such lessons can also open the prospect of something more. A teacher who helps students make a habit out of considering, with each text they encounter, what does it say about the world and why does it say it could lead the class into engaging with the same ideological issues around "mass deception" that Critical Theory so avidly pursued (to use part of a chapter title from *Dialectics of Enlightenment*; Horkheimer and Adorno, 1972). A few of the students may start to question the larger economic and ideological motives behind, say, newspaper editorials supporting America's military actions in the name of freedom and democracy. From such a starting point, the endemic and repeated pattern of biases could become apparent for inspired teachers and students, who would realize something far more systemic and inherently ideological is at work in mainstream media, resulting in, as Horkheimer and Adorno put it, "the stunting of the mass-media consumer's powers of imagination and spontaneity" (1972, 126). The rise today of the blogosphere, as a large-scale alternative media with a substantial segment devoted to taking issue, from its own ideological positions, with this mainstream media, offers educators further opportunities to help students realize just what the culture industry would make of them.

CRITICAL LITERACY

If but the faintest trace of Critical Theory survives in what the IRA and Media Awareness Network make of Critical Literacy, its legacy is far more vibrant and alive among more progressive forces in education. Ira Shor, at the City University of New York, for example, has used Critical Literacy as a concept to apply and extend the work of Paulo Freire in post-secondary education. Freire's (1985) rightly celebrated work on behalf of educating the oppressed has proven an inspiring point of departure for many working in Critical Literacy, with the step from Critical Theory's interest in emancipation taking on the far more educational sensibility with Freire's focus on empowerment (Lankshear and McLaren, 1993; Morgan, 1997; Shor and Pari, 1999).

When it comes to the question of "What is Critical Literacy?", Shor treats it as a means by which we "can redefine ourselves and remake society, if we choose, through alternative rhetoric and dissident projects"; he holds that "this is where Critical Literacy begins, for questioning power relations, discourses, and identities in a world not yet finished, just, or humane" (Shor, 1999). It is also with the questioning of power relations, discourses and identities that Critical Theory begins in Shor's work, and far more so than in his hopes of redefining lives and remaking society. In fact, if Critical Theory begins with such questioning, it is never quite clear where Critical Theory goes next, except on to further critical questioning. This is part of the dilemma of Critical Theory's legacy for Critical Literacy. The IRA lessons on Critical Literacy may not go far enough in their pursuit of critique, or at least would take an inspired teacher, with Joe L. Kincheloe's *Critical Pedagogy Primer* (2004) tucked under his or her arm, to push beyond the superficial identification of bias, and realize the more profound ravages of ideology that are affected by the media. But by the same token, Shor and others need to recognize the risk of assuming that this critical questioning will lead to the remaking of societies. It can have the effect of undermining the value of the critique itself to which Critical Theory so closely held.

Horkheimer and Adorno offer repeated instances of this blunt refusal to step beyond the questioning; they were more than satisfied at leaving things upturned by their aggressive, no-holds-barred critique. They conclude their review of the culture industry in *Dialectic of Enlightenment*, for example, by noting the ultimate hollowing out of our lives in modern times, while not pausing for a moment over what was to be done as a result: "The most intimate reactions of human beings have been so thoroughly reified that the idea of anything specific to themselves now persists only as an utterly abstract notion: personality scarcely signifies anything more than shining white teeth and freedom from body odor and emotions" (1972, 167).

So at one level it makes sense that Shor, Steinberg, and others, inspired by the level of critique sustained by Critical Theory, have seen fit to carry the critical ball into the schools through the development of educational programs and by supporting "alternative rhetoric and dissident projects," to cite Shor again (1999). To their credit, those working today with Critical Literacy have struck something of a balance, in which they have kept distinct both the surviving elements of Critical Theory, in Adorno's sense, and the educational rhetoric of empowered alternatives and the equipping of students with needed skills. There are those who would blur distinctions between critical theory and pedagogical strategies, as suggested by Robert Young's (1996) advice to teachers: "it makes it a little easier to remember that critical theory is more appropriately thought of as a critical *method*" (2) and by the book title *Critical Literacy/Critical Teaching: Tools for Preparing Responsive Teachers* (Dozier, Johnston, and Rogers, 2006).

Keeping these two aspects in peaceful coexistence amounts to an ongoing educational experiment, not just of working from within the institutions – as the Frankfurt Circle had little trouble with that aspect, even as they worked hard to maintain their intellectual and financial independence as an Institute of Social Research – but in how far the weight of this critique can be carried into the lives of teachers and children (something for which Adorno, at least, had something of an appreciation for, with further discussion of this to follow). This is why it is worth reconsidering how themes of Critical Theory and education programs can be brought together in Critical Literacy.

To take one striking example, Shirley Steinberg, a professor at McGill University, provides an analysis of *critical (media) literacy* that in the course of a single paragraph carries with it this movement between the current rhetoric of student preparation and the spirit of Critical Theory. In the preface to a reader on media literacy, she first establishes the collection's educational bona fides. She makes it clear that "our responsibility [is], then as educators, to prepare our students/citizens, to learn how to use [media], consume it, and to have personal power over it" (2007, xiv). That obligation out of the way, she decisively delivers a few sentences later the decisive Critical Theory line: "Media have been and can continue to become the ultimate hegemonic WMD [weapons of mass destruction] to a complacent or ignorant audience" (Ibid.). Horkheimer couldn't have said it any better. But then, Dewey might well subscribe to Steinberg's earlier sense of educational responsibility. Certainly, I would. There is realpolitik and savvy to such a stance, as it is able to make what is critically subversive possible for so many more teachers and students than would otherwise be realized. There is, as well, a distinction to be made here between the practice of theory and the theory of practice, with the traditions of Critical Theory playing a greater role in her scholarly publishing (the practice of theory) than in her work with education students where the theory of necessary educational practices play a greater part in helping these students bring this Critical Literacy into the lives of the students. There are precedents within the Critical Theory legacy, at least in the case of Adorno, as I shall discuss below, for the material and institutional basis for these distinctions. A similar skills-based grounding for lessons inspired by Critical Theory is found when Davies (1997) defines "Critical Literacy" as a "capacity to make language live, to bring oneself to live through language and, *at the same time*, bring to bear on language a critique which makes visible the powerful forces of rationality and linear patterns of thought" (28); she then goes on to conclude that Critical Literacy (and critical social literacy) "are aimed at giving students some skill in catching language in the act of formation and in recognizing and assessing the effects of that formation" (29).

In terms of large-scale implementations of this two-sided approach to Critical Literacy, Allan Luke was able to bring such a program to Queensland, Australia, in his role at the time of Deputy Director General of Education for the state. For him the question was "What happens when a 'radical' idea [like Critical Literacy] moves from the political outlands to become a key concept in a state curriculum" (2000, 448). Under his leadership, Critical Literacy was to form part of a "semiotic 'toolkit'" in a statewide curriculum (449). The idea was to enable students to use "their existing and new discourse resources for exchange in the social fields where texts and discourses matter" (449). His was "a vision of literacy as visible social practices with language, text, and discourse," and he saw Critical Literacy as "an educational project that engages with critique of the worlds of work, community life, media and popular and traditional cultures" (459). Critical Literacy is again part of an instrumental skill-set, as well as the source of specific critiques, whether of "possessive individualism" or "gendered forms of social identity" or on behalf of "disadvantaged students" (452). However, Luke points out, these "'critiques' did not stay critiques for long," and were soon "transformed into practical agendas and materials for teachers across Australia" (Ibid.). Luke again makes clear the back and forth motion of these ideas, the moving within and outside of Critical Theory's particular legacy. The movement back into the sharper legacy of Critical Theory adding considerably, I would suggest, to the quality of this tool, while the moving outside of it, by turning it into skill and method giving it its hold on the classroom. Luke (2000) suggests that, "The accelerated attempts by teachers to transform contemporary academic theory... into classroom practice were and remain quite remarkable among Australian teachers" (452).

TEACHING AND CRITICAL THEORY

In the hands of these educators, teaching remains an act of hope and possibility that was otherwise missing from the philosophy of the Frankfurt School, even as its members continued to teach a distinguished second generation of critical theorists (including Jürgen Habermas, Angela Davis, Andrew Feenberg, and Axel Honneth among others). It might seem the perfect complement, if not the ultimate compliment, to give Critical Theory a bit of a second life in the pages of this work devoted to Critical Literacy. But something else has to be said as well, at this point of reflection. And that is, that Critical Theory's disinclination to move beyond a theory of critique cannot be treated as entirely the result of difficult and dismal historical experiences or a lack of opportunity in exile. In America, rather, the ability to obtain research funding for empirical studies in prejudice became the best means of maintaining the intellectual independence of the Institute of Social Research (keeping it from being absorbed into Columbia University). But in all of that, the critique has its own special claim as a source of knowledge and understanding for Critical Theory. This claim rests on how it engages the gaps and contradictions within existing ideas (in a dialectic), rather than imagining that it has a grip on an external reality. What follows from the critique, whether in the form of educational programs, alternative or experimental models, systematic research projects was a concern to the Frankfurt School insofar as such practical and programmatic matters could, if they began to drive the work, place the theoretical value of critique at risk.

Members of the Institute of Social Research did undertake in Frankfurt and New York social science studies of authority and culture, Nazism and anti-Semitism. The Institute maintained an active publishing program, including a scholarly journal, which brought together theoretical work, intellectual historical studies, and survey results (e.g., German physicians' attitudes toward sexual morality). In America, the Institute undertook a major program of research on the sources of prejudice that was financed by the American Jewish Committee and the Jewish Labor Committee in the 1940s. But still Horkheimer treated the empirical side of this research as itself an experiment, to be approached warily, and saw the challenge, as Director of the Institute, "to present examples of an approach especially aware of the necessity to integrate theoretical thinking with empirical analysis" (1941, p. 365). The degree to which that integration was successful or ultimately helpful to theoretical thinking (as it was for Institute funding) is an important question to ask, as part of what Critical Theory achieved, and what I am drawing attention to with this chapter in relation to the work of Critical Literacy advocates, is how integration may not be the principal issue in the relation between the theoretical and empirical, compared to more distinct forms of co-existence that are possible. The Frankfurt Circle had long rejected "the hypothesis-verification-conclusion model," as Martin Jay points out in his history of the Institute, given how, in his words, "modern empiricism [was seen to have] capitulated before the authority of the status quo" in its positivist attempts to separate facts and values (1973, pp. 240, 62). Adorno, in a section of his book *Minima Moralia* (1951) that he later excised, wrote: "The procedure of the official social sciences is little more than a parody of the businesses that keep such sciences afloat while really needing it only as an advertisement" (cited by Jenemann, 2007, 1).

In the 1940s, Adorno become involved in the major empirical research initiatives on prejudice and authoritarian personality types through the Institute. The Institute's best-known study resulted in *The Authoritarian Personality* by Adorno, Frenkel-Brunswik, Levinson, and Sanford (1950), which Martin identifies as "probably the most deeply flawed work of prominence in political psychology" with its "methodological, procedural, and substantive errors" the subject of much critique, even as he acknowledges "theoretically rich critique of the authoritarians."

THE LEGACY OF THEODOR ADORNO

Adorno later explained, in the sardonically entitled radio talk "Scientific Experiences of a European Scholar in America," that in conducting his work with the Institute's most famous study on authoritarian personalities, involving interviews and questionnaires, "we never considered the theory simply as a hypothesis, but rather as in a certain sense something independent" (1998a, 236). It is the work of theory, for Adorno, which stands, ultimately, as a corrective to the empiricist reduction of experience. Adorno was determined, after returning to Germany, to make up for the lapses: "What I have in mind after all that is a kind of restitution of experience against the empiricists' deformation" (242).

While acknowledging the complex historical exigencies that enabled the Frankfurt Circle, with remarkable adeptness, to hold together as more than just a body of thought, it seems important to step back and review what it attempted to make of critique. This legacy can otherwise be lost sight of as we build, propose and construct school programs, work with teachers in action research settings, as we learn from our students how to use new technologies to develop new forms of Critical Literacy, and as we push the possibilities of critique into the blogosphere, virtual realities, social networks, and global activism.

In making sense of Critical Theory, it needs to be seen what sort of theory it is and is not. It is certainly not a theory in the sense of traditional philosophical theories, such as Platoism or pragmatism. That is, it has not set out to explain how it is we know the world and should act within that knowledge, at least not apart from its sense that a critical engagement with what passes for common sense is where it stands on its surest philosophical ground. There is no presumption within Critical Theory that the goal is to identify any sort of real or ideal world that operates outside of this dialectic engagement with negative aspects of the administered life, the pseudo-reality and activity. And while elements of Marx are at work at many points in Critical Theory – from the class analysis to concerns over alienation and dehumanization – it is not a theory like Marxism, which Horkheimer criticized for presuming to pursue a "knowledge of a 'totality' or of a total and absolute truth" (1993, 129; see also Rush 2004, 9). Critical Theory *qua* theory is all the more removed from natural science theories such as evolution. For all of its work in educational institutions, it was not interested in formulating educational theories, such as John Dewey's theory of the role of art and experience in learning.

Critical Theory is far more a theory in the sense of constantly bringing forward a speculative set of ideas about, in this case, what lies behind this seemingly given reality. It is the theoretical product of imagination, insight, and thoughtfulness. It is a theory that did not seek its fulfillment in practice. Or as Adorno somewhat obfuscates it, it is not given to "consecrating existing conditions by making practical applicability of knowledge its criterion for knowledge; supposedly nowhere else could the practical effectiveness of knowledge be tested" (1998b, 259). Critical Theory is a theory about the value of taking a critical stance, of finding contradictions, of recording losses, as to the economic conditions, aesthetic qualities, and individual expression of our lives. Though ideas were drawn from Freud, Marx, Hegel, Kant, any aspirations these thinkers had to grasp and represent the whole of a phenomenon were treated with deep suspicion. Adorno took this stance to the point of declaring that "the whole is the untrue" (1951, 50). Bonner (1998) identifies this as the basis of an anti-epistemology in Adorno's work. See also, Horkheimer and Adorno: "Explanations of the world as all or nothing are mythologies" (1972, 24).

For all of that, Habermas is right to say that Critical Theory sought a "totalized critique" (1995, 119) even as it worked against such totalities. Those involved in the Frankfurt Circle spoke of their work as fragments, wrote in aphorisms, included notes and drafts in published works (see Adorno, 1951; Horkheimer and Adorno, 1972). However theoretical, the claims never lacked for confidence or assurance, certainly on the part of Adorno, whether his target was art–"Every work of art is an unexecuted crime" (1951 111)–or women–"Women of especial beauty are condemned to unhappiness" (1951, 171). This assurance is worth comparing to what poet John Keats (1817) termed "negative capability, that is when man is capable of being in uncertainties, mysteries, doubts without any irritable reaching after fact and reason".

Despite its anti-epistemological tendencies, Critical Theory still possessed a theory of knowledge, one from which Critical Literacy advocates can draw both in their teacher education programs and scholarly projects. Critical Theory did not pursue a theory of knowledge that had to do with system or method, criteria or checks. In fact, Horkheimer and Adorno saw in such mainstays of modern rigorous inquiry the first misstep of the Enlightenment, tracing the problem back to Bacon's seventeenth-century pursuit of experimental science. As Horkheimer and Adorno saw it: "On the road to modern science, men renounce any claim to meaning. They substitute formula for concept, rule and probability for cause and motive" (1972, 5). The emphasis placed on the development of scientific methods is taken to represent the Enlightenment's failure of nerve, its anxiety over issues of control, knowledge, and power: "Enlightenment has put aside the classic requirement of thinking about thought...Mathematical procedure became, so to speak, the ritual of thinking" (24). Even language has succumbed: "There is no longer any available form of linguistic expression which has not tended toward accommodation to dominant currents of thought" (xii).

Such systems and forms of expression need to be opened and exposed by entering in a critical spirit through the inevitable gaps that persist. To engage in critique is seen as a dialectical process of confronting propositions with counter-propositions based on those gaps, or as Horkheimer and Adorno spin it around and around: "To proceed dialectically means to think in contradictions, for the sake of the contradiction already experienced in the object, and against that contradiction. A contradiction in reality, [dialectics] is a contradiction against reality" (Adorno, 1973, 144-45). Contradictions motivate Critical Theory, and for the sake of contradicting what is otherwise taken for granted, exposing cultural delusions, making apparent how, for example "the misplaced love of the common people for the wrong which is done them is a greater force than the cunning of the authorities" (134).

The danger in such a constant assault on common sense is that it will carry with it some faint recall of the inconsolable crankiness of critique in childhood, if with the highest philosophical guise. Is it to be a critique of everything, and nothing but critique, all of the time? The Frankfurt Circle was driven by a particular dilemma, that at its broadest, entailed the successive loss of humanity in the face of a growing bureaucratic administration and ordering of our lives, which was felt, for example, as "advance in technical facilities for enlightenment is accompanied by a process of dehumanization" that, in Horkheimer's judgment, threatens to "nullify the very goal it is supposed to realize–the idea of man" (2004, v). But as well, those involved in Critical Theory's project saw themselves contributing to, in Marcuse's (1958) words, a "materialist protest and materialist critique [that] originated in the struggle of oppressed groups for better living conditions and remain permanently associated with the actual process of the struggle" (141). For Horkheimer, it was to be philosophy against economy, with the intent of making it clear the transformations underway that were turning "fair exchange into a deepening of social injustice, a free economy into monopolistic control, productive work into rigid relationships which hinder production, the maintenance of society's life into the pauperization of the peoples" (1972, 247).

The turn to Critical Theory, then, could be cast as sufficient in itself, and bound to be something less as it is treated as a starting point or part of a larger program of hope. Adorno, especially, held to the value of keeping theory from practice: "Praxis is a source of power for theory, but cannot be prescribed by it" (1998b, 278). Criticism is cast as crucial for culture: "Culture is only true when implicitly critical... criticism is an indispensable element of culture" (Adorno, 1967, 22). It is as if the act of criticism is the only way to clear a place to stand within what is otherwise cast as "unjust state of life," the only way to rise above "the impotence and pliability of the masses" (Horkheimer and Adorno, 1972, xv). While engaging the contradictions within that state of life is a form of action, or at least reaction, it does not seem, to me at least, to be an instance of Marx's famous call to philosophers: "The philosophers have only interpreted the world in various ways; the point is to change it" (Marx, 1995). Marcuso (2006), for example, cites this famous statement in relation to Critical Theory.

ENGAGED WITHDRAWAL

Such a charged expression might well serve Critical Literacy advocates, in their aspirations to use literacy to remake the world. Critical Theory, on the other hand, has as its goal "utterly critical criticism," in another of Marx's felicitous phrases (2000). If philosophers have only interpreted the world in various ways, the point for Critical Theory is to interrupt those interpretations, and to interrupt them with daring and aggressive interpretations capable of hurtling past the "horizon of untruth that bars the door to real emancipation," in Marcuse's phrase (1968, 151). Such interruptions may indeed change the world, but that prospect–and what would come of it–is not the point for Critical Theory.

The faintness of hope for substantial, life-altering change running through Critical Theory can be discouraging. Simone Chambers calls it "the politics of engaged withdrawal" (2004, 220), and it is fortunate, in that sense, that what Critical Literacy advocates such as Steinberg (2005b) achieve makes critique anything but politically withdrawing (see also Brady, 1994; Fecho 1998). Yet those who have worked this early vein of Critical Theory have demonstrated that the withdrawal affords an ability to bring to the surface just how deeply mired modern life is in a dehumanizing administrative apparatus of technical rationality in which we are offered "enlightenment as mass deception" (Horkheimer and Adorno, 1972, 120–167). To call for developing one's Critical Literacy skills and filling one's semiotic toolkits within such a context can seem a little distracting in its own right. Which is to say that this is not simply a story of mixing and blending elements from Critical Theory and literacy pedagogies, but of preserving something of where and how that critical element plays itself out. Not that this critical spirit won't be compromised and contradicted in moving these ideas into the schools, which are part of the culture industry. This critical spirit was certainly and necessarily compromised within the Frankfurt School, yet without being completely submerged or lost.

To see how this commitment to the critical negative, this great refusal, can turn, within the scope of one man's work, I would conclude with Theodor Adorno's response to questions of political and pedagogical action during the 1960s. At the time, Marcuse was enjoying his standing as something of a rock-star philosopher, never more so than when he appeared onstage with poet Allen Ginsberg and Black Power activist Stokely Carmichael at a Dialectics of Liberation conference in London in 1967 which was recorded on a rather overwhelming 23 LP records (Marcuse 1967). If Marcuse got with the program, Adorno kept to the critical line and the politics of engaged withdrawal to a rather dismal end. Adorno did deliver lectures on philosophical and general topics ("Free Time") on the radio during the 1960s, showing an impressive concern with making his prose more public: "I want to be understood by my listeners" (cited by Pickford, 1998, viii).

It is worth noting that in the course of theses radio talks, Adorno addressed more than once his work with schoolteachers. He was involved in the examinations in philosophy that needed to be passed in order to qualify as teachers (only in Germany, you say?). Adorno quotes from the exam regulations on how they are intended to "determine whether the applicant has understood... the vital philosophical, pedagogical, and political questions of the present" (1998b, 21). He expressed a concern over the quality of teaching in elementary education, proposing that, if anything, soulless teaching of the young "was partially responsible for the catastrophe of National Socialism" (1998c, 28). With this concern, the education of teachers stood as a practical activity for Adorno, a merging of theory and practice that he otherwise resisted. He eschewed, as might be expected, scientific approaches to teaching: "They imagine that their salvation is secured if they follow scientific rules, heed the ritual of science, surround themselves with science" (1998c, 32). One can imagine that the current U.S. government's What Works Clearinghouse run by the Institute of Education Sciences, as the perfect embodiment of instrumental rationality in the overly administered lives of teachers, would not go over well with the Frankfurt Circle (even as it has proven flawed by its own standards; Schoenfeld, 2006). The methodological fetish that Critical Theory worked hard to expose represents another area where critical pedagogy has demonstrated how teachers can, in a very practical sense, exercise methodical resistance to authorized methods (Kincheloe and Steinberg, 1998).

There was, as well, another side to Adorno, the educator of educators. In a starkly entitled talk, "Education after Auschwitz," he opened with the simple and profound declaration that "the premier demand upon all education is that Auschwitz not happen again" (1998d, 191). In facing the ultimate educational question, Adorno did not hesitate to recommend a systematic series of steps intended to prevent any reoccurrence: "One must come to know the mechanisms that render people capable of such deeds, must reveal the mechanisms to them, and strive by awakening a general awareness of those mechanisms, to prevent people from becoming so again" (1998d, 193). It signals his own educational compromise with Critical Theory, given the positivistic, programmatic, and instrumental nature of these recommendations. Sometimes confronting the toughest questions leads us into taking reassuringly confident stands, and, in this case, you can hear the voice of a concerned educator speaking to a radio audience. As I mentioned earlier with Steinberg, there is place for maintaining a healthy distinction between the practices of theory in one's published work and the theory informing practices with educators and, in this instance, Adorno's fails to sustain the necessary connections between the two. Later in the same talk and more promisingly – in terms of where Critical Theory might meet education on its own terms – he holds with the educational principle of encouraging "autonomy" among the students and "the power of reflection, of self-determination, of not cooperating" (195). Adorno describes "autonomy," in this context, as "the Kantian expression," in reference to how Kant held that enlightenment was about people moving out from under the tutelage of others (1970). In this instance, at least, Adorno's position is closely aligned with the Critical Literacy advocates who draw on Critical Theory, with the interest in fostering critical reflection and refusal balanced by their systemic affirmation of the work that schools need to do.

However, for Adorno the teacher and inactivist theorist, it was to end badly in the classroom. In April of 1969, he was subject to a bizarre act of political theatre that took place as he began to lecture on "dialectical thinking" at the University of Frankfurt (Lee, 2006). Students at the university had been protesting the lack of educational reform, as they were in many spots around the world, as well as the particular failure of German society to deal more openly with its Nazi past. In all this, the Frankfurt School was proving a disappointing source of seemingly inert Critical Theory for the more militant of the students. Just a few minutes into Adorno's lecture that day, a student ran up to the blackboard and wrote "Whomever allows the beloved Adorno to do what he pleases will remain under the spell of capitalism forever" (Lee, 2006, 114). This was followed by a commotion in the classroom, as Adorno sought to bring order to the situation, during which three women belonging to the German Socialist Students came to the front of the room and surrounded Adorno. They began showering him with tulip and rose petals while baring their breasts, after which they distributed a brochure entitled, "Adorno as an institution is dead" (Ibid.). Lisa Yun Lee interprets the incident as a direct challenge to his masculinity, as well as the impotence of theory (2006, 115). This bizarrely staged mock funeral was to presage his actual death a few months later from a heart attack that he suffered while on holiday in Switzerland.

In February 1969, two months prior to the disruption of his lecture on dialectical thinking, Adorno gave a very brief radio talk entitled "Resignation." He obviously felt compelled to deal with the general accusation that his refusal to become involved in or support the activities of the New Left during the 1960s was an act of resignation. Adorno had taken a few token political steps earlier that year by sending two essays that defended the rights of homosexuals to the new Minister of Justice in light of proposed reforms on the penal code (Pickford, 1998, ix). He spoke from the perspective of, as he put in his opening line, "we older representatives of that for which the name Frankfurt School has established itself" (1991, 198). He did not pull any punches in this statement: "We are not prepared to draw the practical consequences from this theory" (Ibid.). This stance had been interpreted, he noted, as offering "tacit approval" of current conditions and an unwillingness "to get his hands dirty" (199). He offered a relatively arrogant denial that this is the case. He suggested that "fear" is at the root of the "repressive intolerance toward a thought not immediately accompanied by instructions for action," a fear that "this thought is right" (Ibid.). It is right (or perhaps it is *more likely to be* right, one might want to say) because "thinking, employed only as the instrument of action, is blunted in the same manner as all instrumental reason" (202). The idea is worth pausing over.

CONCLUSION

Could our thinking about education and literacy be blunted by this interest in seeing our work become "the instrument of action?" It speaks to the value of pursuing the practice of theory as a critical activity without always asking whether it is practical enough, whether it can be implemented in classrooms, whether it is what education students need to become good teachers, whether it is sensitive enough to the current educational climate of test-accountability. It speaks, as well, to an interest in working out the critique as itself an integral act that may – once it is fully realized, debated and discussed by others – later have practical implications whether in terms of empirical research (to pick up an earlier point) or teacher education programs. There may be something desperate, as Adorno charges, in reformist efforts entirely focused on taking small steps against "a thoroughly mediated and obdurate society" (1991, 201). Today, with "designated protest areas" (cages really) set up for world summits, there may be something to his charge that activism represents the channeling of spontaneity in an "administered world" (Ibid.). In a similar channeling vein, Michael Crowley has noted how "conference calls and e-mail messages to Congress have mostly replaced antiwar demonstrations and street theater" (2007, 55). But finally, for Adorno, the rejection of activist programs of reform came down to the simple pleasures of intellectual work: "Thought achieves happiness in the expression of unhappiness" (202). In not letting anyone take that away from him, he concludes, he "has not resigned" (202).

Despite Adorno's final pout on the question of resignation and the price he was to pay two months later in the classroom, his insistence on the value of critique being taken on its own terms is well taken. It can indeed seem, as social activism is being carefully staged and orchestrated, while Critical Literacy advocates are developing more elaborate programs, that it is important to continue to create an educational space within Critical Literacy for the culture of critique, a space to work out critiques that can seize hold of the most basic contradictions, broken promises, seeming conundrums and necessary compromises. It is important, in that sense, to treat that critique as the supremely educational event in fostering autonomy and reflection. The intellectual space of refusal and, yes, resignation from, say, reformist efforts needs to be judged for the larger sense and insight that it can contribute to our understanding as one of the valuable forms that critical work in literacy can take.

I say this as one whose work has been moving away over the last decade from writing critiques of literacy programs, linguistic ideologies, imperial legacies, and other acts of seeming Critical Literacy, to developing software programs, with accompanying semi-promotional rhetoric and advocacy research, that are designed to contribute to the economic and political reform of scholarly publishing. See the Public Knowledge Project (http://pkp.sfu.ca), including my related, and freely available, publications (http://pkp.sfu.ca/biblio). This move came out of a time for me when the idea of undertaking another critique, of pursuing another related line of contradiction with the educational legacy of imperialism, seemed too much like doing too little. I wondered if it would not mean more to create an alternative path for at least one aspect of the institutional structures and administered life by which I lived, namely how this academic community unnecessarily and thoughtlessly restricted access to the knowledge it so proudly produced (Willinsky 2006). It is a project that draws, in part, on later generations of Critical Theory, on Habermas's hopes (1991) for improving the quality of rational communication by extending the public sphere and the possibility of a more deliberative democracy (for which he has been accused of leaving Critical Theory behind; Chambers, 2004, pp. 232–235) and on Andrew Feenberg's notions (1995) of the possibilities of democratizing technology. What may be lost in my less-than-critical turn to developing and promoting new publishing models has been part of what this chapter has tried to bring forward, as part of Critical Theory's legacy for Critical Literacy. That is, there remains the need for such work, and Critical Literacy more generally, to be led by the distinct work of engaged critique.

In this time of anniversaries, it seems only appropriate to consider again, the compromises and contradictions, as well as the very charge of a Critical Theory, that continue to provide a reference point for the place of the critical. Fortunately, a number of those associated with Critical Literacy continue to work both the critical and instrumental strands with a distinctiveness that make educational settings interesting and promising and do so without having these two approaches cancel, or unduly blunt, each other. Adorno held that "the only education that has any sense at all is an education toward critical self-reflection" (1998c, 193). If we can look for ourselves in that reflection, in who we were and what we first took hold of, and what we hold to now – especially in thinking about the relation that Critical Literacy holds between theory and practice – we will indeed have something to celebrate, if not in the getting of wisdom finally, then in realizing the weight of critical choices.

REFERENCES

Adorno, T. W. (1998a). In scientific experiences of a European scholar in America. In *Critical models: Interventions and catchwords* (H. W. Pickford, Trans., pp. 215–242). New York: Columbia University Press.

Adorno, T. W. (1998b). Marginalia to theory and praxis. In *Critical models: Interventions and catchwords* (H. W. Pickford, Trans., pp. 259–278). New York: Columbia University Press.

Adorno, T. W. (1998c). Philosophy and teachers. In *Critical models: Interventions and catchwords* (H. W. Pickford, Trans., pp. 19–35). New York: Columbia University Press.

Adorno, T. W. (1998d). Education after Auschwitz. In *Critical models: Interventions and catchwords* (H. W. Pickford, Trans., pp. 190–204). New York: Columbia University Press.

Adorno, T. W. (1991). Resignation. In J. M. Bernstein (Ed.), *The culture industry: Selected essays on mass culture* (pp. 198–203). New York: Routledge.

Adorno, T. W. (1984). *Aesthetic theory*. New York: Routledge and K. Paul.

Adorno, T. W. (1973). *Negative dialectics* (E. B. Ashton, Trans.). New York: Seabury Press.

Adorno, T. W. (1967). Cultural criticism and society. In *Prisms* (S. & S. Weber, Trans., pp. 17–34). London: Neville Spearman.

Adorno, T. W. (1951). *Minima moralia: Reflections from a damaged life* (E. F. N. Jephcott, Trans.). London: NLB.

Adorno, T. W., Frenkel-Brunswik, E., Levinson, D. J., & Sanford, R. N. (1950). *The authoritarian personality*. New York: Harper and Row.

Brady, J. (1994). Critical literacy, feminism, and a politics of representation. In P. McLaren & C. Lankshear (Eds.), *Politics of liberation: Paths from Freire*. London: Routledge.

Bronner, S. (1998). *Dialectics at a standstill: A methodological inquiry into the philosophy of Theodor W. Adorno*. Illuminations: The critical theory Web Site. Retrieved from http://www.uta.edu/huma/illuminations/

Chambers, S. (2004). The politics of critical theory. In F. Rush (Ed.), *The Cambridge companion to critical theory* (pp. 219–247). Cambridge, UK: Cambridge University Press.

Crowle, M. (2007, September 9). Can lobbyists stop the war? *New York Times Magazine*, 56–59.

Davies, B. (1997). Constructing and deconstructing masculinities through critical literacy. *Gender and Education, 9*(1), 9–30.

Dozier, C., Johnston, P., & Rogers, R. (2006). *Critical literacy/critical teaching: Tools for preparing responsive teachers.* New York: Teachers' College Press.

Fecho, B. (1998). Crossing boundaries of race in a critical literacy classroom. In D. E. Alvermann, K. A. Hinchman, D. W. Moore, S. Phelps, & D. Waff (Eds.), *Reconceptualizing the literacies in adolescents' lives* (pp. 75–102). Mahwah, NJ: Erlbaum.

Feenberg, A. (1995). *Alternative modernity: The technical turn in philosophy and social theory.* Berkeley, CA: University of California Press.

Focus on Critical Literacy. (2007). Newark, NJ: International Reading Association. Retrieved from http://www.reading.org/resources/issues/focus_critical.html

Freire, P. (1985). *The politics of education: Culture, power, and liberation* (D. Macedo, Trans.). South Hadley, MA: Bergin.

Habermas, J. (1995). The entwinement of myth and enlightenment: Max Horkheimer and Theodor Adorno. In *The philosophical discourse of modernity: Twelve lectures* (F. G. Lawrence, Trans., pp. 160–130). Cambridge, MA: MIT Press.

Habermas, J. (1991). *The structural transformation of the public sphere* (T. Burger, Trans.). Cambridge, MA: MIT Press.

Hebeale, R. (Ed.). (2006). *Feminist interpretations of Theodor Adorno.* University Park, PA: Pennsylvania State University Press.

Horkheimer, M. (2004). *Eclipse of reason.* London: Continuum.

Horkheimer, M. (1993). On the problem of truth. In *Between philosophy and social science* (G. F. Hunter, M. S. Kramer, & J. Torpey, Trans., pp. 177–216). Cambridge, MA: MIT Press.

Horkheimer, M. (1972). Traditional and critical theory: Postscript. In *Critical theory: Selected essays* (M. K. O'Connell, Trans., pp. 244–252). New York: Herder and Herder.

Horkheimer, M. (1941). Preface. *Studies in philosophy and social science, 9*(3), 365–388.

Jay, M. (1973). *The dialectical imagination. A history of the Frankfurt School and the Institute of Social Research 1923–1950.* Berkeley, CA: University of California Press.

Jenemann, D. (2007). *Adorno in America.* Minneapolis, MN: University of Minnesota Press.

Kant, I. (1970). An answer to the question: What is enlightenment? In H. Reiss (Ed.), *Kant: Political writings* (H. B. Nisbett, Trans., pp. 54–60). Cambridge, UK: Cambridge University Press.

Keats, J. (1817, December 21). *Letter to George and Thomas Keats.*

Kerouac, J. (1958). *On the road.* New York: Viking Press.

Kincheloe, J. L. (2007). *Creating an open scholarly archive on Paulo Freire.* Paper presented at PKP Scholarly Publishing Conference, Vancouver; Blog by Valerie Hodge. Retrieved from http://scholarlypublishing.blogspot.com/2007/07/creating-open-scholarly-archive-on_12.html

Kincheloe, J. L. (2004). *Critical pedagogy primer.* New York: Peter Lang Publishing.

Kincheloe, J. L., & Steinberg, S. R. (1998). Lesson plans from the outer limits: Unauthorized methods. In J. L. Kincheloe & S. R. Steinberg (Eds.), *Unauthorized methods: Strategies for critical thinking* (pp. 1–23). New York: Routledge.

Knobel, M., & Lankshear, C. (2002). *Critical cyberliteracies: What young people can teach us about reading and writing the world.* Paper presented at the National Council of English Teachers' Assembly for Research Mid-Winter Conference, New York. Retrieved from http://www.geocities.com/c.lankshear/cyberliteracies.html

Lankshear C., & Knobel, M. (1998). *Critical literacy and new technologies.* Paper presented at the American Education Research Association. San Diego, 1998. Retrieved from http://www.geocities.com/c.lankshear/critlitnewtechs.html

Lankshear, C., & McLaren, P. (1993). *Critical literacy: Politics, praxis and the postmodern.* Albany, NY: State University of New York Press.

Lee, L. Y. (2006). The bared-breasts incident. In R. Hebeale (Ed.), *Feminist interpretations of Theodor Adorno* (pp. 113–140). University Park, PA: Pennsylvania State University Press.

Leonard, S. T. (1990). *Critical theory in political practice.* Princeton, NJ: Princeton University Press.

Luke, A. (2000). Critical literacy in Australia: A matter of context and standpoint. *Journal of Adolescent and Adult Literacy, 43*(5), 448–462.

Marcuse, H. (1968). Critical theory and philosophy. In *Negations* (pp. 134–158). Boston: Beacon.

Marcuse, H. (1967). *Liberation from the affluent society.* Paper presented at Dialectics of Liberation Conference. Retrieved from http://www.marcuse.org/herbert/pubs/60spubs/67dialecticlib/67LibFromAfflSociety.htm, Audio Clip: http://www.marcuse.org/herbert/soundvideo/67LondonConf.wav

Marcuse, H. (1964). *One-dimensional man.* Boston: Beacon.

Marcuse, H. (1958). *Soviet Marxism, a critical analysis.* New York: Columbia University Press.

Marcuso, R. (2006). "Already the effect of the whip": Critical theory and the feminine ideal. *Differences, 17*(1), 88–115.

Martin, J. L. (2001). The authoritarian personality, 50 years later: What questions are there for political psychology? *Political Psychology, 22*(1), 1–26.

Marx, K. (1995). *Thesis on Feuerbach* (W. Lough, Trans., Orig. 1888). Marx/Engels Internet Archive. Retrieved from http://www.marxists.org/archive/marx/works/1845/theses/theses.htm

Marx, K. (2000). Preface. In *The economic and philosophical manuscripts* (Orig. 1844). Marxist Internet File. Retrieved from http://www.marxists.org/archive/marx/works/download/Marx_Economic_and_Philosophical_Mauscripts.pdf

Media Awareness Network. (2007). *Detecting bias in the news.* Ottawa, Canada: Media Awareness Network. Retrieved from http://www.media-awareness.ca/english/resources/educational/handouts/crime/detecting_bias_news.cfm

Morgan, W. (1997). *Critical literacy in the classroom: The art of the possible.* London: Routledge.

Muspratt, S., Luke, A., & Freebody, P. (1997). *Constructing Critical literacies: Teaching and learning textual practice.* Cresskill, NJ: Hampton Press.

Pickford, H. W. (1998). Preface. In *Critical models: Interventions and catchwords* (pp. vi–xii). (H. W. Pickford, Trans.). New York: Columbia University Press.

Public Knowledge Project. Retrieved from http://pkp.sfu.ca

Rush, F. (2004). Conceptual foundations of critical theory. In F. Rush (Ed.), *The Cambridge companion to critical theory* (pp. 6–39). Cambridge, UK: Cambridge University Press.

Schoenfeld, A. H. (2006). What doesn't work: The challenge and failure of the what works clearinghouse to conduct meaningful reviews of studies of mathematics curricula. *Educational Researcher, 35*(2), 13–21.

Shor, I. (1999). What is critical literacy? *Journal for Pedagogy, Pluralism and Practice, 1*(4). Retrieved from http://www.lesley.edu/journals/jppp/4/shor.html

Shor, I., & Pari, C. (1999). *Critical literacy in action. Writing words, changing worlds/A tribute to the teachings of Paulo Freire.* Portsmouth, NH: Boyton/Cook.

Steinberg, S. R. (2005a). Reading race on film: Critical media literacy. In M. Pollock (Ed.), *Everyday antiracism: Concrete ways to successfully navigate the relevance of race in school.* New York: The New Press.

Steinberg, S. R. (2005b). Using critical media literacy to teach about racism against Muslims and Arabs. In J. Paraskeva (Ed.), *Congress at Manigualte: Education and politics.* Manigualte, Portugal: Municipal Publishing. Translated into Portuguese.

Steinberg, S. R. (2007). Reading media critically. In S. R. Steinberg & D. Macedo (Eds.), *Media literacy: A reader* (pp. xiii–xv). New York: Peter Lang.

Walzer, M. (1977). *The company of critics: Social criticism and political commitment in the twentieth century.* New York: Basic Books.

Willinsky, J. (2006). *The access principle: The case for open access to research and scholarship.* Cambridge, MA: MIT Press.

Young, R. E. (1996). *A critical theory of education: Habermas and our children's future.* New York: Teachers' College Press.

ROBERT E. WHITE

CHAPTER 2

Above and Beyond: Critical Literacies for the New Millennium

There were four horsemen of the Apocalypse; War, Famine, Pestilence and Death. However, had there been a fifth horseman, perhaps that fifth horseman would have been Illiteracy. Numerous researchers (Macedo, 2006; St.Clair, 2003; Wagner, 1993) have linked lack of literacy to poverty and even to a foreshortened life span (Khan and Asaduzzman, 2007; McMullen, 2006).

While this reference to the Apocalypse may appear to be hyperbolic or even iconoclastic, it is nonetheless true that literacy is inimitably and intimately linked with success in whichever terms one wishes to cast personal achievements. Thus, every literacy that will allow for success on an individual or societal level can be considered a Critical Literacy. As an example, writing is an act of meaning making for oneself and for others (Mayher, 1990). As such, because all language is socially situated (Graff, 1987; Street, 1984), writing and, I dare say, any system of meaning making is a form of social action (Cooper and Holtzman, 1989). This chapter will attempt to identify and define new emerging systems of meaning making and discuss how such systems, as forms of literacy, can indeed be critical.

Gene Rodenberry was once heard to comment that his creation "Star Trek" had nothing to do with science fiction. As I pondered this comment, I was struck by the fact that most sci-fi presents its audience with familiar situations in unfamiliar settings. It is within this juxtaposition that new learnings about societies, familiar and unfamiliar, can take place. So it is with Critical Literacy. Our current society makes available a new, textured and ever-changing backdrop against which familiar artifacts, events, concerns and social issues can be explored through systems of meaning making – our literacies, some of which have been with us for a very long time and some of which are only just now emerging.

MULTIPLE MEANINGS OF LITERACY

The term "literacy" began with the Middle English term meaning "to be lettered"; in short, meaning to be able to read and possibly even to write. However, similar to many things that become common language terms, the term "literacy" has been victimized by obfuscation, appropriation and expropriation. Edelsky and Cherland (2006) speak of a similar fate which befell the "Whole Language" movement. They claim that what began as a very clear pedagogical understanding has become so fuzzy and distorted that almost any approach to language acquisition can now be considered to be "Whole Language":

K. Cooper and R. E. White (eds.), Critical Literacies in Action: Social Perspectives and Teaching Practices, 21–35.

At first, it was the designation chosen by some reflective teachers who had read work by Kenneth Goodman (1967) and began to observe their students' learning through the lens of language learning, standing back to note students' hypotheses about written language. These teachers began studying the assumptions underlying their own practice, aiming for student-centeredness (e.g., student choice, student-teacher negotiation of curriculum), and meeting with like-minded others to support their professional, theoretical shifts. Their energy, camaraderie, and enthusiasm attracted attention; in a world of professional burnout, whole language sparkled. Soon, publishers grabbed the label to boost sales, marketing such oxymoronic materials as "whole language workbooks." With a one-weekend workshop behind them, entire schools (dragging along veteran teachers who saw no reason to examine or even acknowledge their own theoretical assumptions, let alone change them) declared themselves "whole language" to show parents and the community at large that they were on the cutting edge. The net effect was that in the larger professional community and also among the public, "whole language" came to be an empty term, signifying just about any educational practice (Edelsky and Cherland, 2006, 18).

Similar to the whole language "cat", the literacy cat is now out of the bag and it is not possible to get it back into the bag. Literacy no longer means simply to be lettered. Due, in part at least, to the passage of time and to many other factors including the Industrial Revolution that created a need for children to find something other to do with their time than to sweep chimneys, education of large numbers of people, specifically school-age children, resulted in the spread of literacy, in terms of reading and writing. At this point, what was meant by literacy was quite specific. Nowadays, however, what is meant by the term "literacy" is subject to the fraying and blurring of a multiplicity of genres. Consequently, a redefinition of new and hitherto taken for granted concepts around what constitutes literate behaviour is desperately required, as representation moves away from writing to embrace a variety of images, opening up a new chapter in literacy research.

In essence, how do teachers learn to become more experienced in order to become more vigilant concerning what conditions truly support literacy, particularly for children of poverty or for those who have been labeled "at-risk"? Although these ideological considerations cannot be dealt with in short order, it may be helpful to look briefly at how definitions of literacy have changed as a result of changing economies, cultures, institutions and possible worlds that we inhabit (Cooper and White, 2006).

– A literate person is a person who can, with understanding, both read and write a short, simple statement on his everyday life (UNESCO, 1951).
– Functional literacy is the ability to engage effectively in all those reading activities normally expected of a literate adult in his community (Hunter and Harman, 1979).

- [Literacy is] using print and written information to function in society, to achieve one's goals, and to develop one's knowledge and potential (Southam Literacy, 1987).
- Literacy is the ability to identify, understand, interpret, create, communicate and compute using printed and written materials associated with varying contexts. Literacy involves a continuum of learning to enable an individual to achieve his or her goals, to develop his or her knowledge and potential, and to participate fully in the wider society (UNESCO, 2008).

Suffice it to say that what has been considered to constitute literacy has expanded over the fifty-odd years that these definitions have been in place. Since that time, however, literacy has evolved along with the evolution of the computer. In effect, it may be insufficient to equate literacy only with print media. As Sefton-Green (2003, 2001) suggests, nowadays, the term "literacy" is in reality a misnomer for it really applies to far more than merely being able to read and write; that is, it applies to more than being able to decode and encode script. This expanded, and quite possibly appropriated, notion of literacy can be problematic when some use the definition of yore, while others are using the term in a more modern iteration, particularly when used to express contexts within subject areas and disciplines which have not commonly or previously been associated with literacy.

In fact, the term literacy can mean many different things to different people, depending on ontological and epistemological cleavages. For instance, if ontology refers to a basic truth or understanding about knowledge, and if epistemology refers to how that truth is represented (Willis, 2007), then one's ontological worldview directly impacts upon one's epistemic beliefs and how those beliefs are to be represented. For example, if literacy means to be "lettered", that is, to be able to read and write, epistemologically speaking, reading and writing are going to be the sole representations of this worldview. Literacy will be tightly tied, then, to print media alone. However, if literacy is understood ontologically as a system of meaning making which can epistemologically be represented through a variety of systems of meaning making, literacy then engenders a multiplicity of ways that meaning can be represented and interpreted.

This chapter uses the broader definition of literacy and takes it to mean any form of encoding or decoding of any system of meaning. As a consequence, a significant portion of this chapter provides examples and attempts to understand these new and emerging literacies in the context of the new millennium.

CRITICAL THINKING AND CRITICAL PEDAGOGY

Definitions are political (Willinsky, 1994), and the following definitions help to reveal and define the political leanings of this chapter. In this section, Critical Thinking and Critical Pedagogy are compared and contrasted. Critical Literacy is then situated as a subset of Critical Pedagogy. The examination of these components of criticality is important in order to clarify the role that each plays in development of a Critically Literate citizenship. Firstly, the term "critical" has generally been defined as an attitude of questioning or skepticism regarding commonly accepted ideas and ideologies. In educational settings, the term "critical" is embedded in three related concepts; Critical Pedagogy, Critical Thinking and Critical Literacy (Cooper and White, 2008).

Critical Pedagogy traditionally and historically has raised questions regarding inequalities of power, issues of meritocracy and how belief systems become internalized. Unlike Critical Thinking, Critical Pedagogy demonstrates an agenda that seeks out potential for change whereas Critical Thinking advocates the analyzing of our individual lives on the basis of choices made; in short, the living of an examined life. Neither Critical Thinking nor Critical Pedagogy is monolithic or homogeneous, although each one evinces some characteristics of the other (Burbules and Berk, 1999). Lankshear and McLaren (1993) recognized that while Critical Thinking and Critical Literacy are regularly and erroneously conflated, each term means different things for different educators with different world views, depending on whether one subscribes to psychological or sociological theoretical models.

CRITICAL LITERACY

Critical Literacy develops the capacity to read and represent, linking the development of self-efficacy, an attitude of inquiry, and the desire to effect positive social change and, not surprisingly, Critical Literacy is frequently described as a theory with implications for practice rather than as an instructional methodology (Behrman, 2006)). Being critically literate, therefore, represents an attitude towards history, politics and social systems in opposition to a dominant power (Shor, 1999). Situating this notion sociologically, Luke (1997) suggests that these critical approaches to literacy necessitate "a shift away from psychological and individualistic models of reading and writing towards those approaches that use sociological, cultural and discourse theory to re-conceptualize the literate subject, textual practices, and classroom pedagogy"(143).

By way of explanation, sociological theories are comprised of complex theoretical frameworks used by sociologists to explain and analyze variously how social action, social processes and social structures work. While cultural theories may be closely related to sociological theories, these theories suggest that cultures exhibit or demonstrate ways in which humans interpret their environment. According to this point of view, culture becomes an integral part of the human environment, and as such, is definitive of human nature. Distinct from both sociological and cultural theories, discourse theory is a framework that offers a representational language for examining contextually dependent meaning in discourse. Individual sentences as well as the context of a dialogue play important roles in deriving meaning from the represented dialogue, conversation or text.

Edelsky and Cherland (2006) believe that Critical Literacy instruction has certain defining features including the critique of social systems of dominance, injustice and privilege. It calls for systemic change and, as a result, Critical Literacy instruction worthy of the name is offered by teachers with strong predilections for noting systemic privilege and engaging students in using literacy to work against systems of injustice (Altwerger and Saavedra, 1999).

Luke, (1997) describes Critical Literacy as "a commitment to reshape literacy education in the interests of marginalized groups of learners, who on the basis of gender, cultural and socioeconomic background have been excluded from access to the discourses and texts of dominant economics and cultures" (143). Gee (1996) and Edelsky and Cherland (2006) support this description of Critical Literacy. Central to this is the notion of dialogue, or in Freire's terms, "reading the word" and "reading the world" (Freire and Macedo, 1987).

However, in order to be Critically Literate in the new millennium, it is not sufficient to be proficient merely in reading and writing; one must be able to truly "read the world". This requires individuals to become not only Critically Literate in terms of reading and writing, but also in other forms of expression and interaction as well. Both Habermas (1990) and Barth (2002) honored individual perceptions and envisioned a multiplicity of perspectives by reducing traditional power hierarchies through equitable discussion. Although, terms such as Critical Thinking and Critical Literacy continue to be used in a technical manner rather than with a sociological perspective, it remains that Critical Thinking is a necessary precursor to Critical Literacy. Critical Literacy may be understood in terms of the dynamics of identity, context and teaching practices as the intimate and recursive relationships between language, representation and power develop within and become part of teachers' professional dialogue. (Cooper and White, 2008).

But how does Critical Literacy differ from plain old-fashioned ordinary literacy? Perhaps this is not so difficult a question after all. Perhaps the real question is not so much, "What is Critical Literacy?" as "What is NOT Critical Literacy?" For example, knowing how to withdraw money from a bank definitely has a critical edge to it, for if one were not able to do this, how would one live? Perhaps the alternative to this is to become a ward of the state and depend on social programs to keep body and soul together. As for the literacy part, this is something that people who have money in banks often take for granted. To illustrate that this is indeed a literacy that is worthwhile practicing, imagine that you are trying to withdraw money from your bank account in a country such as China. Unless you are fluent in the language and can receive instructions, or are fluent in the myriad ways that money can be withdrawn from banks around the world, you could find yourself in serious distress for the simple reason that you are unable to access the system of meaning. As this influences your own well being in a very direct way, the system of literacy that you are attempting to access can rapidly become Critical, in that it can influence your health and welfare.

Or, to use a more dynamic example, driving a car requires that you are both literate in the ways of navigating, reading signs and obeying laws as well as having the disposition to do so (Capper, 1993). It is this disposition that makes good driving an appropriate metaphor for Critical Literacy. Imagine the carnage if you had either no ability to drive or did not care about your fellow citizens. It is this element of literacy then, that makes most literacies Critical – the willingness and the capacity to recognize how these systems of meaning contribute to the betterment of society.

In the manipulation of the multiple systems of meaning-making that people encounter during their daily lives, there is a performance aspect to being literate in today's world that is absent in the traditional sense of merely being able to read and write. In today's society one must be able to not only comprehend the myriad systems of meaning, but one must also be able to manipulate them or perform in order to meet many of our most basic needs or to guarantee the basic needs of others for the general betterment of society. Literacy itself may is passive, but Critical Literacy has an active component to it. In short, we DO Critical Literacy.

In essence, Critical Literacy entails more than an operating knowledge of a vocabulary or a system of meaning; it is also a way of being, doing or performing. As Shor and Pari (1999) claim, Critical Literacy challenges the status quo in an effort to discover alternate pathways for social and self-development. Critical Literacy is, therefore, largely attitudinal:

> This kind of literacy – words rethinking worlds, self-disserting in society – connects the political and the personal, the public and the private, the global and the local, the economic and the pedagogic, for reinventing our lives and for promoting justice in the place of inequity (Shor and Pari, 1999, 1).

All literacies, then, have the potential to be Critical, since all literacies as systems of meaning have the power to include or exclude. All literacies may be viewed as systems of meaning that can provide or deny power in the form of access to equitable and equal benefits, treatments and privileges enjoyed by those who have access to those literacies (Shor and Pari, 1999).

At the end of the day, while there are many literacies that can be noted, they only become Critical Literacies when they are employed for the practice of self empowerment, social justice or the improvement of political, legal and judicial systems.

EMERGENT LITERACIES

Distinctions continue to be made between so-called "traditional" literacy and the aptly named "digital" literacies, distinguished by the fact that digital information is accelerated, media-saturated and automated (Jones-Kavalier and Flannigan, 2006). What these traditional and digital systems of meaning-making share is that they all represent modes of communication (Street, 1995) and use the same skills that have been used for centuries, namely analysis, synthesis and evaluation (Jones-Kavalier and Flannigan, 2006).

There are a number of so-called digital literacies, some of which are subsets of larger domains of computer and information technology (CIT). Computer Literacy refers to the knowledge and ability that is required to be able to use computers and technology efficiently. An associated literacy relates to the understanding of how computers function. Among subsets of computer literacy is Internet literacy. Additional literacies may include photo-visual literacy, reproduction literacy, branching literacy, information literacy and socio-emotional literacy (Yoram, 2004). Given the breadth of the field, it is little wonder that any precise definition of computer literacy can be quite elusive.

Media literacy can be conceptualized as an expansion of computer literacy and, as such, can be considered as part of the digital literacy family. Like most digital literacies, media literacy is an interactive process that entails the accessing, creation, analysis and evaluation of information messages through a variety of media modes, genres and forms. Media literacy also avails itself of opportunities to assist individuals in becoming more critically aware of bias, censorship, propaganda and disinformation in print and digital programming, including how funding and ownership issues contribute to encouraging distortion in information technologies. As such, media literacy lends itself to critical examination. Through the eyes of Wikipedia:

> Media literacy aims to enable people to be skillful creators and producers of media messages, both to facilitate an understanding as to the strengths and limitations of each medium, as well as to create independent media. By transforming the process of media consumption into an active and critical process, people gain greater awareness of the potential for misrepresentation and manipulation (especially through commercials and public relations techniques), and understand the role of mass media and participatory media in constructing views of reality (Wikipedia, 2008b).

Similar to media literacy, multimedia literacy is rapidly receiving recognition through the simultaneous use of a variety of media to convey information. Combinations of text, audio, graphics, animation, video and interactivity are becoming more common representations of multimedia literacy. Other forms of multimedia literacy, such as virtual reality, computer programming and robotics are possible candidates for future inclusion (Wikipedia, 2008c).

Electracy combines "electrical" with "literacy" to describe the facility of being able to explore the communicative potential of a widening range of new electronic media such as multimedia, hypermedia, social software, and virtual worlds. Electracy also encompasses broader cultural, institutional, pedagogical and ideological implications inherent in transitioning between a print literacy to a culture saturated with electronic media (Ulmer, 2003, 1989). According to Inman (2003):

> It is important to distinguish electracy from other terms, such as computer-based literacy, Internet literacy, digital literacy, electronic literacies, metamedia literacy, and even cyber-punk literacy. None of these other terms have the breadth electracy does as a concept, and none of them draw their ontology from electronic media exclusively (52).

Information and media literacy (IML) is a combination of information literacy and media literacy. In order to be able to engage in a digital society; one needs to not only have the ability and the disposition (Capper, 1993), but also the means to use, understand, inquire, create, communicate and think critically. Of equal importance are the capacity, disposition and means to be able to effectively access, organize, analyze, evaluate, and create messages in a variety of forms. The transformative nature of IML allows for creative works and the creation of new knowledge; to publish and collaborate responsibly requires ethical, cultural and social understanding (Wikipedia, 2008a) of a Critically Literate nature.

Perhaps all such methods of communication in the forms of texts, events and practices as they appear across modes and media can be included under the banner of "literacy", misnomer or not. Thus, lettered representation (Kress and Van Leeuven, 2006) could be considered no more a literacy than would other modes of communication, such as oracy, sculpture or sign language. As Jackie Marsh (this volume) suggests, the production and analysis of multimodal, multimedia texts can be embedded within curricular frameworks. In this way, then, emphasis can be placed on developing the learners' skills across all modes and media, obliterating any distinction between traditional or other, more digital literacies. In fact, in response to new literacies and new technologies, along with related theoretical viewpoints, school textbooks have already come a long way in support of this notion.

Design and textual production has taken on a new dimension in view of the fact that children are learning to read differently than they have done in the past. As a result of video game technology, students reveal greater ambiguity about where to begin on the text page. This phenomenon has been noted since the days of "Pac-man", with students attempting to view the page as a "gestalt". This is to say, students no longer necessarily begin to read from the top left corner of the page to the bottom right corner, progressing in a linear fashion. To "map the page" nowadays, students use a variety of methods borrowed from video-gaming that are only just now being recognized as reading strategies. To be fair to video-games, other influences on reading strategies include greater exposure – in this age of diversity and mass human movements to far flung parts of the world and back again – to other cultures that do not necessarily make use of left to right, top to bottom reading strategies and to increasing valorization of visual media over linear, two-dimensional print media as a means of communication in general.

In order to reduce the impact that this must have upon print media, publishing companies have fought back in the only way they can. Their strategy is simple – if you can't beat them, join them. Text features now include many things that hold student interest, guide the progression of the reading selection and provide additional information through sidebars for students who wish to augment their learning. The use of fact boxes, diagrams, charts and tables, as well as photographs, cutaways and magnifications help to inform the process of understanding. Timelines and maps also help to explain data in ways other than through or in conjunction with the printed word. In terms of print features, it is common to find "easements" such as bold or coloured print, italics or bullets. Captions and labels complement large areas of print, and titles and headings are commonplace in helping to break long passages.

Even for the purist, there are a variety of literacies that are taken for granted in today's literacy currency. While not an exclusive list, some of these include reading and writing, oracy, numeracy, encryption and logo literacy (Cooper and White,

2006). Reading depends on the decoding of a system of symbols, the alphabet, which in turn represents a writing system made up of graphemes, representing consonant and vowel sounds. Conversely, writing is the representation, or encoding, of language in a textual, typically two-dimensional medium through the use of a set of the same signs and set of systems that reading makes use of. While reading and writing may be inverse practices relating to one another, the learning of these practices may not necessarily be so and may require quite disparate skills and skill sets.

The term "oracy", coined by Andrew Wilkinson, a British researcher and educator, in the 1960s was formed by analogy from literacy and numeracy (MacLure, 1988) and was intended to draw attention to the neglect of oral skills in education. Numeracy has been with us as a type of literacy for a relatively long time. It originated as a portmanteau word standing for "numerical literacy" (UK Committee on Education, 1959) and refers to the ability to reason with numbers and mathematical concepts. In some areas, numeracy is also known as Quantitative Literacy. There is also substantial overlap between concepts of numeracy and statistical literacy.

Encryption can be considered as another form of literacy and is the process by which information is encoded using an algorithm, or cipher, to make it unreadable to anyone except those possessing the key for the decryption of the information. The process for encryption and decryption is typically a mirror-image process, where one who encrypts possesses the means to decrypt and vice versa.

Logo literacy is a relatively new development as immigration becomes more commonplace. As it became evident that pictures were needed to accompany signs written in the language of the dominant culture, logos have seen a huge proliferation. A logo is a graphical element in the form of a symbol, emblem, picture or ideogram that identifies areas, places, functions, directions or information. Logos are also frequently used to identify organizations and commercial or non-commercial entities.

Sign language is also commonly used as a system of meaning using manual communication rather than sound, text or pictures to convey meaning. One of the more common forms of sign language is American Sign Language (ASL) which combines hand signs with gestures and facial expressions to express thoughts. Sign languages have typically developed in communities of the Deaf and frequently include interpreters, friends and families of people who are hearing impaired. ASL is the dominant sign language of the Deaf community in the United States, in the English-speaking parts of Canada, and in parts of Mexico. Although the United Kingdom and the United States share English as a spoken and written language, British Sign Language (BSL) is quite different from ASL, and the two sign languages are not mutually intelligible (Wikipedia, 2008).

Artifactual Literacy (Pahl and Rowsell, this volume) comes to making meaning through form and its meaning. The power of this literacy focuses on what materials can or can not do. Simply put, materiality lends power to meaning because such powerful artifacts represent strong potential for meaning-making, Artifactual Literacy in the form of two-dimensional and three-dimensional representation can also be included as an emerging form of literacy. Two-dimensional representations commonly refer to paintings and related works of art. Literally, painting means to apply pigment to canvas or other medium that will support the artistic process. A few mediums include, but are not limited to, paper, canvas, wood, glass, and concrete in combination with drawing, composition and other aesthetic considerations that may manifest expressive and conceptual intentions and interpretations of both the represcnter and the viewer. According to Wikipedia (2008d):

> Painting is used as a mode of representing, documenting and expressing all the varied intents and subjects that are as numerous as there are practitioners of the craft. Paintings can be naturalistic and representational (as in a still life or landscape painting), photographic, abstract, be loaded with narrative content, symbolism, emotion or be political in nature.

Three-dimensional representations usually are considered to be "sculptures". Most commonly, sculptures such as statues may be free-standing and can be viewed and interpreted from a variety of angles and perspectives. Sculpture may also be attached to a background to form various types of "reliefs". Site-specific art, or installation art, is a form of sculpture as is kinetic sculpture that involves physical motion. Such variety allows for a multiplicity of experiences both creative and interpretive. As such, artistic endeavours represent systems of meaning, albeit often not easily understood and frequently open to interpretation.

The theory of multiple intelligences was developed in 1983 by Dr. Howard Gardner of Harvard University, and has added significantly to our understanding of intelligences and therefore to our recognition of what constitutes different systems of meaning. Gardner (1983) proposed eight different intelligences, or literacies, to account for a broader range of human systems of meaning-making. These intelligences include the capacity to become literate in print media, such as reading and writing, logical-mathematical endeavours such as numerical literacy and the ability to reason with numbers, as well as spatial intelligence, or a capacity to develop literacy in abstract and concrete dimensions such as two- and three-dimensional art and representations. Gardner has also recognized "intelligences" such as Musical intelligence, Bodily-Kinesthetic intelligence, Interpersonal and Intrapersonal intelligence, as well as Naturalist intelligence. Each and every one of these "intelligences" represents, I believe, the capacity to form a system of meaning that can become a "literacy" in its own right.

Currently, schooling tends to valorize and validate linguistic and logical-mathematical literacy above other forms of literacies, but Gardner (1983) contends that we should also attend to individuals who are gifted in different ways. This concern is expressed by numerous researchers (Eisner, 1995; Greene, 1991; Marcuse, 1964). Many artists, including those in the representational and performing arts, including naturalists, designers, dancers, therapists, entrepreneurs, and others who enrich the world in which we live must often develop their own literacies – their own capacities to develop specific systems of meaning-making – without the benefit of formal education or schooling in these areas of literacy.

Perhaps it is such capacities, dispositions and means as those represented above that Bourdieu and Passeron (1979) are pointing to in their discussion of the sociological concept of habitus as cultural, social and symbolic capital. As a result of the connections between changing social environments facing students and teachers and new multiliteracy approaches to pedagogy, the multiplicity of communications channels and increasing cultural and linguistic diversity in the world today call for a much broader view of literacy than those portrayed by traditional language-based approaches. Such multiple literacies have the potential to overcome limitations that plague traditional approaches. Such innovations emphasize how negotiating multiple linguistic and cultural differences in our society has become central to achieving literacy by creating access to the evolving language of work, power and community, and by fostering critical engagement for students to design their social futures (The New London Group, 1996).

Teachers and administrators are under considerable pressure to meet two goals; to better support all student's literacy development and to be responsive to other learning and literacy needs. These include, but are not limited to linguistic and print-based literacies, such as, reading and writing; technological literacies, such as logo literacy; mathematical literacies such as numeracy, estimation and finances; and scientific, research, media, cultural, family, English and aesthetic literacies (PhD Program Proposal, 2008). Consequently, it can be said that all literacies, accepted as such, are critical since an understanding of each can, in its own way, be critical to one's well being.

SUMMARY AND CONCLUSION

In *Gulliver's Travels*, long a favourite of mine, our hero, Lemuel Gulliver, travels to the land of Balnibarbi where people have opted to relinquish the power of speech in favour of showing one another what they intend. The proposal to substitute objects for words is similar to an actual proposal made by Sprat, historian of the Royal Society of England. Sprat wanted the Society's reports written in a mathematically plain style that would contain pictures of everything mentioned. This style, as a result, would have virtually as many pictures as words (CliffsNotes, 2008).

While this may (doubtfully) embody some of the components of Habermas's (1990) Ideal Speech Situation, such as intelligibility, truthfulness, sincerity and justification, the "speakers" needed to carry with them any items that they wished to demonstrate. Consequently, people were soon seen wandering about with huge packs of things on their backs and eventually were reduced to waiting patiently in one place because they could no longer move about under the weight of all their "words". Unfortunately, no one else could move about either, so the entire populace became islands unto themselves, surrounded by artifacts that no one would ever be able to enjoy, share or use to bring about change. So these people sat, silently, islands of objects surrounded by a sea of silence. Clearly this form of literacy could not survive unsupported by other forms of literacy. It is in this way that literacies can be seen to be *not* mutually exclusive. In fact, the more literacies that one has at his or her disposal, the greater the ability to advocate on behalf of themselves and others. It is also in this way that Critical Literacy can ensure social, political and emancipatory inclusion for all individuals and groups of individuals within any given society.

However, it is essential to recognize that multiple literacies are neither a panacea nor an antidote to cure society's ills. Regarding this caveat, Warschauser (2003) suggests that social relations, human capital, culture and language are all critical for shaping people's access to and use of new information and communication technologies and, I would hasten to add, all existent traditional and historical literacies. While technology and, in truth, all existing literacies can and should act as intellectual and social amplifiers, those who tend to be marginalized through lack of access, benign neglect or systemic exclusion tend to become further marginalized. In the words of Anderson and Irvine:

> Literacy is understood as social action through language use that develops us inside a larger culture, while Critical Literacy is understood as "learning to read and write as part of the process of becoming conscious of one's experience as historically constructed within specific power relations" (1993, 2).

The essence of Critical Literacy is that it takes into consideration how a variety of systems of meaning help to reproduce or transform domination through the provision of access to those methods by which systems of meaning can be decoded or encoded. The goals of Critical Literacy are to incorporate the development of self-confidence and self-esteem, which, in turn, has the potential to benefit not only the individual but also the society in general. Critical Literacy may be viewed as having at least three supporting dimensions; the operational, the cultural and the critical. This has the potential to give rise to a new meta-language inter-playing and interfacing among language, meaning and context (Lankshear and Knobel, 1998) which may have the intended or unintended benefit of democratizing cultural production (Sefton-Green, 2003). Consequently, school curricula, rather than valorizing print-only media, may be in the process of becoming poised to recognize the linguistic, social, economic and cultural capital that students bring to school (Walsh, 2007).

Literacy, then, and Critical Literacy not excepted, has moved from a primarily passive state to being something in which people can engage. People can actively engage in Critically Literate thought processes that exist within the interstices between the mode of literacy practice and its manipulation. Consequently, literacy is no longer an abstraction of skills manifested on paper to be used as a tool for inclusion or exclusion, but has the potential to determine social activity located within interactions between people. Perhaps it is this interaction which has the potential to make all forms of literacy at once more critical.

The more literacies one has, the more literate in the social sense one is. Therefore the more one is able to access and understand systems of meaning, the more successful one will be in negotiating the rapidly expanding diversity of our current social reality. This ability to negotiate the amazing variety of meaning systems is life enhancing. As such, these are necessary literacies and, therefore represent Critical Literacies.

REFERENCES

Altwerger, B., & Saavedra, E. R. (1999). Forward. In C. Edelsky (Ed.), *Making justice our project: Teachers working toward critical whole language practice* (pp. vii–xii). Urbana, IL: NCTE.

Anderson, G. L., & Irvine, P. (1993). Informing critical literacy with ethnography. In C. Lankshear & P. McLaren (Eds.), *Critical literacy; Politics, praxis and the postmodern* (pp. 81–104). Albany, NY: SUNY Press.

Author. (2008). *Doctor of Philosophy program in educational studies.* Unpublished Proposal. Prepared by the Inter-University Doctoral Program Proposal Committees of the Nova Scotia Inter-University Committee on Teacher Education (ICTE) of Acadia University, Mount Saint Vincent University, St. Francis Xavier University.

Barth, R. S. (2002). The culture builder. *Educational Leadership, 59*(8), 6–12.

Behrman, E. H. (2006). Teaching about language, power, and text: A review of classroom practices that support critical literacy. *Journal of adolescent and adult literacy, 49*(6), 480–488.

Bourdieu, P., & Passeron, J. C. (1979). *The inheritors: French students and their relation to culture.* Chicago: University Of Chicago Press.

Burbules, N. C., & Berk, R. (1999). Critical thinking and critical pedagogy: Relations, differences, and limits. In T. S. Popkewitz & L. Fendler (Eds.), *Critical theories in education.* New York: Routledge.

Capper, C. (1993). Educational administration in a pluralistic society: A multiparadigm approach. In C. Capper (Ed.), *Educational administration in a pluralistic society* (pp. 7–35). New York: SUNY Press.

CliffsNotes. (2008). *Gulliver's travels. Book III: A voyage to Laputa, Balnibarbi, Luggnagg, Glubbdubdrib, and Japan.* Retrieved April 6, 2008, from http://www.cliffsnotes.com/WileyCDA/LitNote/Gulliver-s-Travels-Summaries-and-Commentaries-Chapter-5.id-120,pageNum-69.html

Cooper, K., & White, R. E. (2008). Critical literacy for school improvement: An action research project. *Improving Schools, 11*(2), 103–115.

Cooper, K., & White, R. E. (2006). Critical literacy in action: Action research in a grade three classroom. In K. Cooper & R. E. White (Eds.), *The practical critical educator* (pp. 3–16). The Netherlands: Springer.

Crowther, Sir G. (1959). *UK committee on education.* Retrieved April 5, 2008, from Wikipedia http://en.wikipedia.org/wiki/Numeracy#cite_note-0

Edelsky, C., & Cherland, M. (2006). A critical issue in critical literacy: The "Popularity Effect". In K. Cooper & R. E. White (Eds.), *The practical critical educator* (pp. 17–34). The Netherlands: Springer.

Eisner, E. (1995). What artistically crafted research can help us understand about schools. *Educational Theory, 45*(1), 1–6.

Freire, P., & Macedo, D. (1987). *Literacy: Reading the world and the word.* South Hadley, MA: Begin Garvey.

Gardner, H. (1983). *Frames of mind: The theory of multiple intelligences.* Jackson, TN: Basic Books.

Gee, J. P. (1996). *Social linguistics and literacies.* London, UK: Taylor and Francis.

Goodman, K. (1967). Reading: A psycholinguistic guessing game. *Journal of the Reading Specialist, 6,* 126–135.

Graff, H. (1987). *The labyrinth of literacy.* London: Falmer Press.

Greene, M. (1991). Blue guitars and the search for curriculum. In G. Willis & W. Schubert (Eds.), *Reflections from the heart of educational inquiry: Understanding curriculum and teaching through the arts* (pp. 107–122). Albany, NY: State University of New York Press.

Habermas, J. (1990). *Moral consciousness and communicative action.* Cambridge, MA: MIT Press.

Hunter, C. S., & Harmon, D. (1979). *Adult illiteracy in the United States: A report to the Ford foundation.* New York: McGraw-Hill.

Inman, J. A. (2003). Electracy for the ages: Collaboration with the past and future. In J. A. Inman, C. Reed, & P. Sands (Eds.), *Electronic collaboration in the humanities: Issues and options* (p. 52). Mahwah, NJ: Lawrence Erlbaum Associates.

Jones-Kavalier, B. R., & Flannigan, S. L. (2006). Connecting the digital dots: Literacy of the 21st century. *Educase Quarterly, 29*(2), 211–214.

Khan, H. R., & Asaduzzaman (2007). Literate life expectancy in Bangladesh: A new approach of social indicator. *Journal of Data Science, 5,* 131–142.

Kress, G., & Van Leeuven, T. (2006). *Reading images: The grammar of visual design* (2nd ed.). London: Routledge.

Lankshear, C., & Knobel, M. (1998). *Critical literacy and new technologies.* Paper presented at American Educational Research conference, San Diego. Retrieved April 13, 2008, from http://www.geocities.com/c.lankshear/critlitnewtechs.html

Lankshear, C., & McLaren, P. (Eds.). (1993). *Critical literacy: Politics, praxis and the postmodern.* Albany, NY: SUNY Press.

Luke, A. (1997). Critical approaches to literacy. In V. Edwards & D. Corson (Eds.), *Encyclopedia of language and education, Vol. 2: Literacy* (pp. 143–151). The Netherlands: Kluwer Academic Publishers.

MacLure, M. (1988). Oracy: Current modes in context. In M. MacLure, T. Phillips, & A. Wilkinson (Eds.), *Oracy matters: The development of talking and listening in education.* Milton Keynes: Open University Press.

McMullen, J. (2006). *When literacy means life: The link between indigenous health and education.* Address to the UTS Library Market Forum. Retrieved April 5, 2008, from http://www.lib.uts.edu.au/sites/www.lib.uts.edu.au/files/5353_When_Literacy_Means_Life_2006.pdf

Macedo, D. (2006). *Literacies of power: What Americans are not allowed to know.* Jackson, TN: Westview Press.

Marcuse, H. (1964). *One-dimensional man: Studies in the ideology of advanced industrial society.* Boston: Beacon Press.

Mayher, J. (1990). *Uncommon sense: Theoretical practice in language education.* Portsmouth, NH: Boynton.

New London Group. (1996). A pedagogy of multiliteracies: Designing social futures. *Harvard Educational Review, 66*(1), 60–92.

Sefton-Green, J. (2003). Media literacy or media arts? Competing visions for the future? *Telemedium, 1*(Spring), 49–50.

Sefton-Green, J. (2001). Computers, creativity and the curriculum: The challenge for school, literacy and learning. *Journal of Adolescent and Adult Literacy, 44*(8), 726–728.

Shor, I. (1999). What is critical literacy? *Journal for Pedagogy, Pluralism and Practice, 4*(1). Retrieved April 6, 2008, from http://www.lesley.edu/journals//jppp/4/shor/html

Shor, I., & Pari, C. (1999). *Critical literacy in action: Writing words, changing worlds.* Portsmouth, NH: Boynton.

Southam Literacy. (1987). In P. Calamai (Ed.), *Broken words: Why five million Canadians are illiterate.* Toronto: Southam Press.

St.Clair, R. (2003). Poor beyond words: Literacy and poverty in North American social policy. *Canadian Society for the Study of Adult Education – Online Proceedings.* Retrieved April 5, 2008, from http://www.oise.utoronto.ca/CASAE/cnf2003/2003_papers/ralfstclairCAS03.pdf

Street, B. V. (1995). *Social literacies: Critical approaches to literacy in development, ethnography and education.* Upper Saddle River, NJ: Longman.

Street, B. V. (1984). *Literacy in theory and practice.* New York: Cambridge University Press.

Swift, J. (2005). *Gulliver's travels.* Oxford, UK: Oxford University Press.

Ulmer, G. L. (2003). *Internet invention: From literacy to electracy.* New York: Longman.

Ulmer, G. L. (1989). *Teletheory: Grammatology in the age of video.* New York: Routledge.

UNESCO. (1951). *A definition of fundamental education.* Retrieved July, 2005, from http://portal.unesco.org/education/en/ev.php-URL_ID=53553andURL_DO=DO_TOPICandURL_SECTION=201.html

UNESCO. (2008). *Definition of literacy.* Retrieved April 12, 2008, from http://portal.unesco.org/education/en/ev.php-URL_ID=53553andURL_DO=DO_TOPICandURL_SECTION=201.html

Wagner, D. A. (1993). *Literacy, culture and development: Becoming literate in Morocco.* Cambridge, UK: Cambridge University Press.

Walsh, C. S. (2007). Creativity as capital in the literacy classroom: Youth as multimodal designers. *Literacy, 41*(2), 79–85.

Warschauer, M. (2003). *Technology and social inclusion: Rethinking the digital divide.* Cambridge, MA: MIT Press.

Wikipedia. (2008). *American sign language.* Retrieved April 5, 2008, from http://en.wikipedia.org/wiki/American_Sign_Language

Wikipedia. (2008a). *Information and media literacy.* Retrieved April 12, 2008, from http://en.wikipedia.org/wiki/Information_and_media_literacy

Wikipedia. (2008b). *Media literacy.* Retrieved April 12, 2008, from http://en.wikipedia.org/wiki/Media_literacy

Wikipedia. (2008c). *Multimedia literacy.* Retrieved April 12, 2008, http://en.wikipedia.org/wiki/Multimedia_literacy

Wikipedia (2008d). *Painting.* Retrieved April 5, 2008, from http://en.wikipedia.org/wiki/Painter

Willinsky, J. (1994). *Empire of words: The reign of the OED.* Princeton, NJ: Princeton University Press.

Willis, J. (2007). *Foundations of qualitative research interpretive and critical approaches.* Thousand Oaks, CA: Sage.

Yoram, E.-A. (2004). Digital literacy: A conceptual framework for survival skills in the digital era. *Journal of Educational Multimedia and Hypermedia, 13*(1), 93–106.

CHAPTER 3

Critical Alternatives: Solutions to Ease Discrimination, Oppression, and Youth Violence

Historically, discrimination has been defined as unfavourable treatment based on prejudice, especially on the basis of race, colour, or sex. In this chapter, we attempt to raise awareness of another group at the receiving end of discriminatory practices, impoverished youth from large, modern, first-world democracies.

It is easier to portray violent youth as "dangerous others" with individually flawed characteristics or behaviour than it is to accept that we have collectively supported, or failed to address, the conditions of social injustice they endure. For parents, educators, psychologists, researchers, youth workers, and policy writers, violent youth have become the site for a sense of moral panic. From a psycho-analytic perspective, it is not unexpected that anxiety over widespread exposure to youth violence via the media pushes us to suppress acknowledgement of our responsibility for the oppression triggering expressions of violence by youth. For our protection, we resist the moral panic that surfaces when awareness of youth violence becomes inescapable; for example, as we are informed by the media of a mass murder at a school.

Traditionally, it has been easier to view violent youth as "bad kids" or "juvenile delinquents" who need to change their characteristics or behaviour than face the fact that we, as a society, might be neglectful and in need of behavioural change. While it has been observed that it "takes a village to raise a child", we no longer live in villages. For the most part, in large modern democracies, we now live in large urban centres. Thus, there is a need to create a new kind of village in which to raise our children. Collectively, society assumes responsibility for younger generations and must embrace youth violence as a societal concern. Consequently, society must face its own moral outrage and panic, and adjust not only its behaviour, but those social structures that have been created which oppress youth.

Fine and Burns (2003) highlighted the fact that, for poor and working class youth in North America, no social movement exists that could be considered equivalent to the powerful feminist, civil rights, disability rights, or gay rights movements. Yet, youth have less power and autonomy than adults do. Professionals who serve them can help to bring issues that concern youth to a critical level of public awareness. Youth deserve their own movement to develop public awareness and subsequent action to counteract the discrimination and oppression they experience. Alternatively, critical educators and critical psychologists could create a forum for disenfranchised youth to speak for themselves. Such oracy, a form of Critical Literacy, would allow youth to voice their own experiences, tell their own stories,

K. Cooper and R. E. White (eds.), Critical Literacies in Action: Social Perspectives and Teaching Practices, 37–48.

and advocate for social changes in the name of social justice. In much the same way, Critical psychology could, in turn, create community networks of parents, educators, and youth workers to address social problems affecting all of society.

CRITICAL LITERACY

Like critical psychology, Critical Literacy or critical pedagogy refer to the attempt to make invisible assumptions and practices affecting individuals and society visible by identifying what is not working in traditional approaches and structures, then offering solutions and alternatives. Critical Literacy theorists view economic, social, and educational practice as inextricably linked: therefore, "literacy" can be understood only in relation to how it privileges some groups over others (Franzak, 2006). Schools and their policy-makers do not adequately support the role of text analyst, a potential Critical Literacy strategy, which may help all students understand how the text positions them with respect to social patterns of power and language usage. Luke (cited in Cooper and White, 2006, 97) stated that critical approaches to literacy involve helping at-risk learners give voice to their ideas, accepting what they have to say, finding ways to help them tell their stories, and conceptualizing their original life experience. In short, this allows youth to speak, write, and integrate what they read with what they live. This is a proven approach to develop a desire to read and increase self-knowledge, along with knowledge of diverse cultures (Cooper and White, 2006). For a group of urban, inner-city Toronto readers they studied, Cooper and White (2006) found that public expenditures on education were so low that youth were not supplied with adequate resources to develop basic literacy skills, let alone become motivated readers via text analysis.

What insights can Critical Literacy contribute to finding solutions to youth violence? Critical Literacy can be understood in terms of the dynamics of identity, context, and teaching practices employed. Daiute and Fine (2003) note that schools currently reproduce class, gender relations, and privilege. Students may be alienated from an official curriculum that does not include their histories, lived experiences, interests, and backgrounds. After years of exposure to the dangerous memories of exclusion, students learn to mask their fears of inadequacy and alienation through gaining acceptance from their peers, who sometimes form a violent sub-culture (Caruthers, 2005). Critical educators allow and encourage the establishing of positive relationships with students through using students' backgrounds and interests to engage them in school and offer an alternative to validation through identification with peers and a potentially violent sub-culture. However, the majority of teachers work under conditions that cause them to wear "politically correct" straitjackets. Working outside of the traditional curricula and organizational structure is discouraged. Engaged and innovative teachers may be stifled as a result (Cooper and White, 2006). This is unfortunate, as it is this very important relationship between engaged, innovative teachers and potentially alienated youths that can make a vital difference in the youth's toxic social setting. In the absence of such positive interventions, "civilized oppression" (Harvey, 1999) in the form of benign neglect is often an unfortunate result.

THE AVOIDANCE OF AWARENESS

Oppression can be viewed as the experience of repeated, widespread, and systemic injustice (Deutsch, 2006). Such "civilized oppression", Harvey (1999) refers to as vast and deep injustices which are supported through cultural stereotypes, the media, and bureaucracies, as well as market mechanisms. Certainly, youth, particularly those living in impoverished neighbourhoods, suffer from "civilized oppression".

To continue to think and act within the confines of traditional theoretical boundaries, we construct race, class, and gender as "static" or "essential" categories used as a basis to "discriminate" against individuals and groups. However, discrimination can also occur due to age and generation (youth), status (impoverishment), and community and location (such as First Nations members on reserves in the most barren lands in Canada, North African and Black youth in "quartiers sensibles" in France, and recent immigrants in big-city slums in Canada and the U.S). Both public and academic discourse has created restrictive perceptions that often remain unchallenged. Society often allocates blame to violent youth without acknowledging how we have contributed to social conditions leading to such discrimination, social injustice, and oppression that ultimately fuel violent reactions.

"URBAN VIOLENCE" AS A "VOICE" FOR YOUTH

In her paper, "Deconstructing youth violence in French cities", Body-Gendrot (2005) suggested that each time the term violence is used, it serves to reduce a whole range of behaviours to an ambiguous symbolic idea. As the questions surfacing in societies change, the use of the word is reconstructed to serve new purposes. As the social agenda shifts, so do definitions of violence.

In North America, in the 1960s society was concerned with interpersonal violence and all citizens were included as potential perpetrators of interpersonal violence. By the 1980s, the subject of the discussion shifted from "we" to "them". An overriding concern was, "Why are the urban poor involved in so many violent crimes"? This shift permitted construction of the "dangerous other", allowing individuals to defend against having to reflect on their own sins of omission, or commission, in the co-creation and avoidance of dealing with urban poor in their communities. By so doing, mentally and materially, we can keep "dangerous others" at a distance (in "quartiers sensibles" in France and "First Nations reserves" in Canada or inner-city slums in the U.S.A.).

By the 21st century, the terms "urban violence" or "violent urban youth" serve as symbols of multifaceted, and often unexplored, emotional and moral tensions (Body-Gendrot, 2005). Western societies are highly anxious and do not know how to deal with such anxieties, not having fully identified what is triggering these anxieties. In France, the "dangerous other" feeling has been projected on urban male youth—mainly young men from North Africa, or other parts of the African continent.

Body-Gendrot chaired a European network examining the dynamics of violence in Europe and observed that some Western countries construct their "dangerous others" out of soccer hooligans, racial minorities, and asylum seekers. Such "dangerous others" are associated with car burnings and aggression towards their teachers and fellow students. They have been mentally kept at a distance by both educators and psychologists who label them juvenile delinquents (Blatier, 1999a, 1999b). This terminology clearly permits a "blame the dangerous other" social construction.

At a more practical level, educators, in concert with clinical psychologists, have created operational definitions for violent youth. Fortin and Favre (2000) identified aggressive adolescents in Canadian and French secondary schools as sharing the following characteristic or externalized behaviours which include defiance and aggression; lack of social skills; attention and concentration problems; and frequent high levels of anxiety and depression.

SOCIAL TOXICITY: POVERTY AND VIOLENCE

What children live in poverty? In Europe and North America, as in many other parts of the world, the income discrepancy between the affluent and poor continues to widen. The most affluent nations have the greatest differences between the poor and the top earners. Incredibly, in the U.S.A., 40% of all children live in poverty. Poverty is defined as not having enough money to meet the basic needs of food, shelter and clothing (Pagani, Boulerice, Vitaro, and Tremblay, 1999). In Canada, the average rate of poverty across the country is 25% (however, 56% of First Nations children live in substandard conditions) although impoverished children are concentrated in certain large urban centres (a full 60% in Montreal and Toronto combined). 52% of all impoverished children are recent immigrants. By way of contrast, only 8% of children live in poverty in France (average for the EU) (Economic Policy Institute, 2007; UNICEF Innocenti Research Centre, 2007).

How is poverty connected to violence? More specifically, how do the "dangerous others" constructed by society (i.e., the violent urban youth of France and the young offenders of Canada) end up using aggressive or criminal acts as a response to their poverty? According to Garbarino (1999) social toxicity leads to violence. He refers to social toxicity as social environments that are so lacking in all conditions needed for healthy development, that youth do not believe that authorities, institutions, and social arrangements are just. In modern industrialized nations with the highest rates of homicide, child poverty, single-parent families, schools that are dangerous, drive-by shootings, and alcohol and drug addictions, there are also the highest rates of violent adolescent acts, including murder, theft, and vandalism.

Crenshaw and Garbarino (2007) noted that the very children constructed as "bad kids" or "juvenile delinquents" by their parents, teachers, and psychologists, are the same ones who have suffered a maximum amount of discrimination and oppression. They have failed to receive the support needed from the adults in their lives. Often, their parents are affected by extreme poverty, lack of education/work, psychiatric disorders, imprisonment, addictions, and/or exposure to violence amongst others. These burdens mean that children may learn early on in life that the world is a place of privilege for some but not for others. Often, the schools they attend perpetuate this social injustice.

As a result, social toxicity has increased, rather than decreased, in recent generations. Yet, social policy continues to pursue interventions aimed at changing individuals or families instead of pursuing interventions aimed at changing social opportunities. In North America, the culture promotes the myth of meritocracy so strongly that there is an entrenched belief that children need to change themselves in order to rise above their socially toxic backgrounds. In other words, the role of the professional is to help them improve their personal resilience so that social toxicity will not have such a strong impact on them. Of course, this insulates society in general and its citizens in particular from having to address social injustice. Further to this is the underlying assumption that if we could simply identify resilient characteristics, we could promote them. Thus, resilient children can be "self-made" and rise above all harsh conditions they face. At best, this is a naïve approach.

France has a public rhetoric that articulates care and concern towards all citizens. Yet, immigrant youth, specifically those who are Black and of North African origin, are shut out of the upward mobility ladders that count: jobs, economic security, and status (Centre d'analyse stratégique: République Française, 2007). There is a public articulation of care and concern (solidarity), in France. However, at the same time concern is expressed, action and change are barely perceptible. Almost no progress has been made over several generations to adequately integrate, house, and employ North African and Black youth. For generations, youth of North African and Black origin have lived in the same deteriorating social housing complexes, tenderly named, "les quartiers sensibles" (sensitive neighbourhoods). Progress has not been made in changing adult mobility ladders for them. Recent research has clearly demonstrated that such individuals do not even get interviewed for jobs on the basis of discrimination due to their origins (Duguet, Leandri, L'Horty, and Petit, 2007).

In France, social welfare provisions, including social housing, strong monetary stipends for the unemployed, and accessible, subsidized day-care, mean that fewer people live in poverty than in North America. Yet, in spite of their central myth of republican solidarity, the urban poor in France are seen to drain the resources that would be available to other French citizens "paying the freight". In a similar manner, despite generations of well-meaning public administrators and politicians trying to address the problems of First Nations citizens in Canada, a majority continue to live in poverty on reserves, out of sight – out of mind, in cold, barren rural settings. Canadian governments fail to support or adequately address the third-world conditions First Nations Canadians endure, while some citizens harbour negative feelings about "paying their freight" via taxation.

PRODUCTIVE WAYS OF VIEWING YOUTH

Michelle Fine (2006) points out that psychologists, and indeed educators as well, contribute to the social construction of "dangerous others" by promoting and maintaining the myth of meritocracy. This is the belief that life chances are determined by educational achievement, fuelled by the personality characteristics, drive, intelligence, and the disciplined behaviour of the individual. Historically, educators and psychologists have overwhelmingly and blindly endorsed a "God's eye view" (Harding, 1987) in research and practice. Traditional educators and their counterparts in psychology observe the "dangerous others", test them, describe them, diagnose them, and then propose treatment or incarceration based on the fundamental concept that each individual will succeed or fail as a result of their own efforts and merits.

Mainstream efforts have often focused on identifying internal sources of an adolescent's aggressive acts and delinquent behaviours (for example, reading difficulties, low intelligence as categorized by IQ, Attention Deficit Disorder, Oppositional Defiant Disorder, Conduct Disorder, Antisocial Personality Disorder or poor moral reasoning skills). (Prilleltensky, 1994; Prilleltensky and Prilleltensky, 2006). Clinical and forensic psychologists influence decisions by legal authorities in individual cases, via writing psychological reports, potentially influencing incarceration, while often failing to focus attention on social justice issues or attempting to address socially toxic environments (Fox, 1997).

As a result, efforts to locate the sources of an individual's behaviour mainly within the individual neglect both the causal role of the individual's interactions with others and the causal role of the social institutions in which those interactions are embedded. Critical educators and critical psychologists have challenged dominant societal values and the institutions that support them (Fox and Prilleltensky, 1997; Morsillo and Prilleltensky, 2007; Prilleltensky, 1994; Prilleltensky and Prilleltensky, 2006).

In Westernized societies people are generally encouraged to seek meaning through individual pursuits, such as careers, shopping, surfing the web, investing funds, purchasing and renovating homes, which provide benefit to the economic/capitalistic system. Such a philosophy of individualism may lead to a search for purely individual solutions, which generally leaves out the marginalized sectors of society. Therefore, it can be taken that individuals are expected to change themselves, rather than to change society. Thus, a critical approach poses the question, "Does a current neo-liberal stance tend to mislead people into identifying problems as purely individual?"

As Critical educators and psychologists evaluate theories and practices of psychology in terms of how society maintains an unjust and unsatisfying status quo, they find themselves paying attention to the welfare of oppressed and vulnerable individuals and groups, examining the social, moral, and political implications of research, theory, and practice (Prilleltensky, 1994). With such an agenda for change, society may benefit from a greater understanding of how to nurture more resilient children in particular cultural contexts by becoming more involved in the cultural contexts. We could then move from approaches where youth are assessed, labelled, and essentially stigmatised, to entering the setting of the youth, assessing the context, and working with others within it by creating school/community/home networks to change extant social conditions (Prilleltensky and Prilleltensky, 2006).

THE DIFFICULTY IN ADOPTING CRITICAL PRACTICES

Kurt Danziger (2007) addressed the fact that psychology really took off at the turn of the 20th century with the understanding that studying the individual would be the focus of psychology. However, this focus created a psychic blindness around social justice issues.

While both educators and psychologists focus on individual "juvenile delinquents", neither group is able to successfully see and examine the social phenomena that lead youth to violence, and the subsequent failure to promote social justice. Further, at a societal level, we fail to examine whether promoting social justice is a commonly held value. This may be due, in part, to the fact that, as educators and psychologists, we have generally been trained to avoid claiming particular value stances in the interests of remaining "objective" and "value-free" even though education, at least, is a value-laden enterprise.

What hope can a critical standpoint bring to youth to allow them to rise above the discrimination and oppression they experience? One solution described by Michael Unger (2006) consists of nurturing culturally specific hidden resilience. Resilience is a function of the resources children draw on, and co-create, in their environment, just as much as it is a unique intrinsic characteristic of the child. Unger (2006) points out that society can benefit from a shift in focus from conceiving of resilience as a "personality" variable, to understanding resilience as a culturally embedded event.

William Arsenio and Jason Gold (2006) note that positive attachments to adults are healthy and beneficial to children and youth. Children may benefit from an atmosphere of caring and fairness in families, schools, and communities, for they do not thrive in atmospheres of domination and power, chaos and disengagement. Educators and other caregivers impact the development of emotional and moral reciprocity and fairness. Attachment and moral development research has demonstrated that children's attachment status is largely a shared pattern of caregiver-child emotional reciprocity in which adults play the leading role. These patterns lead to children's mental representations of victimization and aggression and, as such, attachment patterns are foundational for children's' models of moral reciprocity and subsequent aggressive tendencies.

Arsenio and Gold (2006) identified two types of aggressive children's patterns: (a) some seem emotionally unmoved and unaffected by the consequences of their actions on victims (more a problem of emotional responsiveness than of social understanding); (b) some children have a relative inability to recognize and understand victims' reactions. For them, interventions to enhance perspective-taking and promote empathy have been demonstrated to have a significant impact.

According to Crenshaw and Garbarino (2007), youth in correctional settings have suffered major losses, often not recognized by others nor properly grieved by the youth. In addition, such youth have often not received adequate emotional support from the adults in their lives. These authors point out that a deep reservoir of sorrow often triggers their violence. They use the metaphor "Fawns in gorilla suits" to help read beneath the aggressive exterior of these youth to see them as the wounded, sensitive creatures they really are, recognizing the aggressive exterior as their emotional armour. Crenshaw and Garbarino make it evident that intervention programs for these youth need to allow avenues for them to safely explore their traumatic grief.

When youth experience a series of disrupted attachments, they disconnect from their affect and emotional expressions of all kinds are blunted. According to Crenshaw and Garbarino (2007), the rate of homicide of young Black youth in the U.S.A, aged 15-19, is six times that of white youth of the same age, and 20-50 times that of other youth the same age in other large democratic nations. How could the survivors of neighbourhoods where Black youth are concentrated not be emotionally wounded, having been exposed to a mix of poverty and neighbourhood violence that has brought about the loss of friends and family? They must do something with the profound sorrow and rage they experience. If their own shattered families are unable to help, professionals such as educators and psychologists can embrace the challenge to address this social toxicity in order to provide adult models of moral reciprocity and fairness.

MEANINGFUL SOLUTIONS

Feder, Levant, and Dean (2007) remind us that traditional masculine socialization leads boys to be enculturated to not express emotions. This socialization isolates many boys from their genuine inner lives and vital emotional connections to others. When the trauma experienced in socially toxic environments is added to this socialization, youth need help in expressing emotions and learning to communicate about them effectively. One school and community program resource that has addressed this need is entitled, "The school-based mourning project: A preventative intervention in the cycle of inner-city violence" (Sklarew, Krupnick, Ward-Zimmer and Napoli, 2002).

The goal of this intervention program was to allow children to safely undertake grief and trauma therapy, informally and in safe settings. Creative arts techniques like drama, drawing, games, stories, working in clay and using musical instruments allowed youth to express themselves and to therapeutically deal with their grief. Many researchers have observed that a turning point for youth growing up in harsh environments occurs when they connect with an adult who validates their strengths, talents and redeeming qualities in such a way that they begin to believe in themselves.

Rebecca Lakin and Annette Mahoney (2006) reported that community service programs can have a powerful impact on shaping pro-social behaviour. Taking part in programs, particularly if they have been designed and led by the students themselves, increased youths' self-reported empathy and intent to be involved in future community action. The following YouTube video-clip depicts the testimony of a young man who incorporated two intervention approaches described above to assist younger members of his community heal from the trauma of experiencing the suicides and deaths of family and friends in his inner-city, Boston, U.S.A. neighbourhood. He created an arts-based, community service program to engage youth in healing and activism, allowing youth to grieve their losses in order to change the stories and social conditions of their lives (http://www.favoritepoem.org/FlashVideo/ulrich.html).

What innovative and collaborative solutions to youth violence have educators and psychologists been part of in school settings? In the majority of cases, learning difficulties are associated with violent behaviour. Often these difficulties lead to dropping out of school (Favre, 2007). By the late 1990s, researchers had identified few programs or approaches that could make a significant difference in changing these behaviours. Currently, however, researchers have stopped treating violent youth as a heterogeneous group. Now, widespread research has created a multidimensional portrait of aggressive youth and improved results from context-specific, targeted interventions have been documented (Favre, 2007).

Favre conducted cross-cultural applied research in France, Canada, and Switzerland, demonstrating that approximately half of all violent youth suffer from high levels of depression and anxiety. Interestingly, no youth in his control groups suffered from similar high (but sub-clinical) levels of these emotional states. In addition, it was observed that violent youth tend to have more closed or "dogmatic" thinking. One difference between groups emerged: French youth in the control groups were more withdrawn and passive than the Canadian group who tended to express themselves assertively. It was also notable that many youth in the control group had committed some delinquent acts. Frechette and LeBlanc (1987; cited in Favre, 2007) have estimated that 93% of adolescents commit some kind of delinquent act. However, for non-violent adolescents, this behaviour disappears from their repertoire over time.

Favre (2007) conceives of violence as behaviour resulting from an acquired need to make someone weaker, impotent, or ill-at-ease, in order to make oneself feel strong, powerful, and comfortable. His systematic research has demonstrated how violence can become an addictive behaviour. Dominating others can have a temporary effect on reducing anguish. Specifically, violent youth have not learned how to distance themselves from negative feelings long enough to put the feelings and associated events into words (partly due to language difficulties). Aggressive youth will act immediately and impulsively in reaction to their angry feelings. Training them in skills to effectively channel their emotions and redirect thoughts and behaviour has been effective in reducing aggressive behaviour (Favre, 2007).

In order to be efficient and long lasting, any violence prevention program must take into account individual complexity. Prevention programming helps to increase one's level of frustration tolerance and offers better opportunities to experience levels of self-affirmation that will decrease anxiety. Youth can benefit from developing their "self-talk" (language intérieur) to learn to deal with violence. Favre's method of intervention does not propose that the violent student remains passive or submissive. Instead, the method encourages violent students to use language to make their needs known and to negotiate those needs to their satisfaction. The goal would be to have them react less automatically to situations and take more control over their actions, using improved and more mature self-talk to do so.

Favre (2007) eventually developed a program to prevent violence, administered partially by teachers (Canada) and psychologists (France). Overall, the approach consisted of training students (and teacher or psychologist-facilitators) in important communication skills that may be missing in violent youth, at least partly due to learning difficulties and a lack of important attachment figures who could model and teach essential skills in processing emotions and controlling behaviours. Much of Favre's program consisted of teaching skills to teachers in order for them to model the skills for students, thus creating more opportunities for empathic communication, caring, and reciprocity for the students. He also held intensive communication workshops for students at-risk. Youth learned to experience, value, and apply empathic listening skills.

CONCLUSION

It is important that students make decisions to take action related to concepts, issues, or problems they have studied. Students can benefit from not only exploring and understanding the dynamics of oppression, but also from a commitment to making decisions and changing systems of oppression through social action. Complex factors co-vary with both low literacy and violence, such as, poverty, inadequate parenting, low school attainment, and learning difficulties. However, there is some data to demonstrate that low literacy, separate from poverty, is associated with violent behaviour among adolescents. Davis, Bird, Arnold, Anger, and Bocchini (1999) observed that literacy skills can prevent development of violent behaviour.

Critical Literacy and critical pedagogy provide some hope-promoting solutions for violent youth. A central solution is to provide adequate opportunities for youth living in socially toxic environments to read, speak, and write their authentic points of view in the process of learning to become more critical regarding power structures and how these structures conspire to disenfranchise youth. Critical psychology provides the solution of working more effectively in communities to create more communication and support networks with students, schools and communities. Community service activities initiated and designed by student participants can evolve to address needs in the students' own communities. Crenshaw and Garbarino (2007) have suggested creating opportunities for students to deal therapeutically with the grief and sorrow that underlie their expressed anger and violence, via therapeutic expressive arts opportunities. An applied example of working effectively in schools includes Favre's (2007) approach of teaching classic listening skills and empathic responding to teachers and students. Teachers who become facilitators of emotional growth and maturity may serve as key models for improved communication. Students demonstrating violent behaviour are encouraged to learn how to communicate their emotional concerns effectively, and key learnings are trained and facilitated by professionals who stay in touch with them as they generalize skills to their school and community lives. At their most effective, these approaches may encourage youth to promote and reinforce growth in themselves and in others.

REFERENCES

Arsenio, W. F., & Gold, J. (2006). The effects of social injustice and inequality on children's moral judgements and behavior: Towards a theoretical model. *Cognitive Development, 21*, 388–400.

Body-Gendrot, S. (2005). Deconstructing youth violence in French cities. *European Journal of Crime, Criminal Law and Criminal Justice, 13*(1), 4–26.

Blatier, C. (1999a). Juvenile justice in France: The evolution of sentencing for children and minor delinquents. *British Journal of Criminology, 39*(2), 240–252.

Blatier, C. (1999b). Towards a constructive response to young offenders: Reparation at the levels of justice and individual psychology. *Journal of Social Work Practice, 13*(2), 211–220.

Caruthers, L. (2005). The unfinished agenda of school desegregation: Using storytelling to deconstruct the dangerous memories of the American mind. *Educational Studies: Journal of the American Educational Studies Association, 37*(1), 22–40. *Special Issue: The Contradiction of the Legacy of Brown v. Board of Education, Topeka (1954).*

Centre d'analyse stratégique: République Française (2007). Analyse: Le *testing*, une méthode expérimentale de mesure des discriminations à l'embauche. La note de veille, no 48, 5 mars 2007. Retrieved from http://www.strategie.gouv.fr/IMG/pdf/03NoteVeille48.pdf

Cooper, K., & White, R. (2006). Action research in a grade 3 classroom. In K. Cooper & R. White (Eds.), *The practical critical educator: Critical inquiry and educational practice*. Netherlands: Springer.

Crenshaw, D. A., & Garbarino, J. (2007). The hidden dimensions: Profound sorrow and buried potential in violent youth. *Journal of Humanistic Psychology, 47*(2), 160–174.

Daiute, C., & Fine, M. (2003). Youth perspectives on violence and injustice. *Journal of Social Issues, 59*(1), 1–14.

Danziger, K. (2007). The holy grail of universality. (Keynote address), *"Theoretical Psychology Beyond Borders: Transdisciplinarity and Internationalization", Conference of the International Society for Theoretical Psychology.* York University, Toronto, Ontario, Canada. June 18–22, 2007.

Davis, T. C., Byrd, R. S., Arnold, C. L., Auinger, P., & Bocchini, J. A. J. (1999). Low literacy and violence among adolescents in a summer sports program. *Journal of Adolescent Health, 24*(6), 403–411.

Deutsch, M. (2006). *The handbook of conflict resolution: Theory and practice* (2nd ed.). San Francisco: Jossey-Bass.

Duguet, E., Leandri, N., L'Horty, Y., & Petit, P. (2007). Discriminations à l'embauche: Un *testing* sur les jeunes des banlieues d'Île-de-France. Centre d'analyse stratégique; République Française. http://www.strategie.gouv.fr/article.php3?id_article=488

Economic Policy Institute. (2007). *Snapshot for June 23, 2004*. Retrieved from http://www.epinet.org/content.cfm/webfeatures_snapshots_06232004

Favre, D. (2007). *Transformer la violence des élèves: Cerveau, motivations et apprentissages*. Paris: Dunod.

Feder, J., Levant, R., & Dean, J. (2007). Boys and violence: A gender-informed analysis. *Professional Psychology: Research and Practice, 38*(4), 385–391.

Fine, M. (2006). Bearing witness: Methods for researching oppression and resistance–A textbook for critical research. *Social Justice Research, 19*(1), 83–108.

Fine, M., & Burns, A. (2003). Class notes: Toward a critical psychology of class and schooling. *Journal of Social Issue, 59*(4), 841–860.

Fortin, L., & Favre, D. (2000). Comparison of the psychosocial characteristics of violent secondary school students from Québec and France/Comparaison des caractéristiques psychosociales des élèves violents Québecois et Français au secondaire. *Revue Canadienne de Psycho-Education, 29*(1), 33–48.

Fox, D. (1997). Psychology and law: Justice diverted. In D. Fox & I. Prilleltensky (Eds.), *Critical psychology: An introduction*. London: Sage.

Fox, D., & Prilleltensky, I. (1997). *Critical psychology: An introduction*. London: Sage.

Franzak, J. K. (2006). *Zoom*: A review of the literature on marginalized adolescent readers, literacy theory, and policy implications. *Review of Educational Research, 76*(2), 209–248.

Garbarino, J. (1999). *Lost boys: Why our sons turn to violence and how we can save them*. New York: Free Press.

Harding, J. (1987). *Probation and the community: A practice and policy reader*. London: Tavistock Publications.

Harvey, J. (1999). *Civilized oppression*. Lanham, MD: Rowman and Littlefield.

Lakin, R., & Mahoney, A. (2006). Empowering youth to change their world: Identifying key components of a community service program to promote positive development. *Journal of School Psychology, 44*(6), 513–531.

Morsillo, J., & Prilleltensky, I. (2007). Social action with youth: Interventions, evaluation, and psychopolitical validity. *Journal of Community Psychology, 35*(6), 725–740.

Pagani, L., Boulerice, B., Vitaro, F., & Tremblay, R. E. (1999). Effects of poverty on academic failure and delinquency in boys: A change and process model approach. *Journal of Child Psychology and Psychiatry, 40*(8), 1209–1219.

Prilleltensky, I. (1994). *The morals and politics of psychology: Psychological discourse and the status quo*. Albany, NY: State University of New York Press.

Prilleltensky, I., & Prilleltensky, O. (2006). *Promoting well-being: Linking personal, organizational, and community change*. Hoboken, NJ: John Wiley.

Sklarew, B., Krupnick, J., Ward-Wimmer, D., & Napoli, C. (2002). The school-based mourning project: A preventive intervention in the cycle of inner-city violence. *Journal of Applied Psychoanalytic Studies, 4*(3), 317–330.

UNICEF Innocenti Research Centre. (2007). *Report No. 6. Child Poverty in Rich Countries, 2005*. Retrieved from http://www.unicef.org/brazil/repcard6e.pdf

Ungar, M. (2006). Nurturing hidden resilience in at-risk youth in different cultures. *Journal of the Canadian Academy of Child and Adolescent Psychiatry/Journal de l'Académie Canadienne de Psychiatrie de l'Enfant et de l'Adolescent, 15*(2), 53–58.

CHAPTER 4

Engaging and Critiquing Challenge in the Process Drama Classroom:
Socio-Economic Status as Topic and Resource

Advocates and practitioners of Critical Literacy are critical, to varying degrees, of three aspects of conventional literacy education (Freebody, 2005). First, they are critical of the ways in which *literacy* is used as an object in public debates and in the mass media. External economic competition and internal cultural and linguistic competition regularly create pressures that lead some politicians and media commentators to blame the teaching and learning of literacy in schools. In this way, attention is drawn away from other systems that sustain structural inefficiencies and inequalities (Apple, 1987). Second, advocates and practitioners are critical of the persistence of the unequal distribution through schooling of powerful literacy capabilities and dispositions (Freebody and Freiberg, 2008). They are critical of how public and professional explanations of these durable inequalities resolutely focus on attributes of those students and communities whom current educational arrangements serve badly. In this way, attention is drawn away from educational training regimes, curriculum contents, and assessment procedures that further privilege certain minorities.

Finally, advocates and practitioners are critical of how students are conventionally taught to read and write in schools, often via "set-texts". The materials have been "set" (in their language, dialect, content, and moral and ideological perspective), the ways of interpreting these materials have been "set" through increasingly standardized pedagogies, the work students have been called upon to produce in order to demonstrate their learning has been "set", and the textual criteria applied to determine whether that work constitutes adequate learning have been "set". It is often this particular kind of literacy education that underpins and legitimates the features of exchanges in which teachers and students engage.

This chapter outlines one aspect of a larger investigation into the critical exploration of social processes in classrooms. It is concerned with the potentially distinctive contribution that process drama offers such an investigation. This work takes place at the intersection of three settings of inquiry: the sociological setting of socio-economic status, the pedagogic setting of educational drama, and the methodological setting of Conversation Analysis. We briefly describe these settings of inquiry below and use them to illustrate and explore the opportunities that educational drama provides for enhancing students" engagement in classroom exchanges that are concerned with ideologically challenging issues.

A focus of our interest here is the interactional negotiation of moral reasoning practices as a key empirical issue for critical educational inquiry. Our discussion of

K. Cooper and R. E. White (eds.), Critical Literacies in Action: Social Perspectives
and Teaching Practices, 49–75.

this is informed by documentations of teacher-student interactions in drama activities conducted in two sites whose socio-economic backgrounds contrast strongly. These dramas were focused on the future opportunities and life pathways of young people (Freebody, Hornibrook and Freebody, 2005). Detailed transcripts of actual classroom lessons are used to illustrate and analyze the various ways in which the drama activities were constructed to provide the teachers and students with contexts for engagement and reflection. We also use these transcripts to demonstrate briefly some comparisons between the two sites with regard to the contents, dramatic scenarios, and the solutions explored. The chapter concludes with a discussion of the ways in which educational drama, through the exchange of moral reasoning practices, provides teachers and students with opportunities to develop both understanding and critical analysis.

Educators with an interest in the teaching and learning of Critical Literacy can now draw on an increasing repertoire of pedagogical strategies, and increasingly well-developed and detailed bodies of knowledge that can be used to analyze textual materials in a range of modalities. Distinctive lines of inquiry into pedagogical strategies that support critical orientations to literacy education have also been documented (Lewis, 2001; Wallace, 2003), along with relevant bodies of knowledge from a variety of disciplinary traditions ranging as broadly as applied linguistics, psychology, sociology, and anthropology (as summarized in Freebody, 2008). What this collection of resources for Critical Literacy education has generally comprised, however, is materials, ideas and recommendations aimed at more engaging and informative analyses of textual materials – still generally print materials, and, for the most part, resources for school subjects English or Language Arts. One of our aims is to supplement these more familiar settings for work on Critical Literacy with an extended inquiry into contributions to that effort that could be made via process drama in the conventional classroom.

One motivation behind this aim relates to the conduct of critical inquiry in schools and, more significantly, as part of standard schoolwork. Schools are institutional settings whose goals, key operating systems and categories, and physical layouts combine to make them difficult places for students to achieve the "ability to think 'critically' in the sense of understanding how systems and institutions inter-relate to help and harm people" (Gee, 2001, 2). This is reflected in Edwards and Westgate's (1987) conclusion to their encyclopedic review of research and theory on classroom interaction:

> [Classroom talk] is certainly not conducted normally on a basis of shared knowledge. Its outstanding characteristic ... is one participant's claim to all the knowledge relevant to the business at hand (124).

This chapter aims to contribute to this latter line of inquiry in Critical Literacy, by exploring another institutionalized form of exchange and its potential for interrupting this "outstanding characteristic" of classroom life.

Many studies of the interactional patterns typically making up the daily lives of teachers and students in these settings reflect the generally unnoticed but nonetheless robust relational structures that make often strict institutional constraints on relationships seem unremarkable. One hypothesis that has guided this investigation is that the particular interactional demands of successful process drama sessions may either make these constraints visible enough for scrutiny, or establish interactional procedures that make possible exchanges that are otherwise improbable in classroom settings. In this chapter we present some initial data and observations that illustrate the implications of this hypothesis.

THE ANALYTIC APPROACH

The analyses that follow generally apply the procedures used in Conversational Analysis and Membership Categorization Analysis (henceforth CA and MCA, for details on the analytic procedures and their rationale, see, Freebody, 2003; Freebody and Freiberg, 2006; Heap, 1997; Heritage, 1984; Hester and Francis, 2000; Schegloff, 2007). This entails detailed examinations of the interactional and conceptual features operating in spoken interactions. A summary of some important premises of this line of analysis follows.

Rather than examining one site or type of site and then describing its features as if they define interaction "essentially" in that site, CA/MCA takes its task to be to compare talk in differing sites to determine the features that are distinctive and common to each. Interactions here are seen as structurally organized through turns at talk. Speakers show through their talk that not all kinds of contributions are equally preferred. Pauses, apologies, excuses, indirectness, or one or more of a variety of "softeners" are used when a dis-preferred contribution is made. For example, acceptances are preferred to refusals, agreements to disagreements, and positive evaluations to negative ones.

Sequences of talk need to be viewed by the analyst as they are used by the speakers – *as* sequences and *in* sequence. Specifically, this means i) that the work done by an utterance depends on *how it is heard* in sequence – its location in the course of mutual action, ii) that any utterance can be heard in many ways and may be taken to have multiple functions and hearings, iii) that there is nonetheless an over-riding assumption among speakers that everything said is pertinent to the business at hand – "sustained relevance" – unless explicit markers to the contrary are evident in the talk, and, critically, iv) that speaker's analysis, understanding, and/or appreciation of a prior turn will be displayed in that speaker's current turn; that is, speakers publicly display and up-date their inter-subjective understandings of what is going on and how they may contribute. Talk is both reflective of and productive of the context of its occurrence; that is, that speakers do not merely act out roles predetermined by community, institutional, or physical contexts, but re-inflect and transform those contexts through the talk.

AN ILLUSTRATION: THE DRAMA AND THE PARTICIPANTS

Process drama, once described by Dorothy Heathcote as "a conscious employment of the elements of drama to educate" (Wagner 1979, 13) is the term used here to describe a particular style of educational improvisatory drama. Key figures in the development of process drama are Gavin Bolton and Dorothy Heathcote; since its development, however, it has become a widely practiced form of pedagogy and practitioners such as O'Neill (1995) O'Toole (1992) and others have had a profound effect on the ways in which process drama has been developed and implemented.

Essentially, process drama is a collection of drama activities over an extended period of time that aims to go beyond short-term, teacher-dominated exercises. The teacher and the students build the drama through negotiating and responding to each other's ideas (Kao and O'Neill, 1998). The specific features of process drama outlined here have been collected from the work of a variety of these practitioners. Some defining features of process drama are:

- The absence of script (O'Neill, 1995);
- Its use of powerful pretexts as a basis for dramatic context and tension (Kao and O'Neill, 1998);
- The provision of opportunities for participants to utilize their context and purposes when negotiating the elements of dramatic form (O'Toole, 1992);
- Its purpose to generate a dramatic "elsewhere", a fictional world, which will be inhabited for the insights, interpretations, and understandings it may yield (O'Neill, 1995);
- The impossibility of exact replication (O'Neill, 1995);
- The involvement of the entire group in the same enterprise, with all participants (teachers and students) both spectators and actors or "specactors" (Heathcote, 1984);
- The collection of drama activities over an extended period of time that aim to go beyond short-term, teacher-dominated exercises, where teachers and students build the drama through negotiating and responding to each others' ideas (Kao and O'Neill, 1998).

The features outlined here, as with much of the theoretical work surrounding process drama, provide only an initial understanding of the work participants do when undertaking these kinds of dramatic events. Importantly, the focus of process drama is not on the end product; rather, it is on the process of discovering, negotiating, exploring and understanding that students embark on when participating in a drama. Wagner has used the analogy of a funnel to represent the different "ends" process and product focused drama may lead to:

> In a theater performance, getting to the particular, the sharp dramatic focus, the small end of the funnel, is the end of the process. It is assumed that the audience can do the reflection for themselves. In a classroom drama, the end point is the discovery of universal human experience, the reaching of a deeper insight about the significance of the act or situation in the drama. (1979, 59)

The key intended products of a process drama are the experience of the drama itself, and the subsequent reflections of the students (Kao and O'Neill, 1998). This shift in purpose allows for students to concentrate their thoughts and feelings as they explore how they see the world, rather than focusing on the perfection of a performance. This shift also allows for other shifts in the classroom. While a classroom is a setting with clear institutional roles and behavioral expectations, in a process drama classroom there are opportunities for those roles and expectations to be blurred; the teacher may become a facilitator or "evoker" of drama (Heathcote, 1984) while allowing students to make decisions and choose which direction they want the drama may take.

The project that informs the discussion in this chapter addressed questions of students' critical and moral understandings relating to socio-economic status (SES). This was achieved through an exploration of the ways in which students in differing SES settings drew upon these understandings as either an explicit topic or an implicit resource in their work in drama lessons. The drama lessons in which data were collected focused on the implementation of a process drama about the future pathways and occupational opportunities of the participating students. The participating sites were:

– Priven School: One year 9 class in a government school in the outer Southwest suburbs of Brisbane participated.
– Chifley School: One year 10 class in a religious-denominational independent school in the inner South Eastern suburbs of Brisbane participated.

The process drama undertaken was planned by the researchers, in line with the curriculum documents that the participating teachers were using, to offer participants as wide a range of interactional choices as practicable. Also built in to the planned lessons were a variety of opportunities to think critically about texts and scenarios, and a necessity for building shared understandings about cultural characters.

THREE TYPES OF TALK-IN-INTERACTION

In the drama lessons studies three distinguishable categories of talk-in-interaction were identified, and these are used here to organize the discussion. These three forms of talk-in-interaction are:

– Pedagogic/logistic talk (PLT): talk relating to the management of students" attention, movements and the props in terms of both general school expectations and specific and lesson activities;
– Socio-cultural talk (SCT): talk engaging the cultural, social and moral potential of the lesson, and creating shared accounts and public reasoning practices; and
– In role talk (IRT): talk in which students demonstrated their understandings of the expectations signaled in the SCT and improvised reactions to scenarios as they display these in role as a character-participant in the drama.

"School talk" was found to have certain structural features that were common across these three categories of talk. For example the well-documented initiation, response, evaluation (IRE) cycle (Sinclair and Coulthard, 1975) was found in the transcripts within all three types of talk. However, as shown below, different purposes and activities were achieved in the different sequences in each type of talk.

The focus of this chapter is on SCT and IRT, even though some aspects of PLT are clearly relevant to teachers" understandings of SES, both in terms of the SES of their students (Freebody, Forest and Gunn, 2001) and SES as a topic of discussion (Freebody and Freiberg, 2000).

SOCIO-CULTURAL TALK (SCT)

The talk-in-interaction included under the heading SCT in process drama classrooms tended to focus on the development of shared accounts of people, events, or characters" actions, as the participants take these accounts to be either prospectively ("for later") or retrospectively ("from earlier") relevant to the drama. The orientation of the exchanges is generally to the cultural, social, or moral aspects of the drama as a socio-cultural event, rather than as an institutionalized classroom event. For example, after a teacher reads out a story and asks students for their reactions, the students are likely to respond with agreement or disagreement with the characters' actions, ideas about the fairness of the events in the story, or what they would have done differently had they been faced with similar events, and why. In this way, students are treating the invitation to express their ideas as an invitation to share their thoughts about the socio-cultural aspects of the story, rather than its institutional importance or relevance. It is also a feature of the SCT found in the particular corpus of data explored here that the teachers did not always behave as more knowledgeable than the students on topics relevant at any given time. Rather, the teacher generally facilitated the discussion and usually managed the turn-taking and topic selection for the group's public production of reasoning practices. The teacher also monitored the adequacy of the students' operational appreciation of the prospective relevance of these reasoning practices – their value to the activities to follow, in particular to the IRT.

IN ROLE TALK

During the IRT sections of the observed drama lessons, students were asked to work in role to produce a simulation of an authentic interaction. The basic elements of conversation (how participants did this) warrant exploration because the students had to work to produce an artifact that would seem to be, and would be evaluated as if it were, an authentic simulation of talk-in-interaction. Therefore, how members demonstrate and share with the other participants even the simplest interaction is self-consciously produced in ways that visibly orient to particular demands (character/role, previous talk, and so on), one of which is authenticity. Although IRT is defined by a conscious employment of role rather than by a common set of specific interactional features, participants nonetheless, through their interactions, generally showed that they held themselves responsible for:

– Producing interactions that are compatible with standard expected norms of conversation; that is, they have to simulate authentic conversation;
– Facilitating rather than obstructing the interactional options of the other character-participants;
– Producing physical (bodily movement, use of space, use of props) and verbal interactions that are recognizable by the other character-participants as plausibly attributable to their character type (e.g., would a mother really say that?);
– Physically and verbally interacting within the power structures of the characters being portrayed (e.g., how would a teacher talk to a principal – not how would Anton talk to Craig);

– Producing interactions that have retrospective relevance to the SCT that formed the pretext and planning phases of the unit; and

– Producing interactions that are appropriate for the institutional context "in-school".

Through these responsibilities, participants used IRT to advance, obstruct, shift or reinstate the plot of a drama. Therefore, a participant could advance the plot using an interaction within IRT by:

– Confirming an element of the plot or action of another participant;

– Challenging another participant or disagreeing with a particular aspect of the situation;

– Querying an aspect of the situation which others have taken to be true; or

– Acting out and making explicit an important element within the context of the drama. Instances of all of these modes of plot advancement were evident in the sessions observed.

The emergence of these three types of talk-in-interaction is significant for this particular exploration of critical analysis and moral reasoning in drama classrooms because it has the potential to disrupt Edwards and Westgate's (2987) formulation cited earlier that classroom talk is defined by one participants *claim to all the knowledge relevant to the business at hand.* Students interacting in SCT phases of lessons are presented with opportunities to critically consider moral reasoning and shared interpretations of socio-cultural concepts, and openings to explore cultural stereotypes and the chance to make and defend opinions. Through their IRT, students are given the opportunity to act out and embody these moral reasoning practices to see if and how they can operate in differing scenarios.

Two dimensions of the data from the sites are explored in this chapter: First is the interactional negotiation of moral reasoning practices of students as they engage with theoretical issues in drama classrooms. Specifically, an exploration of the students moral reasoning practices surrounding understandings of happiness/ sadness, lifestyles of different occupations, and agency and the way in which these particular moral reasoning practices and categorizations were informed by the participants' understanding of SES. Second, this chapter focuses on the interactional features of drama pedagogy that provided opportunities for these participants to build critical understandings of texts and scenarios and to engage in shared moral reasoning practices.

HAPPINESS AND SADNESS

During the drama lessons both sites constructed shared understandings of *happiness* and *sadness*. In many cases, these concepts were debated, particularly in the instances in which *wealth* was included as a relational concept. A discussion that took place at Chifley School used photographs of representatives of occupations as part of a pretext to the process drama. One aim was to focus students' comparisons of the occupations on ways in which the photographs represented happiness and sadness. Happiness was discussed through a demonstrated understanding of the categorizations of people with money, people without money, musicians, CEOs, farmers and hairdressers. The attributions assigned to these categorizations that lead to the evaluation of "happy" were wealth, family, agency, passion, power, contentment, simplicity and having a happy personality. Notions of sadness were introduced through the students' demonstrated understandings of the categorizations of: prostitute, prisoner, soldier, factory worker, and waitress. The attributions assigned to these categorizations to lead to the evaluation of "sad" were desperation, low self esteem and no money, a lack of choice, post traumatic stress disorder, a bad work environment and a state of going "around in circles", presumably a metaphor for a lack of occupational advancement in life.

The discussion surrounding the "sad" pictures was not only substantially shorter than the discussion about the "happiest" picture, but unlike the "happy" discussion, the students did not refer to personality in describing and justifying their choice for the saddest picture. Instead, they went through the motions of discussing why their picture is sad using more descriptive reasoning practices and attributions based on the consequences of specific events or actions that may have occurred to or been undertaken by the characters represented (Eglin and Hester, 1992; Jayyusi, 1984). That is, students were more comfortable discussing external attributions for sadness and viewing causes for sadness as external events or actions. This contrasted with their discussion of happiness, which they believed to be internally achieved regardless of external circumstances, or achieved through a variety of external circumstances. This is expressed in Excerpt 1, recorded at Chifley, the higher SES school.

Excerpt 1.

Sally: I know I'm sitting here but like the poorest people in the world are still happy 'cause they have their family around them so like they're really happy without money and they

Teacher: So there's a balance between them it can't just be one thing or another. Mel?

Mel: Um, just because you have money doesn't mean you can do all the things you like... like ...um ... I can't think of an example (laughter).

Peter: You mightn't be a very good singer.

Much of this discussion drew upon the socio-economic status as an organizing device and the categories *Poor People* and *Rich People* were shown to be highly informative resources in the discussion of happiness and sadness. These correlations between affluence and happiness and poverty and sadness are not assembled as perfect equations in this talk. The exceptions; the content farmer, the passionate musician and the hairdresser fulfilling a simple dream are made to be exceptions, marked instances by their own personal internal resources. The internal resources of the rich people nominated as happy were not discussed as causes for their happiness: Whether the CEO or the people with money loved what they did or were fulfilling their dream was not made to be relevant. Rather, the rich people's happiness was attributed to consumerism and power. In these discussions therefore, part of what has been established is the different logic associated with the experience of happiness and sadness as it relates to socio-economic status.

This experience of *happiness* connected to *wealth* was also explored in the (lower SES) Priven School in both the SCT and the IRT phases of the lessons. An in-role scenario that was explored in the process drama focused on Jacinta, a student who wanted to do a chef's apprenticeship but her mother would not sign the necessary forms because she thought it would be better if Jacinta went to university to become a doctor. As a result of this, Jacinta was not only angry with her mother, but had become distant and unmotivated at school. The students, in role as Jacinta's *teachers* (students in role) were having a meeting with the *school chaplain* (student in role), the *principal* (teacher in role) and Jacinta's *mother* (student in role) in an attempt to help Jacinta re-engage with school. The following excerpt contains the students" (as *teachers*) reactions to Jacinta's mother's comments regarding her reasons for wanting Jacinta to be a doctor, notably a "better lifestyle".

Excerpt 2

Jeff:	Yeah, (a comment) sorry to disagree with you, I think (it's a little bit) about the money made by chefs. I am a qualified chef and I do earn a fair bit of money. I think your daughter has potential in the... even though some of your comments before like you said she's not a very good chef. I think she is, but she just needs to be dedicated to it.
Call:	Yeah. I agree with that. Even if she does get in to medicine she will never be happy because it's not what she wants. You've gotta... you've gotta let her try to do what she wants because other than that even [if she] wants to go to medical school. She still won't be happy...., She...., She doesn't want to be.
Teacher:	My learned friends obviously mean that with the utmost respect. Jacinta, can I just...? Sorry, does she see friends outside of school?
Ann:	I don't know. I didn't know she had friends.
Teacher:	Well I... well... well... It's interesting you should say that because we have noticed that at school. At school I see her when I'm walking around the corridors as the principal and when I'm walking around the school. Every time I see Jacinta, she seems to be on her own... ah ... A year ago as you... you're well aware because you saw her report card. She throws herself fully into her educational activities. That makes Jacinta happy. She's very withdrawn now. She's not happy.

Ant: Um, Mr. Principal, I'll just ask a question. Did you invite...
            um... um... Jacinta's friends to this meeting?

Teacher: Well, we... I... I've spoken to Jacinta's friends previously.

Ant: Yep

Teacher: Um, but... why... why?

Ant: Um, 'cause... um... I was kinda thinking that if we bring
            them in and... um... kind of like have so with the Mum and
            just have a word with them...'cause she said that she didn't
            know that she had any friends, so maybe Jacinta's friends and
            Ann can work something out to better help Jacinta. I think that
            the more people we have to help Jacinta out the better.

As in the students' discussions at Chifley School, we see resistance to students' interpretations of money as an attribution of happiness. We also see a demonstration of the ways in which students can use their roles to alter accepted institutional structures and either dismiss or introduce topics of relevance, demonstrated here by the Chaplain's dismissal of the principal's introduction of Jacinta as a *loner* to an introduction of a new structure for the interview: the inclusion of Jacinta's friends. The roles that the students have taken on have given them the allowance of a teacher, chaplain or mother within the context of a school meeting. This affords them opportunities to introduce ideas while maintaining a "moral safety" because the ideas are not actually their own; they are the ideas of their characters.

The discussion regarding happiness and sadness in both the SCT and IRT phases of lessons tended to be critical of formulations that place happiness as a result of wealth. Students tended to align with examples and formulations that placed happiness in spite of lack of wealth, or happiness as a result of passion, family or fulfillment. It is these demonstrated understandings of the relationship between happiness, fulfillment and wealth or lack of wealth that informed many of the class discussion, particularly those associated with occupations, life pathways, and agency.

The moves made by speakers in role potentially provide moral and sociological problems to those in-role characters around them. The demands of being in role entail high levels of displayed engagement and an actual choice among the plot-advancement options available, not just an exploratory enumeration of those options, as would be more likely in standard classroom discussions. In this way the in-role student can embody a moral or ideological commitment, in this case concerning the relationship between "happiness" versus "sadness" on the one hand and occupational choice on the other. This commitment then becomes an object of educational scrutiny.

OCCUPATIONS

The topic of future pathways was central to the process dramas that took place in the two sites. The students used, formed and shared their understandings of the lifestyles, interests, and consequences of participating in a variety of different occupations. These understandings were often connected by the students to notions of personal freedom, intelligence, ability, wealth and agency. The discussion reported in Excerpts 3 through 5 shows a teacher introducing the students to two similar scenarios about young people facing obstacles while trying to achieve their dreams, and asking students to comment on what they thought about the scenarios. The first scenario focused on "Jason": a young boy who wants to go to university and become a scientist against his parents' wishes, who want him to get a trade and help support the family. The second scenario focused on "Sarah": a wealthy girl who wants to be a mechanic, but whose parents are insistent she attend university and study to be a doctor. In this discussion students developed and shared their moral reasoning practices about the two scenarios in ways that usually recruited notions of SES as resources rather than explicit topics. Conclusions about the ways in which students understand categorizations such as *poor boy, rich girl* and *good/bad parents* can be drawn out from the students' expressed attitudes towards the two scenarios. Throughout the discussion the only mention that the scenarios were structurally related came from Anton who described the similarity in the following way:

Excerpt 3

Ant: Um, well this is kind of exactly like the last... um... last family. It's kind of went from poor to a rich job and now.... the next one is a rich person going to like a ... poor job kind of thing.

Teacher: That's right. Well let me just clarify that Jason really wants to go to college. His family wants him to get an apprenticeship. Remember...

Ant: Yeah, but he doesn't want to.

Teacher: ...and Sarah, what...?

Ant: She doesn't want to go to "Uni". It's kind of like... same situations but different opportunity kind of thing

Teacher: Yes

Ant: Like different ways of going to it

Anton's formulation outlined the similarities of the scenarios, with the one key difference made explicit: one scenario is about moving up the proverbial ladder (*poor to a rich job*) and one is moving down (*rich person going to a poor job*). This one difference drew startlingly different moral judgments from the students. There tended to be moral outrage at Jason's parents for stopping him achieving his dream, whereas students tended to be less sympathetic towards Sarah, the wealthy girl. The moral order of class relations is demonstrated here through one student's differing reactions to the similar scenarios. Firstly Tracy's reaction to Jason's story:

Excerpt 4

Teacher:	I want you to be still and concentrate. I hope you heard all that. Jason is very devastated but is very close to his parents and does not want to cause a rift between him and them. He also does not know where he'll get the five thousand dollars that will allow that will allow him to go. OK, before I read you the next one which is... which is something a little bit different. What do we think of that? What do we think of that? What do we think of that scenario?
Tracy:	His parents are selfish.
Lin:	That's what I was just going to say.
Teacher:	Why? Why do you say that?
Tracy:	...because he's like really smart and he wants to go and be one of those genius people, really smart people, and the parents don't want him to go.
Teacher:	They're encouraging him not to go aren't they? Why?
Tracy:	...because they're...
Teacher:	[just prove] to me you were listening, go on
Tracy:	...because they were poor and they wanted him to look after his brothers and sisters
Teacher:	OK, Brent

Tracy's responses to the scenario introduced the idea that Jason's parents are selfish because Jason is *one of those genius people* and his parents are preventing him from achieving greatness because *they were poor and they wanted him to look after his brothers and sisters*. In contrast, Tracy responded to Sarah's scenario with less conviction regarding Sarah's desire to have a career her parents do not support:

Excerpt 5

Teacher:	Is it? Would somebody else like to talk to me about that...now hang on. Sh! Sh! one at a time.
Tracy:	Um... if she goes along with her parents like she does the... um... doctor thing she might end up liking it, and if she took the mechanic thing and she didn't like it.
Darr:	She does like it.

Tracy:	Yeah, but then if she took the mechanic thing and she *didn't* like it, then she's already disowned so ...
Teacher:	OK, so you're saying... interesting point... so you're saying...
Tracy:	She... like, if she became a doctor and she liked it and if she became a mechanic and she didn't like it....

Distinctive from her interpretation of Jason's parents as selfish, the content of Tracy's turn gave an evaluation of the scenario through an interpretation of Sarah as possibly wrong in her decision to become a mechanic. Tracy did this through a consideration of the consequences of making a faulty choice (*what if she becomes a mechanic and doesn't like it*). Despite the similarities between the scenarios and the realization formulated by Anton that the scenarios were the same, at no time was the question of whether or not Jason really knows what he wants to be or what is best for him considered. Tracy's formulations during this discussion were not unusual of those expressed by the entire group.

We see that a central aspect of the moral reasoning of the categorizations built up and deployed over the course of this discussion involved the question of which characters' views the parties to the discussion see as questionable and corrigible. In Jason's scenario, the views of the parents were questioned and debated, particularly over whether they were "selfish", logistically wrong, or whether they should go and "get a job" themselves. Jason's choices and views were never questioned. In contrast, in Sarah's scenario, Sarah's views and choices were debated persistently. Sarah's parents" actions and views, even though in some ways more dramatic that Jason's parents" actions (they threatened to sue the local mechanic and disown Sarah) were not questioned with regard to their fairness or their appropriateness, although at one point the students do question her level of control. The members of the discussion saw Sarah's views as questionable and corrigible, particularly her ability to make the right decision on her own – the debate was about her versus the parents' soundness as judges of her interests – and her ability to support herself as a mechanic. The questions of whether Jason would perhaps enjoy a trade more than being a scientist, or whether he would not be successful in his preferred career were never posed.

This is an important demonstration of the way the members of the discussion assigned moral attributions to particular categorizations (Rich Family, Poor Family, particular jobs, Rich Girl, Poor Boy). The moral reasoning systems were reversed depending on the social class aspirations of the child character vis a vis the SES background of the protagonist. When the relationship between the aspiration and the background was reversed, the moral reasoning was likewise reversed and the attribution became: the parents are selfish on the one hand, the child is selfish on the other. Clearly, one aspect of SES as resource is that differences in SES can reverse moral polarities.

AGENCY

Across the two sites notions of agency were put to work in differing ways to differing effects. At Chifley School a lack of agency was discussed with respect to every picture chosen as "sad", with the exception of the soldier (but even a soldier might *have to kill someone*), this established an event-consequent category that informed the categorizations in play in the discussion. Excerpts 6 through 10 explore the five "saddest" jobs chosen by the students and the ways in which the subjects' sadness was directed related to their lack of agency:

Excerpt 6

Valerie: most people wouldn't choose to go into prostitution as a job. It's not really something that when you're little you dream of doing (giggles). It's usually because you have to...because, like, usually you have no other option.

Teacher: So you think it's out of desperation.

Sally: Yeah, like if someone's just lost everything in their life, like.

In this excerpt Valerie explores the categorization *prostitute* as desperate and without other options. This establishes the event/consequent category that those without agency, in this case those who have no options and have *lost everything in their life*, are victims and therefore represent sadness. A similar notion of "lack of options" was present in the students' discussion of a jail cell:

Excerpt 7

Teacher: Do you think they're doing anything exploitative. OK, cut that! Let's quickly look at this one. First of all guys, why did you choose this one?

Mick: It's a jail.

Peter: A jail.

Mick: You don't want to go.

Jane: A jail cell.

Peter: You don't really have a choice about where about whether you go there or not.

Jane: Yeah.

Mel: Usually criminals go there.

In these turns the categorization *Criminal*, which was explicitly associated with Jail, was allocated the attributions of a lack of choice, and being somewhere they *don't want to be*. Each of these attributions exist as related to sadness through their lack of agency, the subject's inability to choose their circumstances in order to be where they want to be. The perceived sadness of not being able to exercise agency in one's life leading to a lack of options and victimization of subjects was also present, however slightly more subtly, in the discussions of factory workers and a waitress:

Excerpt 8

Nadine: I had the packaging plant and I thought it would be like. I think those people look really unhappy because they're like in a factory without like windows, you know... obviously not like air circulation...so it's probably really hot and muggy. And they're probably like, it's.... They'd have to do the same thing day after day after day after day after day after day and so on. So it, it wo.... it would just get really boring and like they probably won't have like much of a choice to... um... change their job because they might not have like high qualifications. So this is really the only job that they can have.

Nadine's understanding of the factory workers as the saddest photographic subjects was explicated through the monotony of their work, the stifling physical conditions of the labour and, finally, their lack of ability to exercise choice to change their job because of their lack of qualifications.

Excerpt 9

Bron: Are we explaining why she's unhappy? OK, well she feels really (up) in the same thing like she's just going round in circles in her life (and she's just there to pay the bills).

Teacher: And what's her job?

Allison: Waitress.

Bron: She's a waitress and she... Look at that face! She could have been a model (laughter). She had kids and now she's stuck there paying the bills so they can go to school and get a good education.

Similar to the factory workers, the waitress is sad because she is *stuck there*, implying she could not change her job, and that she was simply *going round in circles in her life*. Although all formulations of how a lack of agency informs sadness in one's life are so far similar, one categorization that was discussed as sad, via a lack of agency for reasons other than choice was the soldier:

Excerpt 10

Kath: Um, I think this is the saddest job because like everyday you'd see horrible images of like people dead on the street or like you might have to kill someone to save someone else and those images would be stuck in your head and like you might lose sleep and stuff.

The bulk of the formulation is concerned with the experience of trauma leading to a lack of control over your own thoughts, the inability to stop thinking about "horrible images" and the inability to sleep as a result. Therefore, although a differing understanding of the event/consequent category of agency (i.e. that without it one is at the mercy of the events in their lives and therefore becomes a victim), all categorizations that were assigned the attribution *sadness* are also categorizations that are assigned the attribution *lack of agency,* with the sadness considered a direct result of this lack. Interestingly when these students were developing categorizations around the attribution *happiness*, agency was also present. Those categorizations that were considered to have agency, such as the hairdresser who is achieving her dream, or the farmer who is content with life, were those who were considered to be happy. Notably, students made the link between agency and happiness explicit even when the subject was poor.

At Priven School, agency was discussed in terms of a set of abilities or competences, than as a consequence of an event or action; rather than being a victim of events, one lacks agency when one is not competent enough to exercise personal power. When exploring the scenarios of Jason and Sarah, discussed above, the agency of Sarah, the *Rich Girl*, was given weight within the discussion through the opinion held by many students that, although Sarah should be able to exercise agency, her reliance on her parents, and the level with which they appeared to control her life, meant that she would be a "goner" without them. Therefore Sarah's lack of agency was derived from her inability to look after herself. The different purposes that the notion of agency brought to the discussions in the two sites demonstrated how different sympathies and alignments were developed for different categorizations. The money and opportunity available to a *Rich Girl* can help avoid the events specified as creating lack of agency by the Chifley School students, and therefore Sarah's lack of agency is determined by her perceived inability to take advantage of her privileged situation by these students. This demonstrates that these students drew on the attribution of SES when making formulations to arrive at different understandings of subjects in similar situations.

From these examples (the rich girl, the prostitute, criminals, factory workers, soldiers and a waitress) the students have demonstrated a critical reading of the visual and aural texts, using discussion surrounding these texts as ways to build shared moral understandings of categorizations in order to inform the possible characterizations that may follow in the drama. Moral praise and blame is allocated among the character-categories, and a critical aspect of the resource offered by SES is the way in which these allocation processes are not consistently or symmetrically applied. (Jayyusi (1984) demonstrated the same asymmetries in media represent-ations of certain national and ethnic groups.) The following section shows some ways in which the teachers and students achieve interactions that allow for this critical analysis.

HOW INTERACTION PROVIDES FOR MORAL REASONING

It is important to recognize, while analyzing the critical and moral responses students made in the work described in this chapter, that the participants in these interactions, particularly the teachers, planned and implemented these lessons in order to allow participants the opportunity to conduct reasoning practices. This section is concerned with exploring the ways in which teachers and students interacted to produce a recognizable thing called a "process drama unit". This recognizability arises from the sequential and categorization analysis, as well as the connections between them. These demonstrate the participants' ability to work together to produce institutionally and morally recognizable events in the real world of the classroom and the imagined world of the drama. The following excerpt took place in an SCT phase of the lessons in which the class at Priven School is discussing their reactions to the "Jason" and "Sarah" scenarios. Towards the end of the discussion, the interaction shown in Excerpt 11 took place. The teacher at Priven School gave students the opportunity to establish, collate, and defend their ideas about a key, but so far relatively unspoken theme of the discussion so far – money:

Excerpt 11

Teacher:	OK, any other points on those two extracts that I've just read out?
Lin:	You've got the answers, don't you?
Teacher:	There are no answers. There's no right and wrong.
Josie:	Put your shoes on, you feral (laughs).
Teacher:	Right, OK, can everyone... can everyone sit up now please? Face me. We're going to stand up in a second. Sit up. Thank you. Jake, sit up. Everyone, sit up. Len.
Ant:	Excuse me, sir.
Teacher:	Thank you. Now a few of you in here, can I have your focus please? Thank you, Brent. A few of you in here might think Mr. (teacher's name) has all the answers. I don't. But if you're asking me what I think... what I think is important, I don't think money is particularly important. It's, you know, it's not the be all and end all of everything... money. You know, we do have to strive to be happy.
Call:	But you need money to be happy.
Ss:	(calling out) No/Yes.
Teacher:	Sorry, could you say that a bit louder?
Call:	Well, you kind of do need money to be happy, I reckon.

Teacher:	What do you mean by that? That's a very interesting point
Call:	'Cause if you're not... If you don't have any money, then you're poor and you live in a... You'll like....
Ann:	You live in a bin.
Call:	Yeah.
Ant:	Well not exactly. If you... if you...
Teacher:	You're talking about.... You're talking about an extreme though, aren't you?
Ant:	No, but....
Teacher:	Extreme poverty.
Ant:	Sir, not exactly. If you..., if you..., if you.... if you're not rich, but you're not poor. but you're kind of like not well off so you're just kind of like just coping, it...um...it puts a lot of stress on the family as your parents have to like pay a lot of bills and, um... like they're always stressing about how they're going to get the money to keep the phone on or electricity or like so and so in order to have no debts and not have to stress about needing to pay bills. Um, I think like having money would make you happy as you don't have to stress about those things.

Lin's "You've got the answers don't you?" points to the diverse state of the class's knowledge and views on and around the topic so far. The teacher responded to dismiss the way she expressed this statement, indicating that the terms of "right" and "wrong" are not the framework of the discussion. Nonetheless he responded to this "call for clarity" in two ways. The first was by indicating the urgency of the discussion with respect to the fact that they would *be standing up soon* and moving on, and that, therefore, they needed to pull the discussion together. Second, he responded to the variety of positions laid out in the discussion so far by refocusing the discussion with a statement of his own position; *it's not the be all and end all of everything money. You know we have to strive to be happy.* The consequence of this was five distinct hearings or interpretations of his statement that students provided without explicitly confronting him with a direct disagreement.

- *If there's no money then you live in a bin and can't be happy:* This first hearing categorized money as a candidate definition for happiness. Moreover, it aligned those without money with those that live in bins, "living in a bin" becoming the category-bound activity of the Poor (and, by direct association from earlier in the talk, unhappy) members of society.
- *If you're just coping you're in constant stress and you can't be happy:* Anton's re-formulation of the first hearing maintained the dependency of money on happiness, but oriented away from "unacceptable" extreme cases. Instead of those without money "living in a bin", Anton classified the categorization of

Not Rich, Not Poor, Just Coping as affording the attribution of stress, family stress, and unpaid or nearly due household bills. This formulation located stress in a cause-effect relationship with the creation of unhappiness within a situation, and money a cure for stress; therefore money became a candidate hypothesis for happiness.

- *You can be rich, but you can't buy a wife/partner:* Kate's turn was formulated before Anton's second hearing, evident through Kate's bid for a turn during Teacher's turn. Therefore this turn can be heard as oriented to Callum and Ann's extreme example considering money as a necessity for the attainment of happiness. In this turn Kate challenged this notion by introducing "partnership" or, more specifically, "a wife" as a second candidate definition for happiness and an attribution of a happy person. Money was thereby dismissed because it cannot buy this attribution.
- *If you are rich you can buy anything "in the shops" that you want:* Liam's formulation reoriented the discussion back to the acceptance of money as a definition of happiness, using "the ability to buy things" as the category-bound activity of those with money that creates happiness.
- *Being rich has nothing to do with family. Love of family is necessary and money is not sufficient for happiness:* Sonia dismissed all formulations made about money and happiness by claiming that "Love and family are totally different to money". This was heard as love and family being attributions of happy people and therefore candidate definitions for happiness, with money being separate from them, and therefore not connected to happiness.

Through these five hearings of Teacher's statement of opinion, Teacher and the students orchestrated a summary of the reasoning displayed in the session so far, stepping back from the stories and trying to reach a set of formulations that could constitute the bridge to the next phase in the unit. This excerpt also demonstrates the ways in which Teacher facilitated what constituted an appropriate critical or moral opinion; not through a judgment of personal views, but through the ways in which he accepted or dismissed particular answers. For example, Teacher's dismissal of Callum's and Ann's elaboration, *"if you don't have any money then you're poor"* as extreme, demonstrated that within this discussion, the justification of a point of view needed to be more refined and arguments or formulations should not be based on extreme examples. This offers a clear modeling of public moral reasoning.

The in-role segments of the drama provided opportunities for students to negotiate their socio-cultural understandings of concepts such as wealth, agency, and happiness through the embodiment of characters reacting to particular events, rather than the discussion of abstract ideas. Therefore ways in which the participants understood their responsibilities and obligations within the in-role activities had implications for the particular moral reasoning that took place. These responsibilities were consensualized by the participants to both further the plot of the drama and to shape and impart the students' critical and moral reasonings about the dramatic scenario. An example of the particular ways in which the students used the dramatic structure of the improvised activities to draw on a consensus of socio-cultural categorizations to enhance the plot of the drama is demonstrated in Excerpt 12.

Excerpt 12

Teacher:	OK good afternoon Mr. and Mrs. (Free). Thank you for coming to see me. Do you mind taking a seat? Look, um… I'm sorry to call you in but we've just noticed… I was just wondering…. We've been having a few problems with Kathy at school, um….You know she's been one of our model students, um…. topping lots of her subjects and I just noticed… and reports from a number of her teachers that she just doesn't seem to be herself. And I was wondering if there's anything. We've had our school guidance counselor talk to her but nothing seems to be really…. She doesn't seem… she seems to almost be hiding something. I was wondering if you might be able to let us know if there's anything you've noticed at home.
Val:	Um… well. Actually my husband and I… We've just split up…and Kathy seems to be taking it really badly.
Teacher:	I see. Um, has she spoken to you openly about it, or…?
Val:	I've tried talking to her but she's… She just doesn't want to say anything about it. She just completely ignores me.
Teacher:	I see. And would you say that she's got a better relationship with you? Has she been able to talk to you about things or…?
Sam:	No. I haven't seen her very much since we broke up.
Teacher:	I see. So at this point, Kathy's actually planning to stay with you. Is that right?
Val:	Um, we told her she can decide, but I don't think she wants to choose and I think if she doesn't she'll probably stay with me.
Teacher:	Now, she's in grade twelve so I guess we have to worry about whether this is actually going to affect her grades. Um, do you see if she's still studying at home (like) she used to do?
Val:	To be perfectly honest, I'm really not sure. She just doesn't talk to me at all.
Teacher:	I see. Um, do you think the guidance counselor's a good way to go or if she's got some friends at school that she's close to?
Sam:	Um, she's got a boyfriend. Joe, or something….

Teacher:	Joe. And do they get on quite well together? Like, is he a responsible sort of person? I don't know him very well. I think he's only fairly new at our school.
Val:	Um, he seems really nice, I guess…
Teacher:	OK, OK… Look, well, I'll see what I can do and obviously we'll get back to you. Sorry, I know this has been tough on your family. Um, what was Kathy planning to do next year?
Val:	She wanted to do journalism. But, um… due to the break up, our financial situation's kind of changed. So we're not sure if we're going to be able to send her.
Teacher:	I see. She was very, very keen. I remember her getting up and talking to all the girls in assembly about focus and so do you think this might be part of the problem as well as the family side.
Val:	I think this will have definitely have a big impact.
Teacher:	OK. Look, we'll do what we can from the school and obviously if you can just keep me informed of what's going on…. Thanks for coming today … Thank you ….and cut….

Structurally, for the drama, the purpose of the 19-turn interaction that took place between the teacher in role as *principal* and student in role as *parents* was to outline and explore the problems Kathy was facing, rather than finding solutions. Teacher began the meeting with the parents by formulating a reason for the meeting, *"We've been having a few problems with Kathy … reports from a number of teachers that she just doesn't seem to be herself."* Teacher also outlined the beginning of a problem to be explored, specifically what parts of the problem the parents may have privileged information about. The latching that takes place between the *principal* and the *parents* demonstrated that, as participants of a role-play, with knowledge of the situation they were discussing in-role, they had an obligation to build a shared, coherent narrative that achieved two tasks:

- To bring the problems discussed prior to the role-play to light in the role-play (despite the fact that Teacher was involved in the out-of-role discussions regarding Kelly's problems at home, her character would not be privy to them and therefore it was part of the "job" of the *parents* to inform her within the in-role talk);
- To expand on those problems, adding the complications that, because of the break-up Kelly is ignoring her Mother and has not had much contact with her Father.

These two tasks achieved by the participants of this role play have their roots in the participants' understanding the dramatic elements. Dramatic tension is created by the withholding or allowing of information that, despite all actors involved being aware of, particular characters in the role-play would not know. If withheld, it is the task of the actor enrolled as the un-enlightened character to either attempt to bring this information into the open or to use the withholding to expand the tension or mystery of the situation. Once the information is shared, it is the task of all participants to use it to further the scenario, by either adding to the complication of the plot or working towards a solution. The fact that the students in role as *parents* understood the need for these tasks, and saw fit to engage them demonstrates that they accepted the task they were given within the context of the drama.

CONTRASTING SITES

While this chapter has not been primarily concerned with a comparison of the work done in the contrasting sites, there was one notable and relevant distinction that warrants mention. Students from the two sites drew upon and expressed their critical understandings of SES as topic or resource in two distinctive ways. At Priven School, a comparatively low SES site, despite demonstrating a more sophisticated use of SES as a resource that can offer candidate solutions for the problem of *lack of money* during their in-role interactions, when asked to explicitly discuss topics related to SES in the student focus groups the students had considerable difficulties interpreting and interacting with the concepts in any abstract form. Excerpt 13 provides an example.

Excerpt 13

Interview:	OK, let's break this question down into two things. Let's talk about Australia, right? In Australia, do you think there are some people who get it easier than others?
Maria:	Yes.
Interview:	People? Young people, yep?
Maria:	The dole payers.
Interview:	The dole payers get it easier?
Maria:	...like the dole people....
Interview:	People on the dole?
Maria:	Dole bludgers, that's it.....
Interview:	They get it easier than everybody else? What about young people?
John:	They'll get it easier. They'll get a job easier cause they think they can handle more work whereas if someone with grey hair walks into a shop and they'll go, " Oh yeah, they couldn't do too much work... might get tired real easy" and give it to the younger person.

Interview:	OK …yep…. What about kids leaving year twelve this year … right? In Australia, do you think everybody gets the same fair go?
Ed:	Probably not because they…. Their mind's not really on the job. They're on schoolies or whatever parties.
Interview:	Yeah, but I mean out of them… all them…. Like, some are going to go to university, some are going to go get jobs. Do you think that all of them have equal opportunity to achieve the same thing?
John:	No, not really. Like, some have a better chance because they like tried their hardest and some will just get through….
Carl:	It depends really….it really depends on your school life and if you paid attention in school.

In this excerpt students are responding to the question: "In Australia do you think there are some people who get it easier than others?" Rather than approaching this as a question about privilege, the students at Priven School approached this question as if it were about the perceived easiness of not working (people on the dole) the perceived easiness of getting a job (young people) and the chance of having difficulties finding a job because of the particular stage of life you are in (leaving Year 12). Once the issue of equal opportunity had been explicitly introduced, the students drew on their understandings of what they had (presumably) been told about achieving, *they like tried their hardest,* and *if you paid attention in school.*

In contrast, students at Chifley school, although having difficulty drawing on shared implicit understandings of SES in the in-role interactions, gave sophisticated responses that demonstrated explicit understanding of SES, and levels of privilege in Australian schools, as a topic of discussion. For example, when asked the same question as students at Priven School (*Do you think some people in Australian society have it easier than others?*), students at Chifley School responded as in Excerpt 14.

Excerpt 14

Allan:	Some people are more fortunate. Like, they can afford more things to help.
Jan:	Yeah.
Interview:	What do you think specifically some people can afford that help? Like, you could say, "Well, you've got lots of money but that doesn't necessarily…."
Allan:	A good high school and tutors.
Interview:	A good high school and tutors.

Allan:	Yeah!
Interview:	What do you think is a good high school?
Allan:	I think…
Edith:	Private school.
Interview:	Why do you think private schools are better than public?
Edith:	Um, I've got a bunch of friends at Wellington Point and like they can't get any higher than a C in math or English if they aren't already in the top math class.
Interview:	So that's an organizational thing, like…?
Edith:	Yeah…
Interview:	They stream the classes.
Edith:	And they can't move up. They're stuck where they are.
Carl:	Private schools have better facilities and stuff.

This not only displayed an understanding of privilege as being able to afford better or more *things to help,* it also delved into the students' reasonings for why the more expensive option is better, allowing them to be organized in ways that allow more movement and opportunity and have better facilities.

The responses to the student focus groups not only displayed this distinction between the ways in which students in the two sites drew upon SES as a topic and a resource, but also had implications for the way in which students demonstrate their explicit understanding of SES in Australia. Students at Chifley School were able or willing to engage in interactions about the nature of privilege in their society, whereas students at Priven School, for all their sophisticated, resourceful, critical shared understandings of SES, displayed difficulties realizing these resources as topics and did not explicitly discuss their understanding of the socio-economic structures of society.

CONCLUSION

The processes and formations that have conventionally been the focus of Critical Literacy and critical inquiry in education more generally (gender relations, race and ethnicity, SES, and so on) can be shown to operate as both topics and resources, and potentially these two types of resources can work against one another's interests at any given teaching and learning moment. A central point is that one connection between Critical Literacy and process drama resides in the opportunity process drama provides for the public exchange and educational scrutiny of moral reasoning practices. These practices, evident in the preparatory and planning work done for the drama and in the in-role elements of the drama itself reveal not just the students' understandings and descriptions of social life; these understandings and descriptions also necessarily show "the normatively and morally organized character of categorization work, accounts, descriptions, predictions and discourse-interactional work in general" (Jayyusi, 1984, 28).

The students who participated in the study from which the discussion in this chapter was drawn showed no hesitation in allocating judgments, even outrage, about apparent compliance and violation of norms and morals attributable to the character-categories. The process drama made those descriptions and allocations of judgments urgent and opened up opportunities for both the teachers and students to produce a different kind of talk-in-interaction from that documented in reviews such as Edwards and Westgate's (1987) discussions.

Finally, we have illustrated ways in which participating students from differing socio-economic settings drew upon their own understanding of socio-economic structures both as an explicit topic and an implicit resource for participating in the lessons. The question of young people's understandings of and engagement in their own personal life trajectories has been a key concern for educationists and sociologists of youth for more than a decade. Features of contemporary socio-economic experience that have informed that concern are individualization, uncertainty, and risk. In this regard, the work of the Becks has been prominent (Beck, 1992; Beck and Beck-Gernsheim, 2002). They have argued that the main contradiction of this moment of history in developed nations is "the yawning gap between the right of self-assertion and the capacity to control the social settings which render self-assertion feasible" (Beck and Beck-Gernsheim, 2002, xix).

Young people are urged to make commitments and decisions from a rapidly increasing array of personal, social, cultural and occupational choices in environments in which they experience a rapidly increasing lack of control, in which the long- and medium-term consequences of choices are both less clear and potentially more dramatic. For educators, a significant component of the Becks' (2002) theorization of the contemporary experiences of youth is individualization. Here they refer to a perceived lack of integration of young people into socio-cultural and socio-economic formations:

> Individualization means dis-embedding without re-embedding ... A decline of narratives of assumed sociability ... It is the individualization ... of growing inequalities into separate biographies that is a collective experience ... Social inequality is on the rise precisely because of the spread of individualization (xxiii-xxiv)

In an important empirical examination of these observations, Ball, Maguire, and MacRae (2000) confirmed this growing sense of individualization of responsibility and trajectory. They conducted a longitudinal study of a varied group of young British people and concluded from their extensive interview data that there was a tendency for crises and exclusions to be seen as personal failings rather than "problems of the system" ... These young people see their lives as "up to them" (Ball, Maguire and MacRae, 2000, 145).

While the lack of perceived support systems (Beck"s "dis-embedding without re-embedding") is common across the diverse backgrounds of the young people studied, Ball and colleagues insisted that the sense of trajectory and possibility is not similarly constituted across SES formations "the possibilities and probabilities of a "future" are constituted differently within the different social-class contexts" (145). But one clear and common feature that struck these researchers was that "the "future" is not all that important to these young people"; a disposition toward the present, a sense of deferral, weave through the narratives (145).

Questions that arise for educators include: What are the environments in which the future can be discussed? In what terms and with what guidance can young people engage in informed exchanges about the relative significance of, for instance, personal versus system failures as they consider their life options? One general suggestion arises from the rich and artfully-managed exchanges exemplified in this chapter: The process drama format can provide a setting in which such concerns can be raised with pertinence, guidance, and moral safety, and embodied in temporary commitments – less than personal but more than hypothetical – that can uniquely animate critical educational inquiries into agency, moral reasoning, and social structure.

REFERENCES

Apple, M. (1987). Foreword. In C. Lankshear (Ed.), *Literacy, schooling and revolution*. London: Falmer.

Ball, S., Maguire, M., & MacRae, S. (2000). *Choice, pathways and transition post-16: New youth, new economies in the global city*. London: Routledge.

Beck, U. (1992). *Risk society: Towards a new modernity*. London: Sage.

Beck, U., & Beck-Gernsheim, E. (2002). *Individualization: Institutionalized individualism and its social and political consequences*. London: Sage.

Edwards, A. D., & Westgate, D. P. G. (1987). *Investigating classroom talk*. London: Routledge.

Eglin, P., & Hester, S. (1992). Category, predicate and task: The pragmatics of practical action. *Semiotica, 88*, 243–268.

Freebody, P. (2008). Critical literacy education: On living with "innocent language". In B. V. Street & N. H. Hornberger (Eds.), *Encyclopedia of language and education, Volume 2: Literacy* (pp. 107–119). Heidelberg, Germany: Springer Scientific.

Freebody, P. (2005). Critical literacy. In R. Beach, J. Green, M. Michael, & T. Shanahan (Eds.), *Multidisciplinary perspectives on literacy research* (2nd ed., pp. 433–454). Cresskill, NJ: Hampton Press.

Freebody, P. (2003). *Qualitative research in education: Interaction and practice*. London: Sage Publications.

Freebody, P., Forrest, T., & Gunn, S. (2001). Accounting and silencing in interviews: Smooth running through the "problem of schooling the disadvantaged". In P. Freebody, S. Muspratt, & B. Dwyer (Eds.), *Difference, silence, and textual practice: Studies in critical literacy* (pp. 119–151). New Jersey, NJ: Hampton Press.

Freebody, P., & Freiberg, J. (2008). Globalized literacy education: Intercultural trade in textual and cultural practice. In M. Prinsloo & M. Baynham (Eds.), *The new literacy studies: Advances in research and theory* (pp. 17–34). Amsterdam/London: John Benjamins.

Freebody, P., & Freiberg, J. (2006). Cultural science and qualitative educational research: Work "in the first place" on the morality of classroom life. *International Journal of Qualitative Studies in Education, 19*(6), 709–722.

Freebody, P., & Freiberg, J. (2000). Public and pedagogic morality: The local orders of instructional and regulatory talk in classrooms. In S. Hester & D. Francis (Eds.), *Local education order: Ethnomethodological studies of knowledge in action* (pp. 141–162). Amsterdam/London: John Benjamins.

Freebody, P., Hornibrook, M., & Freebody, K. (2005). Language, learning to read, and life pathways. *Reading Research Quarterly Online*, ms p. 7. Retrieved from *RRQ Online*, http://www.reading.org/Library/Retrieve.cfm?D=10.1598/RRQ.40.3.6andF=RRQ-40-3-Freebody-supp_1.html

Gee, J. P. (2001). Critical literacy as critical discourse analysis. In J. Harste & P. D. Pearson (Eds.), *Book of readings on critical perspectives on literacy: Possibilities and practices*. New Orleans, LA: International Reading Association.

Heap, J. L. (1997). Conversation analysis methods in researching language in education. In H. H. Hornberger & D. Corson (Eds.), *Encyclopedia of language and education, Volume 8, Research Methods in Language and Education* (pp. 217–225). Amsterdam: Kluwer Academic.

Heathcote, D. (1984). *Collected writings on education and drama*. Chicago: Northwestern University Press.

Heritage, J. (1984). *Garfinkel and ethnomethodology*. Cambridge: Polity Press.

Hester, S., & Francis, D. (Eds.). (2000). *Local education order: Ethnomethodological studies of knowledge in action*. Amsterdam/London: John Benjamins.

Jayyusi, L. (1984). *Categorisation and the moral order*. London: Routledge and Kegan Paul.

Kao, S., & O'Neill, C. (1998). *Words into worlds: Learning a second language through process drama*. Stanford: Ablex Publishing.

Lewis, C. (2001). *Literary practices as social acts: Power, status, and cultural norms in the classroom*. Mahwah, NJ: Lawrence Erlbaum.

O'Neill, C. (1995). *Drama worlds: A framework for process drama*. Portsmouth, NH: Heinemann.

O'Toole, J. (1992). *The process of drama: Negotiating art and meaning*. London: Routledge.

Schegloff, E. A. (2007). *Sequence organization in interaction: A primer in conversation analysis*. Cambridge: Cambridge University Press.

Sinclair, J., & Coulthard, M. (1975). *Towards an analysis of discourse: The English used by teachers and pupils*. London: Oxford University Press.

Wagner, B. J. (1979). *Dorothy Heathcote: Drama as a learning medium*. London: Hutchinson and Co Ltd.

Wallace, C. (2003). *Critical reading in language education*. Basingstoke, UK: Palgrave Macmillan.

SECTION II
CRITICAL LITERACIES IN ACTION

CHAPTER 5

Traveling Objects and Reconfiguring Identities: Meaning-Making and Multi-Modalities

As children come to inhabit the figured world of school, the world offers potentials for meaning-making. They can draw on other figured worlds of practice outside of school, such as home and playtimes, to create meanings within school. Much of children's meaning-making is mediated through artifacts, whether these are books, constructions using blocks and Lego, drawings on paper or models. What is central to our argument is that 'artifacts open up figured worlds' (Holland et al, 1998). We consider a focus on artifacts to be productive in inquiring about meaning-making. Within Critical Literacy curriculum, there is a serious consideration of the role of material objects in learning to open up powerful ways of re-configuring identities, as students take objects across from home to school and reconfigure them within learning situations. By "objects", we mean both created objects (boxes created from shoe boxes to represent an environment) and material artifacts such as drawn and decorated portfolios but also traveling objects, that go between home and school, stones purchased for decoration used for the boxes, or special objects such as a teddy bear much cherished by a teenager and described in a piece of writing. These have resonances that go beyond the confines of school and we want to explore what these objects offer learning. The chapter consolidates an on-going interest that we have in thinking about materiality and the liminality of material practices due to hybridity of identities and cultural practices.

How can children's meaning-making be understood when we take a multimodal perspective? Multimodality implies an attention to objects – to the artifacts and to the material objects that children create in the classroom. Often, words are the focus of teachers' curriculum and the multimodal objects get forgotten. In this chapter, we want to consider the object as the focus of a study of Critical Literacy and consider the implication of privileging objects in the literacy curriculum.

We take a critical approach to literacy by looking at the objects of literacy, which can be regarded within classrooms as artifacts of practice. Objects carry with them the traces of their makers' intentions. We have previously argued (Pahl and Rowsell, 2005; Rowsell and Pahl, 2007) that a focus on the identities of the meaning-maker is the key to understanding these intentions. Here, we begin to unpack what this theory means for those who are involved in working with children, adolescents and adults, and enabling them to make texts. Drawing on our separate research projects, we begin to unravel what happens when an individual

K. Cooper and R. E. White (eds.), Critical Literacies in Action: Social Perspectives and Teaching Practices, 79–98.
© *2008 Sense Publishers. All rights reserved.*

makes a text. This unraveling leads us to look at what happens behind the making of a text. Unraveling the making of a text leads us to an understanding of power.

Artifacts in themselves are important for the meaning they carry, but where the power lies is in the process of artifact creation. What choices do producers make and how does that reflect who they are and what they carry with them? Charting process in relation to product offers an understanding of how a producer thinks, reasons and draws on dispositions. Later in the chapter there is discussion of Critical Discourse Analysis (CDA) (Chouliaraki and Chouliaraki and Fairclough, 1999; Rogers, 2003), which works on similar principles to our approach to artifactual analysis in that CDA excavates how discourses relate back to identity and dispositions of a speaker. In our analysis of materiality, we similarly excavate materials used and how they relate to their producers.

Taking an artifactual approach to the teaching of literacy allows us to frame literacy practices around principles of meaning-making. In the two case studies of practice featured later, we show that multimodal artifacts open up more spaces for students to create and understand narratives. The process of making the artifact-based projects gave them an appreciation for what they know and more identity investment in what they value.

Text-making takes place in social context. These social contexts are infused with relations of power. As children make texts, some texts are more powerful than others and these texts carry more weight. As Bourdieu (1991) has described, linguistic capital has impact within educational structures. However, we argue that material cultural is also subject to these constraints. Just as literacy can be regarded as ideological and subject to discussions of power (Street, 1984; 2000), multi-modality can also been seen as ideological and subject to power (Street, in press).

Texts are created within power structures, which in turn infuse their structures. Material objects as texts can reveal choice: choice of material, choice of function, choice of meaning. As words are riven with powerful discourses, objects also carry within them the traces of practices, discursive and also material, that surrounds them. By making the leap from words, and how words can carry different meanings and sometimes speak with two different tongues, to material objects, we begin to set out a theoretical perspective that sees objects as similarly contested, complex and surrounded by relations of power.

In this chapter, we explore the processes and practices that surround the coming into being of material objects – an environment box project and a portfolio of artifacts and explore what happens when objects or artifacts are interrogated for their meaning potential and are used as sites for learning. The environment box project was a study of one Grade Two (aged six – seven year olds) class and a Spring term's work. The teacher had decided to let the children in the class focus on the making of boxes, using shoeboxes, to reflect the different environments the children were researching. The project was repeated the following Spring. The focus of the research was on the affordances of material artifacts to reflect collaborative voices. The portfolio project began as a pilot study in a secondary school in central New Jersey and has become a longitudinal multimodal inter-vention study going into its second year. The project required twenty secondary students to bring objects to school from home and reflect upon their materiality and write up reflections on their relationships to other objects. The group of teenagers then gathered and archived their materials into a decorated portfolio that they presented at an event at the end of the school year. The focus of the study was on the affordances of materials in their world from their clothes to their cell phones to their thoughts and feelings about their community.

Material objects open up opportunities for different kinds of learning. For example, with the collaborative boxes, children inscribed domains of knowledge from home into the finished artifact, the box. They learned to develop strategies in their material meaning-making to take the box into new realms – that of fantasy play. By offering children a site that is material and has color, depth, texture and spatial qualities, new types of discourses can be allowed in. Often, these artifacts are able to act as a conduit between home and school. They develop new ways of talking and discursive opportunities for students who often have no way of connecting the domains of home and school (Heath, 1983).

These domains of practice can be seen as what Holland and her colleagues have called 'figured worlds' that is,

> Figured worlds in their conceptual dimensions supply the contexts of meanings for actions, cultural production, performances, disputes, for the understandings that people come to make of themselves, and for the capabilities that people develop to direct their own behavior in these worlds. (Holland et al, 1998, 6)

Herein we see that artifacts leverage power for students, as different as they are in the projects (one being primary students in the United Kingdom and the other being secondary students in the United States), yet there is a tacit understanding that materials can do certain kinds of things in one moment but these same materials can constrain content in another moment (e.g., crunchy tissue paper vs. cellotape).

THEORIZING ARTIFACTS

Artifacts can be objects or texts produced by students, such as books of writing, drawings, models, or artifacts can be objects or texts that students value, such as objects from home. Artifacts can also be inscribed with school meanings such as reading scheme books and interactive whiteboards. We consider the history of objects, and draw on theory that historicizes them.

Frequently, artifacts produced by individuals such as drawings can be seen as a process by which identities are sedimented into texts. We have previously described this process as being gradual. A child may watch her mother draw kitchen plans. She might also learn to draw a map at school. As she learns about the social practice of making plans, she creates a new text, a plan of her house. Within this plan, aspects of a child's identity (love of savories and sweets) are discerned and sedimented within the plan (Pahl, 2007).

Our theorizing of artifacts derives in part from the work of Holland and her colleagues (1998), who argued that identities in practice can be seen within texts. Holland and colleagues see all identities as realized in practice and through practice. By providing a practice-focused account of identity, this allows a focus on artifacts as being visible within practice. Domains of practice can be artifacts that lead to these figured worlds. In some cases, artifacts are produced as a result of those identities (Holland et al, 1998). Holland and her colleagues describe how identity is a concept that works to connect intimate, personal worlds with the wider world of social relations. The account of identities can also be made more complex by understanding the layers that make them up. In order to provide a metaphorical model for this process, Holland and Leander theorized identities as 'laminated,' as layered, and multi-dimensional, constructed in dynamic and interrelated ways (Holland and Leander, 2004). Artifacts can be seen as produced through complex interpersonal relations. They carry within them traces of their making and as many of the artifacts were collaborative, identities can be seen to be laminated within these material objects.

From there, it is a researcher's project to identify where identities feature within artifacts. Artifacts featured later in the paper can be studied to understand where students' identities lie. These resulting findings can be useful when constructing a literacy curriculum that privileges students' identities. Artifacts carry what Lemke (2000) describes as timescales. For example, a teddy bear might be as old as the child, but a reading scheme book might carry a shorter timescale. Lemke has argued that the semiotic potential of an artifact is linked to its timescale. For example, a Samurai sword may carry a longer and deeper meaning potential than a conventional sword due to its deeper and richer timescale (Lemke, 2000). We also argue that these kinds of artifacts signify identity. For example, artifacts carry traces of their maker's intentions, as for example, drawings that signify and display identity narratives.

Lemke describes how timescales can be important in considering an object (2000). Timescales can be longer (tied to the past and more embedded meanings) or shorter (tied to present-day moments). Lemke offers the samurai sword, described above, as an example of an object with a long timescale that carries a particular history. We can analyze artifacts on different timescales. Literacy events and practices can also be organized by timescale. A key finding in the study is that concentrating our gaze on what objects occupy individual's attention can help us to understand the principles of their meaning making. As Lemke notes,

> No matter how much we homogenize classroom groups – by age, by social class, by gender, by culture, race or dominant language – for the classroom processes at each timescale there will be considerable differences in affective engagement, in evaluative dispositions, in relevant knowledge and skills, and in resources for integrating the events of the moment into patterns that will persist on longer timescales. (Lemke, 2000, 285)

It makes sense that objects and practices in which we have engaged more and longer than others would carry more ideological weight in our meaning making and language activities than texts and practices confined to a school year or even a succession of years. Home timescales often move more slowly and are tied to different events and practices, such as an Islamic calendar or a family bereavement.

Timescale became a particularly helpful concept when we worked through the data and reflected on how different timescales were presented in artifacts.

THE ENVIRONMENTAL BOX PROJECT

The environmental box project represents a case study of artifacts that is both dialogic and collaborative. This project grew out of a study of the impact of a group of artists on children's learning in an Infants' school in South Yorkshire (Pahl, 2007). The project was an ethnographic study involving classroom observation, teacher interviews, child interviews and parent interviews that took place over three years. One key aspect of the study was on looking at what happened to the teachers' practices as a result of the artists' intervention. The artists had set up a series of collaborative ventures including a photograph project called "Capturing your Community" in which the children photographed their local area, and a magazine project involving an account of the local town in which they lived. In both projects, the children made decisions around what they wanted to photograph and draw.

A number of linked projects were set up. For example, children drew their feelings in abstract paintings and developed a lens from which to view their photographs, and focused on texture or color, or shape. In all the projects, their agency was high and their experiences from home drawn upon. The project was creative in that it harnessed the agency of the children, was relevant to their lives and opened the 'space of possibility' so that teachers let go and allowed things to happen (Craft, 2000; 2002; Jeffrey, 2006). This way of working led to new projects. In this instance, one year two teacher, Sally, decided to try out her own project, which was to let the children design and build their own box environments, using shoe boxes. The children, in pairs or threes, were to choose which environments they wanted to make, design the box, research the animals that lived in the environment and develop this. The aim of the project was to encourage collaborative talk and increase the children's skills in art. The driving force of the project was a focus on the children as agents. As she said:

> I think for me it came from that first ... project that we did with Year Two, and its just you always try new things and never underestimate what they can do but it was a big eye opener for me, that they [the children] were so capable at deciding what they wanted to learn and what they wanted to do in that session and in that project. I try to do that quite a lot now in almost everything. (Sally Bean, Year Two teacher)

The teacher was keen to encourage the children to create their box environments independently, without access to her input. The children created their box environments in groups of three, designed them first on paper, and then created them in three dimensions. The class teacher identified her priorities as follows in her diary:

> The Year Two topic for Spring Term is Environments, looking at plants and animals in both local environments, such as gardens, ponds and hedgerows and more global environments such as oceans, deserts and rainforests. My

year group colleague and I planned the first three weeks of the term with a predominantly Science and ICT focus to the children's learning so that the children could spend time comparing living things and finding out how these are adapted to the environment in which they live. The second three weeks was with an Art and Design Technology focus, where the children would create a model of an environment of their choosing in a shoebox, a project which I call their "Box Environments".

I followed the children as a researcher as they made their boxes in teams of three. As I watched, I recorded their discussions and I also photographed the boxes, often asking children to record the making stage themselves using disposable cameras.

I have identified three different affordances in Critical Literacy education that the box projects provided the children. The first was an ability to creatively focus on material choices, problems and solutions, moving on an understanding of how an artifact is put together and crafted. This then leads to a focus on collaborative talk as an engine for meaning-making. I call this creative problem-solving in the material world.

The second affordance was an ability that the project had to enable a joining up of home and school domains as the researching and creating of the boxes required different kinds of knowledge and domains of learning. I call this home/school knowledge building in the material world.

The third aspect that contributes to a Critical Literacy curriculum is an understanding of how the boxes lifted the children's imaginative play and developed close and complex play rituals that could then become narratives of identity. I call this aspect narrative play creation in the material world. These three aspects, problem solving, home/school knowledge building and narrative play take place within the material structures the children were engaged in making. In that sense, these were artifactual sites for meaning-making.

CREATIVE PROBLEM-SOLVING IN THE MATERIAL WORLD

In the first year, many of the children were intensely focused on the material choices they had to create the effects they wanted. For example, in this box representing the ocean the children were trying to get the seaweed to stand up on their box:

Emma: First we got a box and my partner was Sophie. Secondly we painted our box and then we added some things to it. My partner tried to make seaweed and we couldn't. We tried everything we could think of and then Mrs. Bean had a bolt of lightening and she thought of something and we did it but we haven't tried it yet but I think it will work. I hope so...

Kate: So why didn't it go well when it got to the seaweed?

Sophie: Because we tried some see-through crunchy tissue paper, and that didn't work, we wanted it to stand up and it didn't.

Kate: I remember....

Sophie: And then we tried....

Kate: Cellotape?

Emma: What was it for, the seaweed? We did blutac.

Kate: Blutac!

Sophie: We did blutac to stick it down. Well that's when we thought of the acetate and Mrs. Bean thought of the acetate. We didn't know how to stick it up for itself, because we wanted it to look real, so we....

Emma: Then we painted, like, the acetate and stuck it to the box.

Sophie: But we needed to put glue into it because ...um... paint would just peel off

Kate: It was the glue and the paint together?

Sophie: Because it sticks better.

Kate: Was that the bolt of lightening?

Sophie: Yeah

Emma: Yeah.

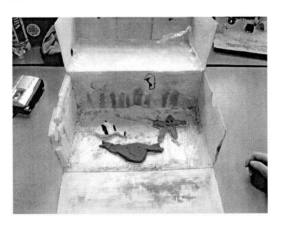

Figure 1. The ocean box year 1

Here, the children talk about materiality in terms of difficulty and solutions. Their focus is on 'wanting it to look real' and their work is entirely focused on what the box environment looks like. They try different solutions until their teacher, Mrs. Bean, comes up with a "bolt of lightening". Here the teacher's role is far removed from theirs – they are very much enmeshed in their own inner world of creative solutions to material problems. The box making throws up problems that the children respond to by creating solutions and the teacher comes in "like a bolt of lightening". By describing the making process so vividly in words, the children re-create and narrate the making process. In this way, the artifact and its affordances are brought into the linguistic domain. As the teacher herself described in an interview:

> They have done tremendously well with the amount of external things they have brought into this project and they have overcome a lot of problems themselves and a lot of difficulties; whether it has been testing out materials or trying something and it not working and I have just tried to be there as a facilitator. (Sally Bean, Year Two teacher)

The teacher's role is changed in response to the children's active engagement with the material process and their need to drive problem-solving independently from her.

HOME/SCHOOL KNOWLEDGE BUILDING IN THE MATERIAL WORLD

In the first year, the children drew on knowledge that they had gained from other domains, notably home. Part of the project was to create animals out of clay or modeling material, to go into the environments. The children had to research the attributes of these animals in order to find out about their characteristics. Some children went to the library or looked up the animals on the Internet. Others used home experience. For example, Carl's experience in his home country of the Philippines governed his making of the King Cobra, while his partner, Francesca, is more focused on material solutions to problems:

Carl: We found a real cobra in the book over there.

Kate: Can you show me?

Francesca: We need more red,

Kate: Have you seen one on the "telly"?

Carl: I have seen one on the zoo. I saw a real one in my cousin's house in the Philippines. He has got a real King Cobra in his house; he has got it locked up in his cage. He's in the Philippines.

Kate: What colours were it?

Carl: Black at the top and steely and brown at the bottom.

Kate: Were you scared?

Carl: He went…"ssss"… like that. (Taped discussion 8.2.06)

Carl translated his own experience of a cobra into a material artifact and created his own cobra out of clay (pictured).

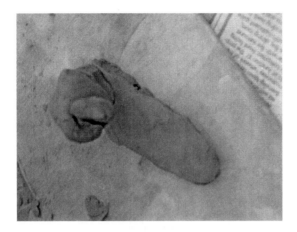

Figure 2. Carl's King Cobra

Carl's actual experience is meshed with the artifact he created and the resulting box reflected knowledge from home as well as school. In some cases, children brought in artifacts from home to decorate their boxes. In the second year, this trend was very evident, as decorative stones and shells were brought in to create ocean environments. Children also brought in 'small stories' from home, narratives that fleshed out their knowledge about the animals they put in their boxes (Baynham and Georgakopoulou, 2006).

This next piece of data comes from the second year – the project was repeated once more with the new intake of children aged six to seven. Here are some children describing their experiences in a group discussion that took place during playtime. A group of girls came up to me and told me about their experiences with the animals they were making:

Taylor:	We are going to go on t' Internet to search on crabs because we don't know how to draw a crab.
Savannah:	No we don't, we have never drawn a crab before.
Taylor:	Well, I have seen them but it's hard to draw one.
Kate:	Where did you see one?
Taylor:	I went on holiday and I went to Skegness and I were swimming in the water, and I saw a crab and I saw about ...four.
Savannah:	When I went to...
Taylor:	And I thought it might – makes pincer movements.
Kate:	Nippy!
Savannah:	I saw one when I went to...I went to Grand Canary you know the Canary Islands on holiday and it took about four hours to

get there and then I saw this crab on the beach when I landed there, and it was about ten of them.

Here, the girls tell me stories that relate to their out-of-school lives, but these stories also tell us about the animals, about their habitat and properties, that can be translated into material artifacts. The Internet was not as useful as actually seeing the crab and observing its movements. Here the material world is brought in as evidence to support the creation of the crab and to provide visual evidence of its qualities.

NARRATIVE PLAY CREATION IN THE MATERIAL WORLD

In this last example of artifactual learning, I describe how a group of girls gradually worked collaboratively on the box to create a play environment for animals. The creation of the environment was, however, determined by the material affordances of the box. As the box developed, it became the site for play, and its material qualities suggested that play. The box started as a basic box, representing the ocean that had a small hill in one corner:

Figure 3. The hill (stage 1)

Taylor: We made a hill with masking tape.

Kate: Masking tape?

Taylor: We are going to paint over it. What we did, we squished paper up and then we...um...added some masking tape on it, and then I got some green paint and just coated it.

Savannah: Are you putting a coat on it?

The children described how the hill was going to be a site for play:

Figure 4. The hill (stage 2)

Savannah:	Here we are going to paint over the masking tape so it makes it look like….
Taylor:	We are going to put some fish in the seabed.
Savannah:	Yes. That's going to be…. These are the seabed under here; we are going to get some over there.
Taylor:	We are going to wrap some of the dolphins under.
Savannah:	Yes we are going to try and get the dolphins to come in here so it looks like they are getting ready to jump up over the water!

The making of the hill created a new material affordance – a place for the potential dolphins to sleep. This discussion, taped about half way through the making process, reveals the girls' complex to and fro discussion about what their box will be and the affordances it provides for imaginative play:

Savannah:	We build the hill because that's going to be where every fish sleeps!
Kate:	You said that about the dolphins peeking through, I like that.
Savannah:	Taylor, I am gonna put that shell there because it looks more nice in there. I am going to bring this little light and I am going to stick it there because it can be light.
Taylor:	Yes, but the light will have to go there because it doesn't look as bright in there.
Kate:	You have a little light.
Savannah:	We could put the dolphins…. we could put the dolphins.

Taylor:	We could put the light in there because it makes it light.
Savannah:	Because the fish will swim into there anyway (higher pitch).
Taylor:	No, they could swim; the dolphins could be peeping through there, couldn't they?
Taylor:	It's gonna have to be ripped a bit like that.
Savannah:	No the dolphins sleep there, Taylor. It can't be like that.
Taylor:	Yes, that's where the dolphins sleep.

Figure 5. The box in its finished state

Two weeks later the box was ready but the play had only just begun. As the children peopled their box with crabs and dolphins, they took on a life of their own. The box became a stage set for a complex play narrative that the girls began to negotiate amongst themselves:

Kate:	Now can you tell me about your box environment?
Savannah:	It's the ocean.
Coral:	We made…we had…
Savannah:	That's the mummy dolphin and that's the baby dolphin!
Kate:	Oh brilliant!
Savannah:	We put them together because the baby has to follow the mummy.
Coral:	We made it out of clay.

Taylor:	Yeah.
Kate:	Are you the ones that had a dolphin school?
Girls:	Yeah! A dolphin school.
Coral:	Because the mummy is going to take the baby to school.
Savannah:	Yes. That's right, because it only lives down here.
Taylor:	We did the jellyfish, ...er.... One's the sister, one's the brother, one's the baby and one's the mum.
Coral:	That's the baby.

The girls told me an unfolding narrative about their school. At times in the narrative, the material affordance of the box creates new opportunities for meaning-making:

Taylor:	We made some children because there is no point making the school if there ain't gonna be no children to go in...
Savannah:	The pond is where they swim sometimes if they want to get cool and if it's hot.
Coral:	Yeah!
Taylor:	And the shallow bit is the sand to make it...um....
Savannah:	We did some shells so then they can pretend they are paper and pencils.
Taylor:	So they can write on it.

The material artifacts created narrative play opportunities and the making of the joint artifact was riven with the discourses of the girls. In some cases, the material object meant different things at different times:

| Taylor: | We did the school because...um...we just wanted to make, ...well we decided that we wanted it to be a rock, but then we changed us mind to put it to a school because there's a door... |

Here, the dolphin school is created through the material affordance of the rock, that has its own meaning-making potential – as Taylor remarks, "We decided that we wanted it be a rock, but then we changed us mind to put it to a school because there's a door". The material affordances of the box created the opportunities for the dolphin school and the girls are led not only by popular culture influences (Finding Nemo, Mermaid stories) but also by the material possibilities they have created for their mini world.

As a conclusion to this data discussion, returning to the idea of artifacts opening up figured worlds, in each case, the affordance of the box creates opportunities for new kinds of engagement with literacy. In the first example, problem solving in the form of the discussion about how to create sticking up seaweed is reflected in complex talk. One of the key aims of the project was to create collaborative talk as the school identified that as one of its core objectives. In the second example, Carl, a shy child, was able to bring his home experience into school. A further discussion could have created a narrative piece of writing upon the box. In the third example the girls created a fully-fledged dramatic world, which could be extended to create a play. While all three examples remain in the material world, the literacy possibilities stemming from this project were immense.

RECONFIGURING IDENTITIES THROUGH ARTIFACTUAL ENGLISH

In another case study, students used artifactual English to remediate identities through the use of common objects and activities. This project grew out of an intervention study to improve the literacy achievement of a group of secondary English students at a high school in Princeton, New Jersey. The study is an action research study with two English teachers and their English supervisor. Students involved in the study take a course called English Plus. The English Plus program enables students to achieve their potential by providing opportunities for supervised completion of their assignments, assistance with skill development, and motivational activities to inspire commitment.

The data collection for the study involved a survey about outside literacy practices, observations of student participants, teacher journals, a portfolio intervention and teacher interviews. A key aspect of the study was a bi-weekly meeting of the research team (Jennifer, Barbara, Julie, and Courtney) and weekly work on portfolios by students. Jennifer came into classes regularly to monitor progress on the portfolios. As with Kate's box project, the project was about creativity and innovation and accessing the students' awareness and appreciation of multimodality and materiality. There were certain research questions that framed our intervention, such as: What is valued by students? What material form do these artifacts take? Why do they value them? Can they articulate why they value them? How do these texts relate to their own learning? Are there inclusions and exclusions in terms of skills? The overall aim of the project was to increase students' motivation in English by invoking their own texts and artifacts.

The student population was a mix of Hispanic, African-American, and White-European students involved as participants. At the beginning of the study, we opted for a survey to get a read on what they engaged in outside of school, which ranged from sports to videogames to music. In light of the information, the research team decided to focus on artifacts as a gateway into learning. Students had class time every week from January to May to write artifact reflections, to gather artifacts and decorate their portfolios.

In an excerpt from one of the teachers' journals, she captured the individual nature of the portfolios: "everyone has become attached to something. Tina (pseudonyms throughout) is enjoying doing artifact reflections; Tyrel is enjoying making each page look special; Katherine misses class for learning lab twice a week…" (May 18th, 2007).

What became clear was that students found their own way into materiality. For some students, they used photographs as central images in their portfolios and for others; they preferred writing narratives to express a strong feeling or sentiment. Creativity was housed in the unique combination of images, written text, or textures students preferred to configure themselves. What surprised me when the portfolios were completed was what each student foregrounded. With teenagers, one might expect MySpace pages, music, and maybe sports, but the artifacts were far more emotional and affective in nature with family artifacts and photos of younger siblings decorating the covers of portfolios. These images were powerful indicators of their identity. Like Kate, I followed the students, worked with them and their teachers as their portfolios evolved over the semester. We all kept journals about the process and shared our findings. In light of the study, I identified three different affordances in Critical Literacy education.

The first affordance in Critical Literacy education deals with the strength of situating identities within materialities. Through the project, the research team and the students became more aware of their identities and the hybrid nature of their lived worlds by reflecting on the materiality of an artifact. I call this "creative process through artifacts of self".

The second affordance was students' ability to see themselves in their artifacts. Much of this category has to do with what artifacts did for students and, what is more, the timescale of artifacts and how they derive a strong sense of themselves through artifacts that have stood the test of time. I call these "timescale artifacts".

The third affordance was students' ability to use the power of expression to transmit parts of themselves through a narrative. Much of this category deals with using the subversive to foreground an aspect of self. I call this "reconfiguring identity through expression".

CREATIVE PROCESS THROUGH ARTIFACTS OF SELF

Students gravitated toward artifacts that represent them. That is, artifacts which positioned their particular perspective. On the covers of some portfolios, students featured hip-hop stars or their boyfriends or girlfriends. Cameron opted for a skateboarder in the middle of a turn on the front of his portfolio.

For Cameron, the image transmitted part of his hybrid identity that does not emerge at school. According to Cameron, the process of gathering objects that he values and uses allowed him to find a voice. Much of his identity is tied to the art of skateboarding and communities of practice (Lave and Wenger, 1991) that accompany skateboarding and he found a voice in foregrounding the image on the portfolio. Cameron's cell phone and skateboard are central artifacts in his life and as such invite invested parts of himself into the creative process of gathering and archiving his portfolio.

TIMESCALE ARTIFACTS

For Paulette, meaning-making centred on objects that have traveled with her. In the image below you see a collage of important images in her life – her teddy bear and a photograph of someone close to her. These visual texts are meaningful because of longevity. Paulette has been home-schooled until mid-high school and, as a result, objects in the home carry so much relevance for her. The phrase 'Things dat mean da most' carries significance with its reference to a vernacular discourse in her life.

Figure 6. Skateboarder Portfolio Cover

Figure 7. Reflection on Things that matter

The image of the bear is a part of her figured world and very much an artifact of self. The materiality of the artifact leads us to its message, with drawn in hearts, cut-out bits of text, and a large photograph of a handsome man. These are all signifiers of enduring importance for Paulette.

RECONFIGURING IDENTITY THROUGH EXPRESSION

Alicia struggled with the portfolio assignment. She did not feel motivated in English class and did not find much meaning in the assignment. However, in the end, she seemed to benefit the most, having found a voice through the expressive nature of her portfolio. Below, you see an excerpt from a letter that she submitted as an artifact that carries great significance for her.

> Sometimes people just don't realize that without the Hispanic community the work wouldn't get done, they are also doing the harder and more complicated jobs that no one else wants to do. It doesn't matter if it's either working at a McDonalds or at a fast-food place that offer minimum wage. They feel proud because of the way they are earning their living and not by seeing if what they're doing is complicated.

Figure 8. Impassioned Paper

In her reflection about her impassioned paper, Alicia said:

I didn't know what to write and say related to the topic but then I figured out that it is worth a try explaining things by how they are and acted upon without making it up and coming from real-life experiences that White Americans might not consider.

Having the freedom to express her feelings about lived experiences gave Alicia a power of expression. In light of writing the assignment, Alicia reconfigured her identity in the English classroom and, as a result, she felt recontextualized into the space of practice. Her transformation over the course of making the portfolio was noticeable and that largely had to do with giving her more room for expression and allowing her own hybrid world in.

BRINGING THE STUDIES TOGETHER THROUGH THE MATERIAL

What gave both projects power and meaning was materiality and reflecting on materiality. Whether it is using cellotape as seaweed or capturing a skateboarder's twist – young and old students think in terms of materiality. Artifactual literacy comes at meaning-making from the text, its form and its meaning. The strength of the data lies in a tacit awareness of what materials can and can not do. Objects that travel to new domains can be seen in a clearer light and can give us more license to open up meanings. They can point to culture or remind us of home spaces. These figured worlds and communities of practice give us power. The intriguing nature of bringing two quite different studies together with the same lens is that they are remarkably similar in terms of how fluent students are about the nature of materiality and the power that materiality gives to meaning.

With both studies in mind, materiality exists in a similar way to James Gee's "bigD" Discourses as parts of self that get interwoven with other parts as sign-makers make meaning and interact (Gee, 1996). Materials as objects reflected upon or brought together to make a box and narrative tells a story about the producer. Artifacts are modal representations of self that provide an understanding of what motivates a meaning-maker. By concentrating the gaze on materialities, identity and the principles of meaning-making can be more fully understood. Being critical about literacy means figuring out the identities of students who make meaning and what motivates them.

Critical Discourse Analysis (CDA) approaches discourse and language as sites of identities, social relations, power, and knowledge (Chouliaraki and Fairclough, 1999). The term 'critical' signals that the approach explicitly deals with how language is used to exercise socio-political control. Interpretation is generated through what is in the text alongside its relationship with the interpreter. Fairclough looks at the dialogic relationship between how analysts interpret texts based on members' resources and social background (Fairclough, 1990). Given CDA's interest in power, we view this method as in line with the work we have foregrounded in the chapter. We believe that we extend this work by looking at how power finds its way into the material. Artifacts featured in the chapter are powerful indicators of identity and fractured identity when the producer is placed in a context wherein they feel they do not have power.

Critical Literacy has focused on language as a site for power (Fairclough, 1990; Muspratt, Luke and Freebody, 1997). In the chapter, we drew on existing studies of multimodality (Kress, 1997; Jewitt and Kress, 2003) and applied a critical discourse perspective to multimodal texts (Chouliaraki and Fairclough, 1999). In doing so, we have opened up a discussion about how material artifacts are themselves contested. For example, the dolphin hill was both a place to sleep and a school and its rip created new opportunities for meaning making. By focusing on artifacts, the portfolio project has involved teachers in finding out about their students' home lives and listening to their experience.

We would suggest the following curricula innovations for Critical Literacy educators:

– To appreciate the traveling nature of objects, as they move between home and school.
– To create opportunities for students to talk about objects.
– To see objects as culturally laden and holding the potential for different kinds of narratives.
– To encourage and support students to discuss material culture as a learning tool.

We would also suggest a focus on material culture within classrooms as a theoretical tool for literacy research. Drawing on work on classrooms as dialogic and riven with complex voices (Maybin, 1994; 2007) we can now extend this analysis to artifacts, their makers and the practices sedimented within them.

Bringing in materials from the lived lives of students and opening up classrooms to different kinds of materials simply allows more students to find a place. As objects travel across spaces, it is possible to let in new, different kinds of discourses and ways of materializing discourses. Our job as literacy educators is to help students think critically about texts and, in that process, enable a broadening of notions of what text is and constitutes. This process then leads us closer to the intentions and identities of the meaning-makers.

REFERENCES

Baynham, M., & Georgakopoulou, A. (2006). *"Big" stories and "small" stories: Reflections on methodological/theoretical issues in narrative research.* Retrieved from http://www.ling-ethnog.org.uk/events.htm#OUMethIss06

Bourdieu, P. (1991). *Language and symbolic power.* Cambridge: Polity Press.

Chouliaraki, L., & Fairclough, N. (1999). *Discourse and late modernity: Rethinking critical discourse analysis.* Edinburgh: Edinburgh University Press.

Craft, A. (2000). *Creativity across the primary curriculum: Framing and developing practice.* London: Routledge.

Craft, A. (2002). *Creativity and early years education.* London: Continuum.

Fairclough, N. (1990). *Language and power.* London: Longman.

Gee, J. P. (1996). *Social linguistics and literacies: Ideology in discourses.* London: Taylor and Francis.

Heath, S. B. (1983). *Ways with words: Language, life, and work in communities and classrooms.* Cambridge, UK: Cambridge University Press.

Holland, D., Lachicotte, W., Skinner, D., & Cain, C. (1998). *Identity and agency in cultural worlds.* Cambridge, MA: Harvard University Press.

Holland, D., & Leander, K. (2004). Ethnographic studies of positioning and subjectivity: An introduction. *Ethos, 32*(2), 127–130.

Jeffery, B. (2006). *Creative learning practices: European experiences.* London: The Tuffnell Press.

Jewitt, C., & Kress, G. (2003). *Multimodal literacies.* London: Paul Chapman.

Kress, G. (1997). *Before writing: Rethinking the pathway to literacy.* London: Routledge.

Lave, J., & Wenger, E. (1991). *Situated learning: Legitimate peripheral participation.* Cambridge: Cambridge University Press.

Lemke, J. L. (2000). Across the scales of time: Artifacts, activities and meanings in ecosocial systems. *Mind, Culture and Activity, 7*(4), 273–290.

Maybin, J. (1994). Children's voices: Talk, knowledge and identity. In D. Graddol, J. Maybin, & B. Stierer (Eds.), *Researching language and literacy in social context.* Buckingham: Open University Press.

Maybin, J. (2007). Literacy under and over the desk: Oppositions and heterogeneity. *Language and Education, 21*(6), 515–530.

Muspratt, S., Luke, A., & Freebody, P. (1997). *Constructing critical literacy: Teaching and learning textual practice.* Melbourne: Allen and Bacon.

Pahl, K. (2007). Creativity in events and practices: A lens for understanding children's multimodal texts *Literacy, 41*(2), 86–92.

Pahl, K., & Rowsell, J. (2005). *Literacy and education: Understanding the new literacy studies in the classroom.* London: Paul Chapman.

Rogers, R. (2003). *A critical discourse analysis of family literacy education.* Mahwah, NJ: Lawrence Erlbaum.

Rowsell, J., & Pahl, K. (2007). Sedimented identities in texts: Instances of practice. *Reading Research Quarterly, 42*(3), 388–404.

Street, B. V. (1984). *Literacy in theory and practice.* Cambridge: Cambridge University Press.

Street, B. V (2000). Literacy events and literacy practices: Theory and practice in the new literacy studies. In M. Martin-Jones & K. Jones (Eds.), *Multilingual literacies: Reading and writing different worlds* (pp. 17–29). Amsterdam/Philadelphia: John Benjamins Publishing Company

Street, B. V. (in press). New literacies, new times: Developments in literacy studies. In N. Hornberger (Ed.), *Encyclopaedia of language and education* (2nd Rev. ed.). New York: Springer.

CHAPTER 6

Uncomfortable Positionings: Critical Literacy and Identity in a
Post-Apartheid University Classroom

"Is truth that closely related to identity? It must be. What you believe to be
true depends on who you believe yourself to be." (Antjie Krog, *Country of
my Skull*, 1998, 99)

In this chapter I present classroom-based research conducted in a first year English
and Cultural Studies course at a South African university. In my pedagogy, as well
as my analysis, I attempt to answer the questions:
- What does it mean to take student identity seriously in Critical Literacy
practice? and,
- How does one engage productively with student resistance to critical pedagogy?

While the dominant view of resistance to critical pedagogy has been that this
resistance is a problem, which needs to be overcome, my data supports a more
positive view. I argue that student resistance can create potentially productive,
albeit uncomfortable, spaces for Critical Literacy work and that our aim should be
to engage with student resistance rather than to avoid or attempt to overcome it.
Resistance as theorized in my study refers to intransigence or opposition to the
knowledge and identities, as well as the values, which are constructed or presented
and sometimes imposed in the classroom. Using transcripts of classroom discourse,
I document one of my attempts to engage productively with student resistance and
analyze the effects of my teaching strategies: consciously positioning students
differently and attempting to teach them to deconstruct binary oppositions. In the
first part of this chapter, I begin by defining my approach to Critical Literacy and
then discuss research on student resistance to critical pedagogy. I go on to outline
the post-structuralist theorizing of identity that I am working with. In the second
part of the chapter I turn to a discussion of classroom data focusing on an analysis
of classroom discourse and examining the students' constructions of identity.

WHAT IS CRITICAL LITERACY?

Since Critical Literacy has come to assume a range of different meanings in
different contexts, I will begin by briefly sketching what I mean by "Critical
Literacy". Critical Literacy work can be strongly text-focused involving linguistic
analysis of ideologies in texts. For example, there is much work in Critical
Language Awareness in the UK (see Wallace, 2003) and South Africa (Janks,
1993), Critical Literacy drawing on systemic functional linguistics in Australia (see

*K. Cooper and R. E. White (eds.), Critical Literacies in Action: Social Perspectives
and Teaching Practices, 99–115.*

Comber, 1993), or more loosely text-focused, drawing on definitions from critical pedagogy, especially the work of Freire and Giroux (see Bee, 1993).

Giroux argues that Critical Literacy offers "the opportunity for students to interrogate how knowledge is constituted as both a historical and social construction" (1989, 33-34) and should provide them with the "knowledge and skills necessary for them to understand and analyze their own historically constructed voices and experiences as part of a project of self and social empowerment" (Ibid.). Key to critical pedagogy and related Critical Literacy work, then, are the notions of emancipation, through the rational process of increasing students' knowledge and understanding, and empowerment. My own work draws on this broader approach to Critical Literacy that is rooted in critical pedagogy and Freirean ideas of "reading the word and the world" (Freire and Macedo, 1987), although, as my discussion will show, I problematize notions of empowerment and of learning as an emancipatory and rational process.

STUDENT RESISTANCE TO CRITICAL LITERACY

A challenge to critical pedagogy and related Critical Literacy work is found in the problem of student resistance or opposition to critical teaching, that is to the knowledge and identities which are constructed, and possibly imposed, in the classroom. Discussions of such resistance in North America and South Africa suggest that the extent to which students participate in or resist Critical Literacy is bound up with their identities, and thus with how they are positioned or identified through the texts under study (Britzman, Santiago-Valles, Jiménez-Muñoz, and Lamash, 1993; Granville, 2003; Janks, 2001, 2002).

In South Africa, Hilary Janks (1995) remarks on her research into secondary school students' responses to Critical Language Awareness (CLA) materials that "Interpreting the interview data is like disentangling a knot of identity investments" (330). Reflecting on students' responses in this research some years later, Janks writes: "While I recognized the power of identity investments, I failed to realize how helpless rationality is in the face of them" (2002, 19-20). She relates a more recent example where students were involved in deconstructing print advertisements, critically analyzing sexist representations of women. While the female students were well able to produce critical deconstructions of the texts, this did not prevent them from desiring to be like the female models represented as sexual objects in the advertisements. Janks thus argues, "Where identification [with the text] promises the fulfillment of desire, reason cannot compete" (2002, 10). Janks positions Critical Literacy as an "essentially...rationalist activity" and challenges educators working within this frame to explore the territory "beyond reason" (2002, 22).

Writing about student resistance, researchers have drawn on feminist and post-structuralist perspectives which deconstruct critical pedagogy as an enlightenment project and which problematize the notion of the fully rational and unified subject (Britzman et al, 1993, 1991; Ellsworth, 1989; Janks, 2001; Lather, 1991). They problematize the assumption underlying most Critical Literacy approaches that revealing social inequalities to people will necessarily bring about change, whether personal, or collective. As Elizabeth Ellsworth indicates in one of the most-well known critiques of critical pedagogy, this assumption ignores the way in which people have investments in particular social positions and discourses, and that these kinds of investments are not lightly given up (Ellsworth, 1989).

More recent work in Critical Literacy (Ferreira and Janks, 2007; McKinney, 2005; Moffat and Norton, 2005) thus foregrounds issues of student identity, and considers what students' investments might be and how students are positioned both inside and outside the classroom. As the focus on investment and positioning implies, such work brings together critical theory and poststructuralist theoretical frameworks. While critical theory maintains the focus on teaching for social justice and foregrounds issues of power and inequality, poststructuralism signals multiplicity and complexity, a move away from a dogmatic approach to the deconstruction of binary oppositions: For example, oppressor/oppressed; masculine/feminine; advantaged/disadvantaged; and white/black.

THEORIZING IDENTITY/SUBJECTIVITY

In theorizing student identity, I draw on the post-structuralist work of Chris Weedon (1997), Bronwyn Davies (1990, 1997) and Stuart Hall (1996). In particular, I use the key concepts of *representation* and *interpellation* (looking at how we are positioned), *identity investments* and *desire*, as well as subjectivity as a *site of struggle* to analyze and interpret my data. Drawing on the Foucauldian notions of discourse and historical specificity, identity in post-structuralism, or subjectivity as it is often called, is understood as discursively constructed and is always socially and historically embedded. It is thus always in process, "neither unified or fixed" (Weedon, 1997, 87). However, while subjectivity may be always in process, individuals can and do invest in particular identities or identifications which have better or worse effects. Henriques, Hollway, Urwin, Venn and Walkerdine gloss investment as "the emotional commitment involved in taking up positions in discourses which confer power and are supportive of our sense of continuity" (1998, 205). Weedon argues further that subjectivity as a site of struggle enables individuals to resist being positioned in particular ways and to construct new meanings from conflicting discourses.

Along with Weedon, Hall focuses on identity as in process, 'becoming', and, significantly for Critical Literacy, stresses the importance of representation in the construction of identity:

[I]dentities are about questions of using the resources of history, language and culture in a process of *becoming* rather than being: not 'who we are' or 'where we came from', so much as what we might become, how we have been represented and how that bears on how we might represent ourselves. Identities are therefore constructed within, not outside representation (Hall, 1996, 4; my emphasis).

As Hall points out, how we are represented is intimately related to "how we might represent ourselves" (Ibid.). Of course we may not accept certain representations of ourselves, though these will still influence our identities and thus such undesirable representations may be resisted. Finally, in theorizing desire, Davies also emphasizes the centrality of representation arguing that "Desires are constituted through the narratives and storylines, the metaphors, the very language and patterns of existence through which we are 'interpellated' into the social world" (Davies, 1990, 501).

In relation to my pedagogy, I have considered how my students are represented and positioned in and by the curriculum materials that are on offer in the course, as such representations may affect the way that students respond to these inter-pellations. I have also considered the questions: What identities are constructed for students in the classroom and what identities do they construct for themselves? I have thus analyzed evidence of their investments and desires in relation to self and other positionings.

RESEARCH CONTEXT

I turn now to a discussion of the research itself. The project was conducted in 2001 at a university which can be described as a privileged institution, historically linked to "white", Afrikaans culture. At the time of my fieldwork, it still had a large majority of "white" students, who mostly spoke Afrikaans as a first language, but with an increasing number of English first language students and a minority of "Black" students. Among these, there was an even smaller minority of "Black" African students. This predominance of "white" students is unusual in South Africa where universities generally have a minimum of fifty-percent "Black" students enrolled.

I researched my practice, teaching a group of 17 first year undergraduate students, all but two of whom were "white" and most of whom were Afrikaans first language speakers. I taught two South African fiction courses in a small tutorial program as part of the general English studies curriculum followed by all first year students: South African short stories and South African poetry. For the most part, I followed the same syllabus of short stories and poetry as other tutors, but in some classes I had the opportunity to design my own content. At the same time as they were studying South African literature, students also completed two modules taught through large group lectures, one on persuasive language in advertising and another on introductory socio-linguistics. I collected data by video-recording my tutorial classes, later transcribing significant moments from these; keeping a teaching journal, which included field notes; and collecting students' journal writing and more formal written assignments completed during the course.

In my teaching of the South African literature, I aimed at a critical analysis of the social issues and representations of South Africa raised in the texts as well as of the socially constructed nature of students' reading responses. Of course, dealing with social inequality in South Africa inevitably means dealing with the oppressive apartheid past and its continuing effect in the present. However, many of my students, though not all, found it difficult at times to deal with the apartheid past as represented in the prescribed South African literature.

Early on in the course, a heated discussion arose about why students had to study South African literature. Elsewhere, I have analyzed moments of resistance in this class, arguing that students' resistant responses are tied to the undesirable ways they feel interpellated by the texts under study and that they resist such representations because these contradict that aspect of their identities that they attempt to construct for themselves as new, post-apartheid South Africans (McKinney, 2004). During this classroom discussion, I promised my students that we would return to their concern about studying South African literature and that I would take their concerns seriously. The data I consider in this chapter is from a class later in the course in which I gave students the opportunity to discuss at length their feelings about studying South African literature and difficulties in dealing with the apartheid past. This was my attempt to get students to reflect on the reasons for their own resistance to, or desires regarding, representations of the apartheid past in the fictional texts we were working with. The class was thus designed both to develop my understanding of students' resistance as well as to intervene in this. One of my strategies was to connect the students' uncomfortable positionings to the past in relation to other people outside of the classroom. I was fortunate in that earlier in the year Michael Gardiner had written about the crisis in the study of the past in South Africa and the Minister of Education had commissioned a working group to prepare a report on this topic (Gardiner, 2001; Ndebele et al, 2001).

EXTRACT FROM THE HANDOUT FOR TUTORIAL 22

I used Gardiner's (2001) article and the working group report (Ndebele et al, 2001) in a dual move: firstly to position students as not exceptional but similar to many others in South African society and, secondly, to position them as part of the solution in thinking of ways we might address the "crisis", rather than as resistant.

- The crisis in South Africa within the study of the past is, as the report suggests, ironic. Instead of an excited upsurge of interest in the opportunity to explore the past in a freed environment, and despite the belief that "the humane influence of history education would lay claim to a secure and distinctive place in the learning system...the cumulative effect of relevant government policy...has been to de-emphasize history not merely in schooling but also in tertiary sectors (Gardiner, 2001, 10).
- Why do you think there is a 'crisis' in 'the study of the past'?
- Then there are also the subtler forces of aversion to learning about a history of pain and humiliation...as well as the recoil away in young people from overtly political issues (Gardiner, 2001, 10).
- Do you agree that there is 'pain and humiliation' in the study of the past? Are there other feelings?
- A study of the past can serve a range of important and enriching social, political, cultural and environmental functions. Its general potential is particularly pronounced in our own society, which is consciously undergoing change – in historical terms, we are living in a country that is presently attempting to remake

itself in time. In these conditions, the study of history is particularly urgent as it helps to prevent amnesia, checks triumphalism, opposes the manipulative or instrumental use of the past, and provides an educational buffer against a "dumbing down" of our citizens (Ndebele et al, 2001, 7).

– According to the report, what is the value of studying the past? Do you think this is valid? Can you think of other purposes?

The extract of classroom discussion that I present below took place soon after the students had read the selected quotations from Gardiner's (2001) and (Ndebele et al, 2001) report in their handouts.

Extract from Tutorial 22: 16/05/01

I have attempted to use conventions of punctuation to make the transcription of spoken language into writing more readable, conveying my understanding of the spoken words. Overlapping speech and interruptions were common. Italicized words or phrases indicate the emphasis of the speaker. All students are given pseudonyms and gave written consent to their involvement in the research. Alistair, Eric and Keith are "white" English first language and Herman, Riana and Trevor are "white" Afrikaans first language.

CM:	[Asks whether the students, as the post-apartheid generation, can view the struggle positively]
Alistair:	It depends who you are, because if you're looking at the people, I mean, it's obviously.... It's amazing for them to have struggled, but the people who struggled were struggling against the people who you are associated with. But, or, in my case, you understand what I mean...? It's the humiliation factor, because if you look at that positively, they were actually fighting against..., they were struggling against the people who you were..., are....
Herman:	Ja, I don't think if I had to go back these days, I can't associate now..., Well, I can't see the struggle as being positive for me. It..., it's..., it's positive for the country, yes, but... um..., I can't turn against my grandfather's grandfather because it's just..., *wrong*. I can't say that the struggle was positive if I look at it because....
CM:	Because of some family connection that you feel you must be loyal to?
Herman:	Ja, something like that
CM:	Maybe. OK, Eric.
Eric:	I think that perhaps over a longer period of time we could begin to see a broader history, but all..., all these negative things happened such a short time ago it's still, like, eating us.

CM: That the time isn't long enough.

Eric: Ja, and the change was so radical that…, um….

Keith: I think we've also been taught to sort of feel that it does affect us. But I don't feel in any way affected by it. Maybe it did for my father and my parents, my grandfather. But to me…, to me, you know, it's just a story. I don't feel like *I'm* (CM: right, so) a white person and I oppressed Blacks. It's not like I personally took part, so….

CM: Right, so that's interesting in the sense that you feel you can dissociate (Keith: Ja), not dissociate yourself maybe. That's too strong; but separate yourself.

Keith: …like a new generation…from the history of these people, whereas other people feel it's more difficult, or more complicated…. Maybe older people….

CM: And some younger people. Herman is saying he's finding it more complicated than that, perhaps, [Herman nods] which is understandable. [Alistair] Ja.

Alistair: …um…I went to a very much more multiracial school and I did history and this section comes up and it's…it's very difficult in a school like that because the change is so new, this…. The struggles just come (CM: Ja) The change has just come (CM: Ja) They feel that it's still to do with them as much as I feel that I've got absolutely nothing to do with apartheid. Some of them do feel that they've just come out of it and it's still connected to them….

CM: Well, some people… For them they're still living it.

Alistair: And they…, ja…, and they've won it. And they've won the struggle and now they're on top, so there's a big superiority complex that comes into it as well, as if it's almost reverse apartheid. "Look what you did to us now", and it gets like that in some of the classes. You…, you can see them; how they feel; how certain members feel….

CM: [to Riana] OK.

Riana: We went to Robben Island and… um… on a history *uitstappie*…uh… (Hannelie: expedition; CM: outing) outing and it was a very, very racist day because we… we felt…., um… almost uncomfortable because the people who did it with us was, "Here the whites put…." (CM: you mean the tour guides?) Ja, the tour guides, "Here the whites killed the Blacks with telephone wire". Here the whites threw the Blacks with rocks". "Here the whites...". And this really... um..., in..., unhuman way of telling the stories and I remember when we came back, obviously all of us was feeling a bit [pause] .... "Whoa, it was really not me. I'm sorry". And when we got back one of the... uh... [hesitation] coloured girls [soft] in our class just made a comment, "Ha, now you know how we feel". (CM: Uh, right) And I remember thinking that's so sad because it really shouldn't be like that. It's really not how we feel overall, but just the way the tour guides..., y'know..., presented... y'know.... Our history caused that division between the two groups (CM: Mhmm, nods) and I don't think that's right. I don't think it should be like that. [Keith: hand up]

CM: Ja, in the sense of accusing. [Riana: Ja] It was really accusing, ...ja...that they're doing the work of accusing people, right?

Keith: I agree with Alistair. You sort of..., you almost get the feeling you're trying to get put on a guilt trip or something.

Riana: Ja..., y'know, I didn't do anything.

CM: Mhmm, mhmm

Alistair: I feel that the fundamental problem is the teaching. It's not the students who want to learn, it's the teachers who need to be taught how to teach it and you know... not that this massacre took place on this day and that massacre and this is how many they killed and.... We don't want to know..., we..., cos, almost you *do* feel kind of responsible because *you're made to* feel that you have the same colour skin as the people who did it, so it is somehow connected to you and you do feel guilty because the person next to you's thinking "Ja, look what they did to my grandfather... and it's vicious". That's why you must rather learn how they..., they..., y'know....

CM: Ja, I mean, it is a difficult one because if..., if it's..., if our history continues to be taught and thought about by us.... Sorry. Trevor [I didn't see his hand up]. Before I go on....

Trevor: I just wanted to tell about a strange thing that happened when I was overseas. I attended a course for German and these people from overseas, from Germany, from Japan, from Singa..., all over the world..., and you have to tell name, school name, where are you came from and so on. And I said I came from South Africa and there were four people who came from North Africa, somewhere in the Congo and something like that. They suddenly... [gets up from chair and turns round to show turning his back] They turned their backs on me and I said, "What is *wrong*? I have no experience of the apartheid. I have *nothing* to do with that". And they said to me, "Well you were part of it. Now, what I'm saying, the Black community are seeing the white community as part of the apartheid system. And then I told them, "Well, I feel ashamed about it, my past and my country. But I also must feel proud that our country has tried to get in, to be democratic." But if people are seeing another picture that thinks we are cruel, we are hurt *mens* [people]. I feel more ashamed about my past and I have…, I have… [looks to me].

CM: Because of the way that… how people are positioning you basically as being part of that…

"IT DEPENDS ON WHO YOU ARE": RELATING TO THE APARTHEID PAST

I want to focus on two inter-related issues in analyzing the extract above: the first is how students feel positioned by others and how they position themselves in relation to the apartheid past; and the second concerns their feelings of guilt and accusation. We can see a strong discourse of racial division in the extract; 'us' versus 'them' is a recurrent way of talking about 'white' and 'Black' and they are set against each other as opponents. Not only is South African history very clearly divided along racial lines, but deracialization of the history is seen as impossible. In Alistair's contribution at the beginning of the extract, the "people who you were, are" are clearly 'white' people. Alistair's words later in the extract that "*You're made to* feel that you have the same colour skin as the people who did it…," illustrates how he feels positioned into whiteness. In Alistair's expression of being made to feel 'white', he accuses his history teacher of provoking such feelings along with hostility from the 'Black' students. From his account however, it seems that his teacher is presenting particular 'facts' which make him feel uncomfortable because of his own racial connection to the 'white' perpetrators, and this causes him to assume that his 'Black' classmates are thinking ill of him. For some of the students there is thus a complex interaction between being positioned by others as 'white' and positioning themselves as 'white'. Such positionings have profound significance for how they relate to the past, and prevent a positive engagement with this. It is precisely because identities continue to be so strongly racialized and group-based that a young 'white' South African in 2001 could still feel that the struggle was against him, even if he disagrees morally with the view of 'white' apartheid South Africa.

Hall's notion of identities as "being about questions of using the resources of history, language and culture in a process of becoming" (1996, 4) is significant here. Hall goes on to signal the importance of "how we have been represented and how that bears on how we might represent ourselves" (Ibid.). How the students feel they are represented in texts, and by other people, especially young 'Black' people, has a profound effect on how they in turn represent themselves. While the "resources of history, language and culture" might more usually conjure up celebratory and positive connotations, this is not necessarily the case for these students.

Herman's response, "I can't associate...I can't see the struggle as being positive for me," reinforces Alistair's position, although their perspectives are not exactly the same. While Herman chooses to identify with apartheid perpetrators ("...I can't turn against my grandfather's grandfather"), Alistair points out that he is prevented from identifying with the struggle because of the way he feels positioned by the 'Black' students in his history class who have "just come out of it [apartheid]." It is interesting that in showing his family links, Herman goes far back in time and way beyond his parent's generation. In fact during his "grandfather's grandfather's" time (in the 19th century), British colonialism, rather than its offshoot apartheid, characterized the historical period. Herman's reference then suggests that he may even be thinking beyond apartheid, and referring to what his ancestors fought for in South Africa through the Anglo-Boer wars and wars with indigenous people in order to claim the land itself. Perhaps identifying with the struggle for him then would mean a disavowal of his reason for being in South Africa and a complete displacement of that part of his identity which is Afrikaaner South African.

Herman's response later in the class (quoted below) is again, like Alistair's, explicitly articulated in terms of 'race', and gives evidence for my argument that the way in which the students racialize history prevents them from identifying positively with the anti-apartheid struggle. His argument relies on the view that 'race' is the most salient feature in identifying with South African history, rather than moral or ethical values. His speaking of not being able to 'associate' [identify] with Black people because he is 'white', shows how Herman views 'race' as the defining feature in who he is ("being" and "feeling" 'white').

Herman: ... every story in history you take from any country in the world has..., um... two sides and even if you look at both sides objectively, you still..., you still tend to choose that you think right. So how is it possible for anyone living in our country looking at our country's story and also *still being* different races and still feeling that in a way, you can't really look at this story of apartheid without choosing sides, associating with either side and um... I..., I can't..., I can't see how I could associate with... with the side of coloured people because I'm not. So I tend to associate with the white people's side, not that I still share their opinion, but I still feel that I still.... (his emphasis).

While Herman's statement of actually choosing or feeling obliged to choose the side of 'white' oppressors is extreme and drew whispering among some students, it nevertheless expresses a view which is more common: that because one is 'white', one cannot identify with the struggle of 'Black' people, whether one agrees with this or not.

Herman's binary division of only two sides to history (here 'Black' versus 'white') further closes down any opportunities to identify with the struggle. This discussion emphasized for me the powerful role which 'race' plays in the students' identities and indeed their investments in 'whiteness'. Their belief in the apartheid myth that 'race' exists so strongly, traps the students in old ways of seeing and being. While Herman's political views may in any case prevent him from identifying with the struggle for democracy, for many other students (such as Riana and Trevor in the extract) this is not the case. They value this struggle and see it as a positive aspect of South Africa's history, but by virtue of their whiteness, they still feel they represent the people who the struggle was waged against.

CONTRASTING RESPONSES FROM ERIC AND KEITH

In contrast with Alistair and Herman's responses in the classroom extract quoted above, Eric and Keith do not explicitly use "race" in their arguments regarding the difficulties in dealing with the past. For Eric, time is the issue and he argues that it is too soon for them, as 'white' people, to view South African history more positively: "… it's still, like, eating us." This image of the memories of apartheid atrocities 'eating' the current generation is a powerful one, indicating the role which apartheid continues to play in the lives/identities of this "new generation". That aspect of their identity, which is "new", post-apartheid South African, thus struggles to emerge. In Eric's response we see the contradiction which arose in several class discussions: apartheid is both unnecessary to deal with because it's "in the past" and yet it is also too close temporally and thus still too painful to deal with.

While also not placing apartheid in the distant past, Keith's statement seems to contradict that of Eric. Unlike Herman, Eric and Alistair, he is arguing that he can separate himself from the past. But like Eric, Keith is more realistic in his historical placing of apartheid. It is his father, his parents and his grandfather who are affected by apartheid (but significantly, only "maybe" affected), he points out, and not himself. Keith argues that young 'white' people have "been taught to sort of feel that [apartheid] does affect us," but explicitly rejects being positioned in this way. What is interesting here is that unlike many of the other students, Keith does not seem to feel interpellated as a 'white' oppressor. His statement "…I don't feel like *I'm* a white person and I oppressed Blacks," is evidence of this. This is also confirmed by his statement that he is part of "a new generation". Keith seems unable to understand the responses of Herman, Alistair and Eric before him, as when I point out that some people find it "more difficult, or more complicated" to separate themselves from our history than he does, Keith says "maybe older people", thus excluding anybody in his peer group from this problem. It is perhaps significant to note that Keith was schooled at one of the most elite private boys' schools in the country and seems to have mastered a post-apartheid discourse which cuts the "new generation" off from any ties with the apartheid past, including acknowledgment of privilege linked to apartheid.

C. MCKINNEY

"UNHUMAN WAY[S] OF TELLING THE STORIES": NARRATIVES OF ACCUSATION

Apart from the clear (and) binary racialization of history, the most dominant theme of the extract seems to be that of accusation and guilt. Alistair is at pains to point out that the problem in their (i.e. young 'white' people) not being able to identify with the struggle and thus with the positive in South Africa's history, is not that they don't want to do this (like Herman). It is rather that "Black" people still accuse him and other "white" people of involvement in apartheid, thus forcing them to take responsibility for what happened during apartheid: "...look what you did to us...." Again Alistair uses a strong othering discourse in his reference to "Black" people as "they" and "them", and assumes that the rest of the class (including the "coloured" students) will know he refers to "Black" people:

> ...They feel that it's still to do with them. As much as I feel that I've got absolutely nothing to do with apartheid, some of them do feel that they've just come out of it and it's still connected to them.

However, if we remember Alistair's statement, discussed above, regarding the thoughts (rather than the words) of his "Black" classmates, we must recognize that his own feelings are not so clear cut as he suggests here. This notion of being positioned, forced to take on a particular undesirable and uncomfortable identity through the accusations of other "Black" people, is taken up by Riana who offers her own narrative of accusation to the discussion.

RIANA'S STORY

Riana presents a personal narrative, or remembering of a history excursion to Robben Island while she was at school, in order to argue that the way history is represented can cause division between "Black" ("coloured" here) and "white" students. It is significant that the outing was to Robben Island, a powerful symbol of apartheid oppression and one could argue that, regardless of the tour experience, just being on Robben Island may position "white" South Africans in an uncomfortable way. Earlier in the discussion, Riana was the only student who could identify with the positive in South Africa's history by identifying with the success of overcoming apartheid:

> I think the thing is that eventually we got through that and eventually things turned around and there has been a lot of changes, so I think we, that can be said *more*, and I think that should come in as well.

Here Riana chooses to avoid an othering discourse dividing "us" from "them" and to discursively construct a unity of all South Africans in her statement, "*We* got through that". Despite this, her story of the Robben Island trip shows that she is also not so easily able to dissociate herself from the negative in our history at other times. Riana's emphasis in her description of the day as "a very, very racist day" gives some indication of the strong emotion with which Riana told this story; she was clearly upset by the outing and the memory of it is vivid.

Riana's use of the pronoun "we" from the beginning of her story to mean only the "white" people who went on the history outing is also significant. This is more ambiguous with the first use in "we felt..., um... almost uncomfortable" until she continues with her account of the tour guide's narrative and tells of their return to school. Here, it is clear who felt uncomfortable in Riana's "we": "and I remember when we came back, obviously all of us was feeling a bit [pause].... 'Whoa, it was really not me, I'm sorry'". Of course it may well be that the "Black" students did not feel comfortable during the trip either. Riana is thus clearly telling the story from her perspective as a "white" person and, in doing so, positions herself as "white", while at the same time rejecting the positioning of "white" imposed by the tour guide and the "coloured girls" in her class, which she represents as that of "white" oppressor. Her response to the "coloured" student's comment, "Ha, now you know how we feel", is in itself interesting. Her interpretation of this comment was that she, along with the other "white" students, was being blamed for, or at least accused of, apartheid atrocities by virtue of being "white", on account of the way in which the tour guide had told the story of events on Robben Island. Perhaps this was the case, or perhaps the "coloured" student was merely expressing a belief that the "white" students did not really know or understand the experience of oppressed people under apartheid. The statement reported of the "coloured" student could be read in several ways and, of course, it is impossible to reconstruct the "factual" details of the event from Riana's telling of the story. In telling a story like this, there is inevitably a reworking of memory going on, but in many senses what actually took place on the outing and at school afterward does not matter. It is clear that the outing made Riana feel defensive, accused and very firmly positioned with the undesirable, and uncomfortable (as Riana points out) identity of "white" oppressors.

TREVOR'S STORY

Trevor's story of the reaction of African students from the Democratic Republic of Congo to him as a "white" South African is similar to Riana's in that it is also a tale of accusation. In this story, Trevor is positioned by the African students as "part of it [apartheid]" despite his own feeling that he "had nothing to do with that". Trevor told this story with strong emotion, clearly demonstrating how upset and "hurt" he felt at this rejection by the African students. His physical demonstration of the African's turning their back on him and his emphasis in his question "what is *wrong*?" ("wrong" was almost shouted by Trevor), indicated both his distress and disbelief at being treated in such a way. The accusation, "Well you were part of it," which Trevor reports for the African students (and, again, how factual or accurate these words are is not the issue here) is an unequivocal positioning of him alongside the people he describes as "cruel", "white" oppressors under apartheid, from which these students do not allow him to escape. Trevor makes a clear argument for why he finds it difficult to identify with the struggle for democracy: In his view, the "black community" will not allow the "white community" to do this. Trevor's response to the African students shows his desire to identify with the struggle, and to a certain extent he is identifying with this in his statement: "I told them, 'Well, I feel ashamed about it, my past and my country; but I also must feel proud that our country has tried to get in, to be democratic.

But Trevor goes on then to show how this pride is undermined by his being positioned as an oppressor. It is not that he has no desire to identify positively, but he feels he cannot and is left with a feeling of despair, "...but if people are seeing another picture, that thinks we are cruel we are hurt *mens* [people], I feel more ashamed about my past and I have..., I have... [looks to me].

This expression of despair and of helplessness echoes that of Alistair in his explanation of how "...*you're made to* feel that you have the same colour skin as the people who did it, so it is somehow connected to you and you do feel guilty...." In both of Trevor's statements here, the apartheid past of which he is ashamed has become a personal history – it is "my past." It is also interesting to note that when he speaks of shame, he speaks of "my ('white') past" and "my (apartheid?) country" but, in speaking of the new democracy as a source of pride, he switches to "our [all South Africans, 'black' and 'white'] country." Understandably however, accusations from other Africans increase Trevor's feelings of being ashamed about the past, and position him in such a way that he feels forced to accept the shameful apartheid past as his personal history, and to feel distanced from the new democracy.

DECONSTRUCTING BINARIES

In an attempt to disrupt students' essentialist notions of "white" and "Black" in relation to the struggle, I asked the students which part (i.e. "white" or "Black" as these were the categories they were using) of our history the "white" ANC activists Albie Sachs's or Joe Slovo's children were likely to associate with. The students told me that they had no knowledge of Albie Sachs or Joe Slovo and I briefly related their stories.

Albie Sachs was a 'white' African National Congress (ANC) activist who survived a car bomb attack by South African security forces in Maputo, Mozambique on 7 April 1988. In the attempted assassination he lost his right arm and the sight of one eye. He is now a justice of the Constitutional Court of South Africa and, as an expert in constitutional law, played a crucial role in drawing up the post-apartheid constitution.

Joe Slovo (1926-1995) played a leading role in the ANC (as one of the early leaders in the armed wing Umkhonto we Sizwe) and in running the South African Communist Party (SACP). He went into exile in 1963 and returned to South Africa in 1990 to participate in the negotiations for a post-apartheid democracy. He was the first Minister of Housing in democratic South Africa and was national chairperson of the SACP and on the National Executive committee of the ANC at the time of his death.

Alistair then argued that they had never learned about any positive 'white' figures in the struggle in their school history and how necessary this was if they were to be able to identify with the struggle:

Now, you see, that's a positive thing for… just a simple positive thing for say white…, is for looking at people like Joe Slovo and Albie Sachs, y'know. They…, they help us identify with the struggle…

My strategy in attempting to offer alternative and more positive representations of whiteness with which students might identify could be seen to be partially successful in this moment. Since the power of racial identification with white people was so strong, I attempted to work within this framework by identifying and inserting positive "white" role models into the class discussion. I also attempted to make visible to students the range of positions amongst "white" students in the class itself, another tool in deconstructing their homogenous representation of whiteness. We can see this in my attempt to explain to Keith that some people, like himself, feel able to distance themselves from apartheid perpetrators while others, such as Herman, cannot. Such strategies however will have mixed responses and thus mixed success. Ultimately, as the teacher, one cannot control students' self-positioning and processes of identification though one can certainly attempt to influence these. Even in the analysis of one extract from classroom discourse, it is clear that resistance is not a homogenous or unitary experience. Students will resist different texts in different ways depending on their identifications, investments and desires.

CONCLUSION

In this paper I have explored a few significant moments from a class in which I attempted to engage with students' resistance to Critical Literacy pedagogy. I have analyzed the complexities of their being and/or feeling positioned alongside 'white' oppressors, focusing here on such (perceived) positioning from "Black" people, and by the students themselves. I argue that the students' continuing racialization as "white" and emotional investments in whiteness make it difficult to deconstruct their responses to representations in the curriculum materials of the apartheid past and of white people. It was clear to me that I needed to help students deconstruct binary divisions they and many others set up between "Black" and "white". Key pedagogical strategies include offering examples which unsettle binary constructions of "race" in South Africa, both by foregrounding the different positions among these young people themselves (e.g., Herman and Keith) and thus emphasizing difference amongst them as well as by inserting examples of "white" struggle activists to destabilize their racialized logics and illustrate how one's ability to identify with the struggle would not always be tied to 'race' in fixed ways.

Using a post-structuralist theorizing of identity as a tool for understanding actual moments of resistance and for analyzing classroom interaction that engages with this has significant implications for how such resistance can and should be viewed. I would argue that in working with relatively privileged students, the aim is not one of empowerment, though to the extent that it still involves working towards self- and social change, the aim is emancipatory. In order to understand students' resistances and to work productively with these, we need to recognize and analyze what they are invested in, their hopes and dreams, and how they are embedded in the socio-political and historical moment in which they live. While the dominant view of resistance to Critical Literacy pedagogy is that it is a problem that needs to be overcome, I have argued for a more positive view. Resistance does not necessarily prevent productive engagement. On the contrary, it can provide powerful teaching moments. Resistance is a complex, rather than homogenous process and is uneven – that is, students can resist different texts in different ways, and can return to accept texts that they previously resisted. But resistance is also not an arbitrary phenomenon and, in better understanding our students, their fears and desires, we can begin to predict what texts they are likely to resist, though this would not be an argument for excluding such texts. While not part of a linear progression, resistance may be a necessary process for some students and may be the only way that they can engage with particular texts at particular moments. Our aim then should not be to overcome resistance, but rather to engage with it. We need to give students, and ourselves as teachers, the space to explore how and why they resist particular texts and to take their positions seriously. This view does not ignore the fact that engaging with resistance can be extremely challenging for teachers and students (see McKinney, 2005). While it is important to acknowledge the limitations to what is possible in the classroom, it is also important to acknowledge the potential productivity in uncomfortable pedagogic spaces and uncomfortable positionings.

REFERENCES

Bee, B. (1993). Critical literacy and the politics of gender. In C. Lankshear & P. L. McLaren (Eds.), *Critical literacy: Politics, praxis and the postmodern*. Albany, NY: State University of New York Press.

Britzman, D., Santiago-Valles, K. A., Jiménez-Muñoz, G. M., & Lamash, L. M. (1993). Slips that show and tell: Fashioning multiculture as a problem of representation. In C. McCarthy & W. Crichlow (Eds.), *Race, identity and representation in education*. New York and London: Routledge.

Britzman, D., Santiago-Valles, K. A., Jiménez-Muñoz, G. M., & Lamash, L. M. (1991). Dusting off the erasures: Race, gender and pedagogy. *Education and Society, 9*(2), 88–99.

Comber, B. (1993). Classroom explorations in literacy. *Australian Journal of Language and Literacy, 16*(1), 73–84.

Davies, B. (1990). The problem of desire. *Social Problems, 37*(4), 501–516.

Davies, B. (1997). The subject of post-structuralism: A reply to Alison Jones. *Gender and Education, 9*(3), 271–283.

Ellsworth, E. (1989). Why doesn't this feel empowering? Working through the repressive myths of critical pedagogy. *Harvard Educational Review, 59*(3), 297–324.

Ferreira, A., & Janks, H. (2007). Reconciliation pedagogy, identity and community funds of knowledge: Borderwork in South African classrooms. *English Academy Review, 24*(2), 71–84.

Freire, P., & Macedo, D. (1987). *Literacy: Reading the word and the world*. Westport, CT: Greenwood Publishing.

Gardiner, M. (2001, February 2–8). History and archaeology in education. *Mail and Guardian*.

Giroux, H. (1989). *Schooling for democracy*. London: Routledge.

Granville, S. (2003). Contests over meaning in a South African classroom: Introducing critical language awareness in a climate of social change and cultural diversity. *Language and Education, 17*(1), 1–20.

Hall, S. (1996). Introduction: Who needs Identity? In S. Hall & P. du Gay (Eds.), *Questions of cultural identity*. London: Sage.

Henriques, J., Hollway, W., Urwin, C., Venn, C., & Walkerdine, V. (1998). *Changing the subject: Psychology, social regulation and subjectivity* (1st ed., 1984). London and New York: Routledge.

Janks, H. (1993). *Critical language awareness series* (Ed.). Johannesburg: Hodder and Stoughton and Wits University Press.

Janks, H. (1995). *The research and development of critical language awareness materials for use in South African secondary schools*. Unpublished Ph.D. thesis, Lancaster University.

Janks, H. (2001). Identity and conflict in the critical literacy classroom. In B. Comber & A. Simpson (Eds.), *Negotiating critical literacies in classrooms*. New Jersey and London: Lawrence Erlbaum Associates.

Janks, H. (2002). Critical literacy: Beyond reason. *The Australian Educational Researcher, 29*(1), 7–26.

Krog, A. (1998). *Country of my skull*. London: Vintage.

Lather, P. (1991). *Getting smart: Feminist research and pedagogy with/in the postmodern*. New York and London: Routledge.

McKinney, C. (2004). "A little hard piece of grass in your shoe": Understanding student resistance to critical literacy in post-apartheid South Africa. *Southern African Linguistics and Applied Language Studies, 22*(1, 2), 63–73.

McKinney, C. (2005). A balancing act: Ethical dilemmas of democratic teaching within critical pedagogy. *Educational Action Research, 13*(3), 375–391.

Moffat, L., & Norton, B. (2005). Popular culture and the reading teacher: A case for feminist pedagogy. *Critical Inquiry in Language Studies, 2*(1), 1–12.

Ndebele, N., Odendaal, A., Mesthrie, U., Jordan, P., Nasson, B., Esterhuyzen, M., et al. (2001, February). *Report of the history/archaeology panel to the minister of education*. Retrieved February 12, 2001, from http://AReportoftheHistory-ArchaeologyPanel.htm

Wallace, C. (2003). *Critical reading in language education*. Basingstoke: Palgrave Macmillan.

Weedon, C. (1997). *Feminist practice and poststructuralist theory* (1st ed., 1987). Oxford: Blackwell.

VIVIAN VASQUEZ AND SARAH VANDER ZANDEN

CHAPTER 7

Outside More Common Spaces for Critical Literacy: Exploring Issues of Language and Power

Ann Haas Dyson (2005) talks about the long-standing mantra of childhood education: start where the child is she says, "Often, those usual places are in neatly contained geographic locales and along well-marked literacy paths, as the child accrues an ever-increasing basket load of knowledge and skills."(2005, xi) In this chapter our intent is to take readers outside more common spaces to locate the child, in what Dyson refers to as "an imaginative re-interpretation of this long-standing mantra" (2005, xi). More specifically we will take readers outside more common spaces for talking about Critical Literacy and focus on such work with English Language Learners (ELLs). What you will witness however, are not specific teaching strategies for working with ELLs but rather you will be introduced to a group of students who you may not recognize as being ELLs and who participate in taking up social issues with their classmates.

This chapter will describe work that comes from participating in a Critical Literacy study group consisting of approximately eight elementary school teachers and a university professor, who supported their work, in researching their classroom practices over a period of five years from 2001-2006. Vivian was the university professor, and Sarah was a fifth grade teacher.

During this time period, as a group, we attempted to meet at least once a month, at first at the school where the teachers worked and then at different study group participants' houses. Our meetings consisted of sharing articles and other publications on Critical Literacy, new literacies, new technologies, and other related theoretical perspectives. We talked about how these theoretical perspectives work to inform Critical Literacy teaching and learning. We also shared and tried out strategies for engaging with Critical Literacies by sharing instances of learning from our classrooms. As part of this we shared artifacts of learning that represented the Critical Literacy work we were attempting. To our meetings, we also brought texts from our everyday lives as artifacts to analyze from a Critical Literacy perspective. Outside of our discussions and sharing of teaching practices we also agreed to write about what was going on in our classrooms and it became an expectation for each of us to share our writing when we met.

During our meetings we discussed potential venues for publication and venues for presenting the work we were doing. Over the years we have given presentations at various conferences including the National Council of Teachers of English (NCTE) annual convention, the Literacies for All Summer Institute, and the

K. Cooper and R. E. White (eds.), Critical Literacies in Action: Social Perspectives and Teaching Practices, 117–126.

American Educational Research Association. We also wrote together and published articles in NCTE publications. Some study group members even wrote books (Fay and Whaley, 2004; Vasquez, 2004). At the time of this writing, as a group, we were completing a book manuscript on Critical Literacy across the curriculum. Not only did Vivian encourage the group to read and discuss together, she also wanted them to have a chance to dialogue with the authors of published work they had read. Over the years she organized face to face conversations with such researchers as Hilary Janks, Barbara Comber, Peter Johnston, and Jerome C. Harste. These meetings often took place at conferences in which we were presenting our work. This intense participation in our study group helped the teachers become more informed decision-makers when it came to their work in Critical Literacy. They also became skilled at articulating their thinking and sharing their thinking in the field.

As a group we worked from the position that everyday worlds of the classroom are populated by people who have migrated from somewhere else, and their circulating texts are pulsating with rhythms, images and words that have crossed borders (Dyson, 2005). Kathleen Fay and Suzanne Whaley (2004), participants in the study group, in the opening chapter of their book on reading and writing with English language learners, state:

> Seeing each child as an individual is at the heart of what we do. We would never assume that all students with learning disabilities or that all gifted students are the same, and we should do likewise with English language learners. They are a diverse group of children as any (2004, 9-10).

In their diversity, they bring with them multiple identities and multiple perspectives. In this chapter those diverse perspectives come to life as a group of fifth grade students and their teacher, Sarah Vander Zanden, together work to understand how texts, both social and written, work to position them in particular ways as well as unpack the position from which they engage with texts, as they explore issues of language and power. The work is both deconstructive and re-constructive.

WORKING WITH A CRITICAL LITERACY TOOL KIT

The key tenets of Critical Literacy with which we operated stem from the theoretical toolkit that framed our work which included Freebody and Luke's Four Resources Model (1999), Manning's "Literacy As" Model (2004), Kress and Van Leeuwen's Grammar of Visual Design (2000), Gee's work on Discourse Analysis (2002), and Video Gaming (2003), as well as Janks, Interrelated Model for Critical Literacy (2000). Larson and Marsh (2005), do a nice job of summarizing these tenets in a chapter in their book where they focus on Critical Literacy as it unfolded in Vivian's pre-school classroom. Here is a version of those tenets:
– Literacy is not a neutral technology and texts are never neutral
– Learners are differently positioned by texts and learners differently position texts

Therefore while we think about the ways in which texts position us, we also need to think about the position from which we engage with texts.
- Critical Literacy practices can foster political awareness and social change and involves an exploration of the relationship between language and power.
- Critical Literacy involves having a critical perspective.
- Learners' cultural and semiotic resources should be utilized.
- Text design and production can provide opportunities for critique and transformation.

THE SCHOOL CONTEXT

The elementary school where the instance of learning we will be describing took place, houses 900 students from pre-kindergarten through fifth grade. Over 78% of the population speaks a language other than English (English Language Learners, ELL). Forty nations and twenty languages are represented. Fifty percent of the students are native Spanish speakers. The student mobility rate is around 30% and 80% of the students are on free and reduced lunch.

The school accesses Title I funding intended to ensure that all children have a fair, equal and significant opportunity to access high-quality education in order to attain proficiency on challenging State academic achievement standards and state academic assessments. Despite this, however, the school has on several occasions, through letters to newspaper editors and letters to the school community, made it's stance on the limitations of standardized testing very clear in spite of the negative press this stance has received in the local media.

DISRUPTING A NORMALIZED ARBOR DAY PRACTICE

During one of our study group meetings, Sarah shared her experiences in working with her students to focus on class discussion as both a means to articulate their opinions and advocate for their needs and as a way of promoting access to the school curriculum for her fifth grade students who may struggle in academic settings. The class was her first "official" experience with an inclusion classroom. However, she had always had seven or so students with learning disabilities in her class, along with many English Language Learners at varying levels of second language acquisition. Over 60% of the class is on free or reduced lunch, whose family incomes fall below the poverty line.

In her journal she wrote:

> … my goal was for all of the students to be active participants in class, so we spent a great deal of time cultivating a classroom community devoted to listening to one another and learning how to accept that different kids have different needs and that was OK. I explicitly taught kids how to disagree in the classroom and on the playground, as well as how to notice what others were doing so that we could be more respectful of our classmates and be better peer supports in academic settings.

We had many practices in the classroom that emphasized individual roles within our whole class that contributed to the community. For example, we held weekly class meeting and kids could put notes in what we termed "The Discussion Box" and then we could discuss them as a group. These were not sorted as compliments/complaints but items to discuss. There were parameters surrounding the kinds of things that were needed for the whole class' attention vs. smaller group discussion with only those involved. We addressed unfair tag games, class cafeteria jobs not being done, outstanding demonstrations of friendship, and peer pressure. I also had two students involved in a school wide Peer Mediation program and they led many problem-solving discussions.

We had a weekly celebration board where the kids could decide what would go up on the large bulletin board in the back of the classroom. My co-teacher, an LD specialist, suggested this and it became an important classroom ritual. The work that went into the decision surrounding what would go up on the board was important and at first kids were hesitant to walk up and put the drawing, writing, project or whatever they had chosen on the board. After two or three weeks, the kids were prepared and had selected ahead of time what they would put up.

There were many Civics-oriented projects that developed over the year, from writing letters to the principal about a school-wide bathroom rule deemed unfair by the students to a fund-raising initiative. The fund-raising project spun off from a conversation with a group of girls who heard about a project my former students had done, collecting pennies to buy toys for kids in the hospital. This group of girls, led by one student who strongly advocated for animals in daily conversation, wanted to focus their attention on raising money for an animal shelter. When their plan was not approved by the principal (because of the fund raising aspect, not the project itself) they redesigned it to collect materials for the shelter instead of money.

The four girls included other students in the class to create an ad for the in-house School News and in making posters. They went around to classrooms to explain their project. They were thrilled to see the animals at the shelter and proud of their work when we delivered all of the shoeboxes, pet toys, sheets, and towels they had collected; but as one student said, "We did it for the animals we will never see, not for the ones already in the shelter." This active participation in a larger societal organization, the shelter, led by a small group within the class fostered an awareness of things going on around the kids on a day-to-day basis.

Of course, I also read lots of literature that sparked deep thinking and conversation. In my mind multiple perspectives was a big focus.

As a group Sarah and her students read books like *Stand Tall Molly Lou Melon* by Lovell and Catrow (2002), which dealt with issues of difference; *Seed Folks*, by Fleischman (2004), which focused on participation in community; and *The Wump*

World by Peet (1991), where aliens use up the earth's resources. This last book, in particular, sparked lots of discussion about the impact our everyday actions have on the world around us and heightened the group's awareness for observing the world from an environmentalist perspective.

As part of her work with the Critical Literacy study group, Sarah was taking notes, thinking about larger issues her student's were raising and how what she was focusing on in class enriched the set county curriculum in many areas. Throughout this chapter we highlight conversations that demonstrate how the precursors Sarah noted in her journal entry contributed to her attending to a particular statement made by an individual student and the other students' responses.

In Spring 2005, the Student Council sponsored an Arbor Day Tree Planting Ceremony where a few kids from the class were invited to a special dedication service as student representatives to plant a tree for Arbor Day. The following conversation took place upon their return to class:

Francisco: If they are trying to save trees, then why would they give us pencils?

Shena: What?

Francisco: Pencils. Duh???

Apparently the ceremony participants were given pencils at the conclusion of the tree planting. In her journal Sarah noted:

I kept thinking about what Francisco had said. His question was a generative question; it would propel the discussion forward. I knew this because the kids were learning about conservation and we had read books about this. I expected that they would be able to grasp Francisco's observations about the contradiction in handing out a wooden pencil to celebrate trees. It was the contradiction, the thought process and observation that mattered.

PLANT A TREE AND MAKE THE WORLD A BETTER PLACE

Sarah wondered what the other kids thought about the incident and hoped that Francisco's comment would generate topics for study. Conversation, during class meeting, had been a successful venue for the majority of kids in class to participate throughout the year and she wanted to take the opportunity to explore how much some of the kids had grown in this respect. The comment came from Francisco, a student who had become less engaged in the class since the beginning of the year. Despite how hard Sarah tried to keep the curriculum practicable to him, there were many times when he found it difficult to participate and seemed disinterested in the topics under study. Nevertheless, Sarah continued to work with him on re-positioning himself in the classroom to make learning more accessible for him. That is, she tried to help him find classmates with whom he shared common interests and tried to draw out of him what topics and issues he was interested in pursuing.

Regarding Francisco's participation in the Arbor Day Event, Sarah wrote:

Francisco had noticed a contradiction and was raising questions about this observation in a respectful way. He was a "special" participant, one of a select few who could attend this dedication. We had read a lot about conservation in the weeks building up to this event and discussed them as a class. We had studied erosion, weathering and human impact on the Chesapeake watershed through field trips, in class experiments and research in the first quarter of the school year. I included some texts that would reinforce key curricular ideas surrounding land forms and human impact on the land, as specified in the Fairfax County POS (Program of Study) and Virginia Standards of Learning (SOLs) because it was now the third quarter and the year end high stakes tests were coming.

I brought the kids together for discussion, sitting in a circle, and started it off by restating what Francisco had said the day before. The kids were used to discussion and had often sat in the circle for class meetings, book discussions, content lessons, etc. This was not new. I said, what do you think about what Francisco said? Immediately kids had something to say, either to clarify or comment.

Ansony: So what if they give you a pencil? I didn't get one.

Sanya: They could have given you a paper to share at home, I would share it.

Milton: Maybe they thought that if they gave papers, kids would throw them and they won't throw pencils.

Ansony's comment and the response by Sanya and Milton are representative of the 'normalized' treatment of Arbor Day in many school settings where students participate in set rituals as passive observers. It is easy to see how this normalization comes into being when looking more closely at resources available to teachers regarding celebrating this day. For instance phrases like "Celebrate Arbor Day and take positive action" or "Celebrate Arbor Day to make the world a better place", represent the sorts of sentiments that pepper resource documents on Arbor Day. In an Internet search on "Studying Arbor Day" or "Unit of Study on Arbor Day" for instance, I found resources like the Arbor Day Alphabetic Order Worksheet from www.teachnology.com and Activity #2273: Clozing the Deal on Arbor Day, a cloze activity located at www.teachers.net, where students are asked to identify twelve words having to do with Arbor Day, learn to recite and use these words and then use the words in context by means of a class sentence bee.

Neglected are opportunities to historicize and unpack the day as one with political roots whereby people who moved into the Nebraska Territory in the 1800s proposed the holiday at a meeting of the State Board of Agriculture and where eventually what has come to be known as Arbor Day came into being as a result of an official proclamation. Lost are opportunities to explore reasons beyond 'greening' as the impetus for such a day. For instance, Heger (2000) notes that J. Sterling Morton, who founded Arbor Day in 1872, was an ardent opponent of the tariff protecting the U.S. lumber industry from foreign competition and that he had another motive behind his Arbor Day advocacy. According to Heger (2000):

> Morton detested the protective tariff that enriched the U.S. lumber industry and depleted native forests. He wanted to break the power of the tariff. So his secondary Arbor Day message was: Plant a tree and strike a blow for free trade.

This is a far cry from the passive save the world through celebration rhetoric in "Celebrate Arbor Day and make the world a better place".

RE-DESIGNING EXISTING PRACTICE

As the conversation continued, the students began to come up with alternate solutions in a "re-design" of what could have been handed out at the event as one way to get the message out to more than just the special group who was allowed to attend.

Francisco:	We need to save trees, save the environment, not cut down trees. They are lying.
Teacher:	Who are they?
Rustom:	Professionals who protect trees, probably.
Shena:	The PTA
Teacher:	Why?
Shena:	They got the tree.
Francisco:	The government.

As the children continue to unpack the context in which the event took place, they began a conversation about the larger systems in place and how things are decided. They recognize that things don't just happen, there are decision makers out there and there is nothing natural or neutral about the process of deciding the way the day is celebrated and what memento might be appropriate to represent the day. This lends to the development of a worldview that is more active than reactive. If you can identify the decision-makers, those in power, you can then think in a different way about the decisions being made, generate new ideas, and contribute to disrupting the problematic practice.

Meylin:	Yeah, maybe they have so much extra wood that they made pencils for the kids.
Shena:	Yeah, it could be recycled wood. (Examines pencil).
Jonny:	Well, where do they [pencils] come from? Why not use plastic instead of wood?
Cesar:	Well, when they cut down the trees, they have to plant another one. So maybe they did that. But they could just make a commercial and not cut down any trees and everyone would

see it, not just Cheto and Shena. I mean, flyers and pencils both use wood and we don't even know what they wanted now…because we weren't there.

As the group considers alternate perspectives, and seeing his classmates struggling with the issue of 'the Arbor Day pencil', Cesar begins directly teaching about tree conservation, which was something he read about earlier. He talks about access to information and to help spread the word regarding one way to help save the environment. He suggests the use of a commercial rather than distributing pencils, or flyers as suggested earlier.

Oscar: I disagree, factories have to make pencils, and they use energy so they might cut down more and just use the extra wood to do the pencils.

Rustom: I disagree with Jonny, because we can't sharpen plastic pencils. Mechanical would be better.

Fatima: You can sharpen plastic pencils.

Milton: Yeah, lead is better, mechanical…

Rustom: Wait, I disagree with Milton now, even though they wouldn't use wood, they are using other resources. Which resource is better? It's like Wump World. Wait – how do you get lead?

In this exchange, the students begin to stray from the underlying social issue as they discuss whether plastic or mechanical pencils would be better. Eventually they return *to The Wump World* highlighting the human impact and making connections to information previously learned through class work about resources and energy. Since the beginning of the school year, the children had gotten better at using one text (e.g. *The Wump World*) to read another text (Arbor Day as a social text). They have learned that in order to better critically analyze a situation, one needs to frame it differently using a different discursive perspective. Wump World created a space for them to do this thereby returning the conversation to the Arbor Day issue.

Kimseng: For real, if they gave mechanical pencils they would waste more money for them. It's just a dumb reminder; they wouldn't waste that much money on us.

Kimseng had been most disappointed over the distribution of the pencil, the subsequent conversations with his classmates and some of their lack of concern while unpacking the event. His comments during the class meetings on this topic focused on different possible realities; were pencils distributed as an inexpensive token as a money saving technique, or did the organizers take the attitude that "pencils are good enough for the kids"? When he says, "...they wouldn't waste that much money on us", he is referring to any memento that might cost more than a pencil. Either way it was clear to him that little thought was given to the event as a whole, thus his reference to the pencils as "dumb reminders".

Cristina: Who decided it anyways? Maybe we should write a letter.

To get responses to some unanswered questions regarding the decision making process around Arbor Day, and as a form of social action, Cristina, suggests writing a letter. She made this recommendation based on her past experiences and success in getting issues resolved through letter writing. For instance, in the past, she had written a letter in order to be included in the yearly Special Education conference her parents attended at her school regarding how to best support her learning. Francisco, Shena and Kimseng, who first noticed the ridiculousness of distributing pencils on Arbor Day, took up Cristina's suggestion and wrote a letter to the Parent Teacher Association. Further, they submitted comments on a couple of websites focused on Arbor Day. Shena also met with the Student Council Association president and staff representative about making the Arbor Day ceremony accessible to all students instead of limiting the event to a chosen few.

The Arbor Day incident took place at the end of the school year when the fifth graders were about to leave the school to attend a middle school nearby. Sarah, the classroom teacher also left the school to pursue doctoral studies. Unfortunately, as a result, there was no follow up on what resulted form the letter writing and meeting with the student council president and staff representative. After the fact, Sarah did hear that the staff representative, who eventually took on the role of assistant principal at another school, disagreed with the students' concerns and found nothing problematic about privileging some students by inviting them to attend the Arbor Day event while marginalizing others who were flatly denied an opportunity to do so.

CRITICAL LITERACY AS CHANGING PARTICIPATION

Barton and Hamilton (1998) note:

Literacy is primarily something people do; it is an activity, located in the space between thought and text. Literacy does not reside in people's heads as a set of skills to be learned, and it does not just reside on paper captured as texts to be analyzed. Like all human activity, literacy is essentially social, and it is located in the interaction between people (1998, 3).

The interactions engaged in by Sarah's students provided for them space to imagine how existing social practices could be otherwise. This work, not only addresses the School District's Standards of Learning 5.7f, but surpasses the identified key concept; human impact (on the environment). Within the context of attempting to disrupt problematic Arbor Day practices at their school, they began to consider how what they come to know and believe is shaped by "specific participants in a literacy event and the context itself". (Larson and Marsh, 2005, 11) In their letter writing and subsequent meetings with the student council representatives, they began to interrogate the decisions made by these participants as well as the notions associated with the normalized Arbor Day celebration. At the same time they were gaining experience in re-imagining a problematic school practice which helped them to consider ways they could participate differently in the world of school and beyond. As suggested by Janks and Comber (2005), involving young people in the process of text production, editing, and design demonstrates to them that texts are not neutral or natural. This work also helps young people to understand that language does particular life work and that how we constitute things and how we are constituted through social practice makes a difference in the ways we are positioned in life and the positions from which we are able to speak or participate in the world.

Larson and Marsh (2005) note that people learn by participating in culturally valid activities. Even though the letter writing and the meetings may not have worked to accomplish the work the children had imagined, the experience provided a space for them to participate differently in school as active players rather than passive recipients of school and everyday texts.

REFERENCES

Author. (n.d.). *Arbor Day alphabetic order worksheet*. Retrieved from http://www.enchantedlearning.com/alphabet/alphabeticalorder/holiday/10arbordaywords/

Author. (n.d.). *Virginia Standards of Learning (SOLs)*. Retrieved from http://www.doe.virginia.gov/VDOE/Superintendent/Sols/home.shtml

Author. (2007). *Fairfax county program of study*. Retrieved from http://www.fcps.edu/DIS/pos/

Barton, D., & Hamilton, M. (1998). *Local literacies*. London: Routledge.

Fay, K., & Whaley, S. (2004). *Becoming one community: Reading and writing with English language learners*. Portland: Stenhouse.

Fleischman, P. (2004). *Seed folks*. New York: Harper Teen.

Freebody, P., & Luke, A. (1999). Further notes on the four resources model. *Reading Online*. Retrieved from http://www.readingonline.org/research/lukefreebody.html

Gbur M. (2001). *Clozing the deal on Arbor Day*. Retrieved from http://teachers.net/lessons/posts/2273.html

Gee, J. P. (2003). *What video games have to teach us about learning and literacy*. New York: Palgrave McMillan.

Gee, J. P. (2002). *Introduction to discourse analysis*. New York: Taylor Francis.

Haas Dyson, A. (2005). Foreword. In J. Evans (Ed.), *Literacy moves on: Using popular culture, new technologies and critical literacy in the primary classroom* (pp. ix–xi). London: David Fulton/New York: Heinemann.

Heger, D. (2000). *The other meaning of Arbor Day*. Retrieved from http://www.mackinac.org/article.aspx?ID=4126

Janks, H. (2000). Domination, access, diversity and design: A synthesis for critical literacy education. *Educational Review, 52*(2), 175–186.

Janks, H., & Comber, B. (2005). Critical literacy across continents. In K. Pahl & J. Rowsell (Eds.), *Travel notes from the new literacy studies: Case studies in practice*. Clevedon: Multilingual Matters.

Kress, G., & Van Leeuwens, T. (2000). *Reading images: The grammar of visual design*. London: Routledge.

Larson, J., & Marsh, J. (2005). *Making literacy real*. London: Sage Publications.

Lovell, P., & Catrow, D. (2002). *Stand Tall Molly Lou Melon*. New York: Putnam.

Manning, A. (2004). *"Literacy As" model*. Presented at the International Literacy Educators Research Network. Toronto, Ontario: Canada.

Peet, B. (1991). *Wump world*. New York: Houghton Mifflin.

Vasquez, V. (2004). *Negotiating critical literacies with young children*. New Jersey, NJ: Lawrence Erlbaum Associates.

JONATHAN ARENDT

CHAPTER 8

Countering the Rhetoric of Warfare: A Framework for Practical Media Criticism and Curriculum on the War in Iraq

"Unthinking respect for authority is the greatest enemy of truth."(Albert Einstein).

"But the issue still struck her as unimportant. 'Who cares?' she said impatiently. 'It's always one bloody war after another, and one knows the news is all lies anyway'" (George Orwell, *1984*).

War is not only now. History has long attended violent conflict and the present will not be its last witness. A key realization to combating uncritical consumption of media coverage is to recognize the educational sites of practice as the Critical Literacy opportunities they represent; a chance to teach both students and educators to better deconstruct the myriad media messages and the oft inherent contradictory representation of spectacle versus reality. A quarter century ago, early pleas were made to encourage students to "view TV critically, with intelligence and discrimination. *Television criticism*, whether under that title or another, should become a basic subject of instruction in schools from the earliest grades" (Esslin, 1982, 112) and ask such important questions as:

> who, in the end, is authorized to appear but above all authorized to show, edit, store, interpret, and exploit images....or whether about the right to know who owns, who is able to appropriate, who is able to select, who is able to show images, directly political or not (Derrida and Stiegler, 2002, 33-34).

The current war in Iraq is one such moment for critical intervention on the part of teachers and schools. The success of the around-the-clock barrage of news coverage from broadcast corporations began with the first Gulf War (Morris, 2005) and, since then, these national and international crises have received substantial news coverage. Students and non-students alike have found themselves immersed in the reportage as, once more, "daily twists and turns of a fast-paced war [are] almost simultaneously transmitted back to the American public in vivid detail" (Morris, 2005, 59).

The school curriculum, as a result, can be more critically designed to give students the tools to take them beyond the dichotomous, "reifying schema" which opposes "production to consumption, that is to say: by putting analysis on one side (production) and synthesis on the other (consumption)" (Derrida, 2002, 163).

K. Cooper and R. E. White (eds.), Critical Literacies in Action: Social Perspectives and Teaching Practices, 127–141.

Teachers, then, are tasked with providing students with a critical awareness, taken from Giroux:

> Educators have an important role to play in encouraging such an examination of American history and foreign policy among their students and colleagues. Equally important is the need for educators to use their classrooms not only to help students to think critically about the world around them but also to offer a sanctuary and forum where they can address their fears, anger, and concerns about the events of September 11 and how it has affected their lives. The events of September 11 provide educators with a crucial opportunity to reclaim school as democratic public spheres in which students can engage in dialogue and critique around the meaning of democratic values. (2002, 1141-1142)

As a high school teacher in Houston, Texas from 2000 to 2005, I made – with varying degrees of success and failure – many attempts to "reclaim school as a democratic public sphere" and "help students critically think" about the urgency surrounding the government's call to the war in Iraq. The tools at my disposal were limited and I often found myself quite powerless to counter the inundation of packaged thought being distributed to the students in red, white and blue emblazoned news reports.

It wasn't until my last couple of years in this district that the school board decided to implement a "media studies" section of the English curriculum, comprised of pre-packaged units with pre-selected news clips, pre-selected articles, pre-selected lesson plans and questions. It was a veritable instant dinner complete with entrée and sides, but frozen in time and of questionable nutritional value to mentally starving students. While the long overdue inclusion of media studies and awareness into the curriculum was appreciated, its execution was far too superficial and socially disconnected and I found myself working hard to augment and change the curriculum in order to create the classroom environment that Giroux calls for.

These classrooms with young and impressionable minds are important grounds for exploring ways to interrupt history so, as students move into adulthood and occupy decision-making positions, they are more prepared to critically evaluate the media messages – both government official and non – for themselves. Reflecting back on my own attempts, I find a resonance in Banks' (1998) discussion on varying models of inclusion of culturally sensitive and vibrant multicultural works. By successfully reaching students to empower and enable them when issues of violent conflict and national justification arise again (assuming it will be relatively "absent" in the future in the first place), they will have a critical mindset at their disposal for arriving at their own decisions and each, individually, interrupting history in his or her own way.

Five years ago, teaching in a suburban west Houston school district, I received a package of media literacy materials from central administration. Preliminary moves were being made to integrate media literacy with formal objectives that were specific to broadcast media, particularly television and cinema. The goal was admirable but the curriculum implementation was far from what I would term "authentic." The package included one videocassette to be used across four grades by over 30 English teachers. It included one photocopy-ready packet of materials that matched district curriculum goals.

The lone videocassette itself offered little more than news reports and contained little of substance in the way of analytical or deconstructive opportunities. The move was reminiscent of the manner in which the district sought to incorporate more diverse works into the instructional canon despite sparse inclusions found in the recently adopted textbook anthologies. That is, the onus was placed on teachers to find spaces in the curriculum and calendar where they could present the students with materials and resources that were contemporary, relevant, richer and more diverse than what was accessible through district adopted books. Without focusing too much on the anthologies themselves, I can say that they were a marginal improvement from what Hutchins (1953) established as a canonical standard in the introduction to *The Great Conversation* despite the fact that the anthologies themselves carried a late 1990s publication date.

I was seeing first hand evidence of Applebee's (1989) work that distinguished between a canon of availability and a canon of practice; despite the fact that there were increasingly diverse resources being made available to teachers, syllabus after syllabus showed no change in twenty-five years of high school literary instruction. And in the ten years that lapsed between Applebee's study and the anthology's adoption in my school district, little had changed. The same titles were being taught. Many of the same novels occupied the shelves of the department's office and bookroom. This all despite the fact that for years critics had been calling for the inclusion of more postcolonial works (McCarthy, 1998b); de-centering the dominance of western works (Said, 1983); more feminist works (Fox-Genovese, 1989; Smith, 1989); challenges to the inherent class/power issues in canonized works (Murphy, 1991); more works by non-whites (McCarthy, 1998a; Craige, 1989; Banks, 1993; Garcia, 1993; Chiu, 1997); and more contemporary, socially relevant works (Israel, 1997), including those of television and non-print texts (Skretta, 1997).

We are in the midst of the same conversation, with a slightly different media spin; the heart of this matter is broadcast media and, more specifically, the tenor and content of the news reports surrounding the coming conflict in Iraq. Even though Skretta's (1997) essay was partially tongue in cheek, as he pleaded the case for the inclusion of two animated suburban revolutionaries without filter or conscience, Beavis and Butt-head, in the high school canon, his premise is exceedingly important: Students are consuming mass amounts of media, particularly television and internet, and we have a responsibility to equip the students with textual deconstruction skills with the same fervor that we teach literary analysis. And we have to fight to change a media curriculum that is far too superficial and too narrow, just as the critics cited above managed to make strides in the curriculum canon of possibility, with strides being slowly made toward actuality and realization. For these are all texts and merit inclusion and analysis as such.

It is here where adaptation of Banks' model for inclusion (1998) becomes so important. Just as Banks provides teachers and schools with a framework to move beyond superficial approaches for diversity, we need to provide them with a framework to begin critically evaluating the manner in which we instruct students to understand the media that they consume daily. This is merely a framework and, as such, should not be considered an ends; I submit anecdotes from my own experience as I moved through the four steps of inclusion in my senior literature class in west Houston, as I tried to move my students toward a position of agency so that they might not grant, as Einstein warns against, the "unthinking respect toward authority."

THE CONTRIBUTIONS APPROACH

This approach is also commonly referred to as the "heroes and holidays" approach and I saw examples during the month of February, Black History Month and Cinco de Mayo, a Mexican holiday. During Black History Month, the morning announcements would include a short biography of a famous Black figure – musicians, inventors, politicians, athletes, and others. One morning our principal, an African American, played "Lift Every Voice" – the African American national anthem, after the morning's Pledge of Allegiance. This act set off quite an exchange between teachers who vehemently objected to the act and refused to stand during the anthem as a form of protest to the perceived equality of one national pledge to a cultural anthem. The uproar over such a seemingly benign inclusion and concession demonstrates the nature in which even this step, considered superficial and preliminary, can evolve into something more significant and politically charged. The act of the objecting teachers became an entry point into a dialogue of inclusion. Unfortunately, the conversation did not last long and the "heroes and holidays" approach suffered a setback. Cinco de Mayo, meanwhile, one of the most celebrated of Mexican and Chicano holidays, was the only day of the school year in which there was any broad, campus-wide recognition of Latin culture, which is especially discouraging when the campus contains at least one-third of students classified as "Hispanic."

The equivalence of the contributions approach to media analysis can be found in packages such as the one I received from the district; an all-in-one kit that can be used and consumed in a short time period before being passed on. There is little done with such deconstruction "before or after the event, nor is the cultural significance of the event explored in any depth" (Cumming-McCann, 2003, 10). The events selected on the videocassette were recorded and any sort of social immediacy or relevancy had been removed because the event had become anesthetized and was more fiction than reality, an event without import or consequence. Even though, for example, a selected news report covered an event that actually happened but because of time and editing and packaging, the event had become a *simulacrum* (Baudrillard, 1988) because it had become so far removed from the event it ceased to have any visceral impact or meaning. The factual news reports that had been selected for the media unit had joined the realm of the hyper-real, an event "without origin or reality." (Baudrillard, 1988, 166).

The included questionnaires and quizzes and guidelines for lesson planning also did not call for much imagination or insight on the part of the students or teacher. Some of the questions called for a bit of analysis but these questions, on the news report of a crime for example, looked more at the manner of broadcast and cinematography than the manifestation of profiling and the reliance on stereotypical depictions of criminality. There is little doubt that broadcast media representations are instrumental in the forming of ideas and opinions. In fact, Gilliam et al. concluded that:

> in modern society the media are perhaps the most pervasive of [impersonal influences]. Most Americans are bombarded by a steady stream of mass media information, from a variety of channels.... The persistence of racial segregation means that impersonal influences such as the media are likely to play a significant role in the development of racial attitudes (2002, 757)

despite the fact that this "fausse consciousness in Sartre's sense, that television produces, which results in attitudes toward the real world that are unrealistic, illusionary, and even harmful" (Esslin, 1982, 72).

With the current war in Iraq, the twenty-four hour news stations stand to gain even more influence, continuing a trend and repeating a phenomena in the first Gulf War. CNN's success, as illustrated earlier, is indebted to the Gulf War (Morris, 2005). These major news broadcast companies search for "the sensational and the spectacular. Television calls for dramatization, in both senses of the term: it puts an event on stage, puts it in images. In doing so, it exaggerates the importance of that event, its seriousness and its dramatic, even tragic, character" (Bourdieu, 2001, 248). Any curriculum that includes media criticism and literacy must address these sensationalist aspects and examine the nature in which official statements and edited news reports might be affected by more than a strict objectivity to present all sides to an event.

If there is going to be any constructive, authentic deconstruction of the media it is clear that prepackaged curricular content, extricated from dated reports and presented in accordance with a dictated, easily reproducible format does not afford the students or teachers enough analytical opportunity. In times of national crises, such as those surrounding the call and legitimacy of aggression, the news reports do not come with a questionnaire or a pause button with a prepackaged set of guidelines for analysis. The rhetoric put out by the administration created a great deal of debate, among experts and scholars alike; how can we expect students to develop agency and a position of informed response when academics struggle? The curriculum has not changed and even the incorporation of media literacy retains the same structure and goals as conventional "literacy" learning and we know that the struggle over the latter is perpetual, so too must the advocacy for strengthening the former be perpetuated.

THE ADDITIVE APPROACH

The next step in this model is the additive approach, which "allows the teacher to put content into the curriculum without restructuring it" (Cumming-McCann, 2003, 10) and, while teaching in Houston, I worked with an existing curriculum piece, Orwell's (1983) *1984*, and added a novel to the syllabus, Tim O'Brien's (1998) collection of Vietnam War short stories and vignettes, *The Things They Carried*. Using these titles, I tried to link the course content to images of war and the rhetoric of aggression students were reading about in papers and online and were seeing nightly at home.

Orwell's dystopian novel was the summer reading assignment and, as a result, was the novel which we were reading when the September 11 attacks took place. The decision to react, swiftly and decisively, was not questioned by many, including myself. After all, the nation had just suffered an attack on its civilians such as had previously not been seen. Consequently, I did not push the students to deconstruct the retaliatory rhetoric because striking at the heart of the terrorist organization responsible seemed justified for I was as caught up in the emotional need for retribution as many others; I am not condoning it nor do I take personal pride in it. However, once the administration began turning its attention to Iraq, the less convinced I was in the authority the bureaucrats possessed in targeting Iraq on such questionable terms.

It was on a plane ride months later where I read an editorial piece in a magazine that examined the manner in which the United States was building a case against a foreign leader, Saddam Hussein, through mainstream media manipulation. I realized then that I could never teach *1984* the same way again. I endeavored to spend time on the sections that dealt with the depiction of an enemy and Orwell offers several poignant passages through which students could empathize with Winston Smith as he begins to adopt a more interrogative, critical position.

At one point, during a rally, Winston recalls that there was a change in the nation's target that was swift and deftly handled but the switch did nothing to diminish the national ire being provoked. Similarly, the United States declared Iraq a front on the war on terror and the focus switched from the mountains of Pakistan and the search for Bin Laden to the deserts and palaces of Iraq, despite the questionable nature and amount of evidence linking Bin Laden to Saddam Hussein and terrorists to Iraq and the presence of weapons of mass destruction.

Orwell describes the speaker's oration and its effects: "His voice, made metallic by the amplifiers, boomed forth an endless catalogue of atrocities, massacres, deportations, lootings, rapings, torture of prisoners, bombing of civilians, lying propaganda, unjust aggressions, broken treaties." (Orwell, 1983, 160). Though the scene might not have been repeated in the streets of America, the accusations were certainly similar on nationwide news broadcasts and the most disturbing part in the passage, for me as a teacher, occurs as Winston witnesses that "the most savage yells of all came from the schoolchildren" (Orwell, 1983, 160). The importance of helping my students to analyze these messages from authority figures only hastened in urgency. I used *1984* and passages such as these as opportunities to work into the curriculum the news broadcasts that they were watching. I was fortunate enough to have a television in my room with a cable connection, so I was able to watch the news stations with the students in real time and ask them questions, comparing what they were seeing on television with what they were seeing Winston experiencing in Oceania as a citizen and an employee of the Ministry of Truth. Because of a faculty disagreement and vehement criticism of the "liberal" bias of CNN, the classrooms were only able to access FOX News for much of the time before the middle ground of MSNBC was made accessible. So even trying to add mainstream news broadcasts to my classroom was not without political conflict.

With these broadcasts we continued to run into the problems that Baudrillard discusses. War footage shot from the front lines resembled the video games my students were playing, echoing a point Baudrillard (1995) makes. My students could move from watching a news report from Iraq and then play cooperative war games together over a computer network seamlessly. As a result, the war is removed further and further from the actual events and violence taking place and resembles the video game simulations as much as the actual events. Fortunately, Orwell includes in his novel a reference to this distance between event and viewer when he states that "the fighting, when there is any, takes place on the vague frontiers whose whereabouts the average man can only guess at, or round the Floating Fortresses which guard strategic spots on the sea lanes" (Orwell, 1983, 165). The students struggled mightily with what they were reading and tried to reconcile that with what they were seeing and with the opinions shared at home and among friends. Despite the attempts I was making, many students did not engage with the deconstruction on meaningful levels and when they did, their observations were clumsy, but the fact that initial steps were being taken were encouraging.

Buoyed by even the limited success I had with *1984* I decided to add another title to the curriculum, one that had not been taught in the district, Tim O'Brien's (1998) *The Things They Carried*. I was only able to add this book to the course because I was teaching a College Board-sanctioned Advanced Placement Literature and Composition course and O'Brien's piece had appeared on AP Exams previously.

O'Brien is a Vietnam War victim and puts together an often visceral and moving collection of stories drawn from his impressions and memories but which are, ultimately, fictional. I did not have the students read the book from front to back but instead guided them through stories in such an order that O'Brien's delayed confession that the book was fiction was the last thing they read. The response of the students was overwhelmingly one of resentment at being lied to and manipulated and, moreover, I was accomplice and party to the deception even though many of them probably purchased the book in the *fiction* section of their bookstore. The publication information page of the book states "This is a work of fiction. Except for a few details regarding the author's own life, all the incidents, names, and characters are imaginary" (O'Brien, 1998). The students, though, accepted it as truth because it is printed matter and the storytelling is managed with such expertise and clarity that these events *must have* happened. I used this reaction, tried to apply it to the media reports and encouraged students to question the validity of those reports, reminding them how easy it is to be duped, despite the fact that the fictional nature of the book was not hidden by the publisher or the author, although the "truth" was delayed through the order in which the students read the selections. It was uncomfortable for the students and the terrain was difficult for me as a teacher, trying to tread the line between the perception of a teacher pushing them to question all they were seeing and hearing and that, in the position of authority, I was condescendingly manipulating them myself.

O'Brien's novel offers the insight of a veteran reflecting back to a time in his own life when he was the same age as my senior literature students facing the same possibilities and anxieties (*e.g.* was the draft going to make a return?) and he raised questions over the course of his storytelling that intensified the critical posture the students were taking. One of the questions that students reflected on most was the personal stake that anyone in the government had in the war and what risk, if any, they were facing. Many of my students had seen Michael Moore's *Fahrenheit 9/11* and discovered that there were no enlisted family members putting their lives on the line. So, as we read the following excerpt, the students began asking tougher questions and seeking more complicated answers:

> There should be a law, I thought. If you support a war, if you think it's worth the price, that's fine, but you have to put your own precious fluids on the line. You have to head for the front and hook up with an infantry unit and help spill the blood. And you have to bring along your wife, or your kids, or your lover. A *law*, I thought. (O'Brien, 1998, 42).

For seventeen- and eighteen-year old students, this provoked a lot of emotional responses and students began to question everything from the motive to the validity of the claims made against Iraq by the administration. Of course, the critical stance was not adopted by all, but over the course of the year, as *The Things They Carried* was read late during the Spring semester, usually about six months after we started with *1984*, more sophisticated questions were asked, more challenges were made and more skepticism crept into the minds of students, most of whom had begun the year parroting what local politicians and parents were saying and which happened to be predominately conservative and reflective of the political climate in and around Houston.

THE TRANSFORMATIVE APPROACH

The approach to the curriculum becomes "transformative" when it has undergone a complete re-evaluation and reconstruction and "in some cases, a conscious effort on the part of the teacher to deconstruct what he/she has been taught to think, believe, and teach" (Cumming-McCann, 2003, 11). Although I had my first inclination toward such a transformation, I never put anything into effect from a curriculum perspective because I was anxious as to how such changes would be received. My hesitancy stemmed from having my proposal for a Multicultural Literature elective denied at the district level because it was seen as redundant; I worried that such changes to the media literacy curriculum in light of the current political climate would be seen as objectionable. I looked for a couple of non-canonical pieces that would serve to illuminate the side of the argument my students didn't seem to get. Working with *1984* and *The Things They Carried* afforded me opportunities, but even these examples were strained because there wasn't the same non-fictional urgency. I decided to add Chomsky's *Propaganda: American Style* (1987) and excerpts from Lipschutz's (1995) *On Security* which, in part, discusses the notion of national security and how administrative rhetoric can be constructed, however false or disingenuous the "threat" might be, in order to sway public opinion, create a fear and squelch opposition, whether it be media, academic or otherwise. I had more success with the former book because it was more accessible than the latter, which I found I could only use with selected classes or selected students.

When Chomsky (1987) writes in his first paragraph of President Woodrow Wilson's "historical engineering" the students readily identify the concept with Orwell's "memory holes" and other bureaucratic methods for "designing the facts of history so they would serve state policy." In the course of the essay, Chomsky makes several comparisons to the United States policymakers and the manipulative nature of *1984*'s Ministry of Truth and then explains how both follow Lippman's (1922) description of democracy as effected through the "manufacture of consent." Using the Vietnam War as an example, Chomsky analyzes the nature in which the debate over the war in Vietnam wasn't really a true debate but rather a discussion of to what extent the involvement in Vietnam should be, not whether or not the U.S. military belonged there at all. Many of the students saw the similarities in the call to war in Iraq as different sides and primarily discussed how the United States was going to exert its presence on foreign soil using spurious allegations of weapons of mass destruction and not whether or not they had the right to be there. As Chomsky (1987) points out, the debate was essentially over tactics.

The two most striking parts of the article, though, that my students found the most disturbing were his discussion of an El Salvadorian siege and a claim about the vulnerability of the educated when it comes to state propaganda and media. Chomsky describes how, in 1980, the powers in El Salvador renewed their "state of siege" and began torturing and killing civilians and this violence came at the hands of a military force that was trained and funded by the United States. The connection to the U.S. support of the Afghans against the Russians and the Iraqis against Iran were aspects of the discussion that the students had not realized. This discovery of U.S. aid to forces that were now enemies was uncomfortably Orwellian for many of my students and reminded them of the passage in which enemies became allies and allies became enemies, through rhetoric as well as action. And in some cases strictly through words with no viable threat to security, a notion further explored in Lipschutz (1995).

The other alarming comment in Chomsky's essay relates to the nature in which the students may be putting themselves at increased risk by consuming more media, by watching more news. He cites that:

Studies show that among the more educated parts of the population, the government's propaganda about the war is now accepted unquestioningly. One reason that propaganda often works better on the educated than on the uneducated is that educated people read more, so they receive more propaganda. Another is that they have jobs in management, media, and academia and therefore work in some capacity as agents of the propaganda system – and they believe what the system expects them to believe. By and large, they're part of the privileged elite, and share the interests and perceptions of those in power (Chomsky, 1987, np).

The comment on academia certainly has bearing on the nature of this special edition and the academic response. Even though my students are not as academic, perhaps, as the target audience for the call, that does not meant that they are no less discomfited by the accusation – some students, clearly frustrated, said that they would simply be better off not knowing anything, like Huxley's (1998) ignorant Deltas, Epsilons, and Gammas. After all, what point does it serve to consume media in order to try and learn more but in reality, they are only putting themselves more at risk of being more easily manipulated.

This is precisely the point where I see the urgency of such aggressive media curriculum attention, and change. I certainly don't believe that I am capable of changing the students' minds or effecting sweeping change; I was just learning myself along with the students and there was great anxiety and doubt for all of us. But I think this framework, the adaptation of Banks' (1998) model, at least helps teachers and students alike in creating increasingly complex scenarios and opportunities in which intra- and interpersonal interrogation can take place.

The Lipschutz (1995) article I only had limited success with and I think that if presented with a high school audience again, I would probably approach the matter in a different way. After reading the Chomsky essay and comparing it to passages in *1984* that dealt with war and national security, the students asked tougher and tougher questions about how secure our nation truly was; after all, a planned attack was effected on several different sites on domestic soil. How secure were we and what does it mean to be secure? In an effort to answer the questions, I looked for academics who tackled the topic more clearly than I. One of my students mentioned some work of Lipschutz that she had come across in her debate preparations so I began looking at his work. Lipschutz asks, on the topic of the first war in Iraq:

Even the Gulf War, arraying international coalition against renegade state, now is seen to have been somewhat inconclusive. In the midst of such conceptual and practical confusion, against whom or what is anyone to be made secure (1996, 4)?

We revisited, and continue to revisit in the current war, the "inconclusive" nature of the legitimacy of aggression as well as the confusion of both the conceptual and the practical in this conflict as well. My students asked, researched and attempted to identify risks and weighed immediate personal risks with speculation that seemed to merit such drastic responses as battles fought on foreign fronts to attacks on rights to domestic privacy. Their concerns became a chorus: at what price security? It's hard to settle on a "price" when no clear value can be placed on what it means to actually be secure and from whom.

The difficulty in establishing a context for such abstract discussions with a twelfth grade Literature class was profound and, at the same time, both encouraging and discouraging. The students began to associate power with the ability to declare a state as secure or insecure and recognized that this ability to define security "provides not just access to resources but also the *authority* to articulate new definitions and discourses of security, as well" (Lipschutz, 1995, 8). That led the students to wonder why one nation was declared a threat and another nation was not. We had the case of Iraq with questionable destructive capabilities (in terms of WMDs) and the case of North Korea whose official statements included the active pursuit of arming a nuclear device; one received an armed, aggressive response and the other was pursued through more diplomatic means. All of the nuclear ambiguities associated with Iraq drew national security attention, a reflection of the case of a nation

> with the clandestinely assembled and crude atomic device, and not the thousands of reliable high-yield warheads mounted on missiles poised to launch at a moment's notice, that creates fear, terror, and calls for greater surveillance and enforcement (Lipschutz, 1995, 9).

We recognized this in class, on the broadcasts we watched and White House statements we listened to. So there were some practical examples that helped the students understand the complexities of "national security" even though much of the selected article was beyond our collective and instructive grasp.

I regret that I did not incorporate more works of this nature. To my surprise, I did not face much criticism or conflict from the campus administration or parents; the largest group against whom I had to defend myself most was my fellow teachers, typically conveyed through students that we shared. The most common accusation was that I was trying to indoctrinate my students with anti-establishment views. The views were certainly anti-establishment and, although my intent was not to indoctrinate, I've no doubt that my own biases affected the works that I chose and how I presented them to the students and these were clearly contrary to much of what the students had been exposed to. I tried, as best I could, though, to present the students with information and sources that they were simply not exposed to regularly. This third step in the framework is one I know that I barely scratched the surface of but even those few opportunities yielded results.

THE DECISION MAKING AND SOCIAL ACTION APPROACH

The final step is the hardest to implement and requires the most work on the part of the teacher but, if success is to be realized, students have to become advocates for themselves. This was, by far, my least successful area. The approach

> ...requires students to make decisions and to take action related to the concept, issue, or problem they have studied [and].... Requires that students

not only explore and understand the dynamics… but also commit to making decisions and changing the system through social action (Cumming-McCann, 2003, 11).

I have no doubt that many of my students explored the "dynamics" but I can only think of one example of an active attempt on the part of a small group of students who showed such committed, independent acts of social agency and awareness.

And it had nothing to do with the war in Iraq. Instead it dealt with the national celebration around Columbus Day and the veneration our nation has for this explorer. Columbus Day was approaching and I had added some narratives and histories of Columbus's "discovery" of the continent and his treatment of the natives he discovered in these lands, not included in their American history texts. The students were shocked to hear an alternative view that included violent conversions to Catholicism, torture, rape, theft and other acts the allegedly civilized perpetrated against the supposedly savage. One group of students was so incensed that they had not ever been presented this information and decided that they would try to educate others as they had been.

The school district has a staff development day on Columbus Day, so while teachers are on campus for various reasons, students have the day off. In advance of their holiday, these students researched Columbus further, on their own, and created information pamphlets. They then asked permission from the management at a nearby mall to hand out the pamphlets as part of a school project; the mall management complied. These students spent their day handing out their pamphlets and trying their best to answer questions. They were very surprised to find that many people with whom they spoke had never been presented with this side of the 'civilization' of the New World. Ultimately, I have no idea how successful they were or even how accurate some of their answers to passersby might have been, but I take some satisfaction knowing that they felt empowered enough to take it upon themselves to research the topic and "acquire a sense of political awareness and efficacy" (Cumming-McCann, 2003, 11). I do know that I probably didn't reach this stage of media analysis often, if ever. I also know that it would be a primary goal, and should be a primary goal, for any teacher at any level, for more and more students are tuning in and turning on devices that can connect them to the world around themselves.

There is a scene, though, in *The Things They Carried* that speaks to the type of response I would like, ideally, to see from my students. The narrator's impassioned criticism of war and the complicity of those around him reach a crescendo as he describes the silent arguments he has on sleepless nights with these people in his head:

I'd sometimes carry on fierce arguments with these people. I'd be screaming at them, telling them how much I detested their blind, thoughtless, automatic acquiescence to it all, their simpleminded patriotism, their prideful ignorance, their love-it-or-leave-it-platitudes, how they were sending me off to fight a war they didn't understand and didn't want to understand. I held them responsible. By God, yes, I *did*. All of them – I held them personally and individually responsible – the polyestered Kiwanis boys, the merchants and farmers, the pious churchgoers, the chatty housewives, the PTA and the Lions Club and the Veterans of Foreign Wars and the fine upstanding gentry out at the country club. They didn't know Bao Dai from the man in the moon. They didn't know history. (O'Brien, 1998, 45)

History, in this context, is not the archived and canonized compendium of facts and events and dates in high school textbooks. It accounts for the sociopolitical milieu surrounding the narrator and his anger over receiving his draft notice. In many ways, this fictionalized account is just as "factual" as any table found in a mainstream American history anthology. This is also history students need to be presented with, alternative views and contradicting thoughts on contemporary issues which offer much more than a prepackaged curriculum. There is no doubt that the result will probably be unsettling and confusing, but it is precisely these perturbations to the system that allow for more authentic curriculum (Doll, 1993). Doll manages to find such space in a science and math curriculum; surely such openings exist in history and language courses.

CONCLUSION

Recently I was reminded once more of the urgency of the issue and the necessity for meaningful media literacy at levels even below my high school seniors. My wife teaches at a nearby K-8 school, nestled in a small community west of Toronto and over the Christmas holidays one of the eighth grade students lay in a coma before passing away due to complications from what doctors believed was an aneurysm. It was a tragic episode that saddened an entire campus and was on the news, but it did not end with this student's passing. There were soon allegations that the head trauma the boy suffered might have been the result of an attack that happened away from campus, after school hours. Information and misinformation alike began to be broadcast in papers and news reports, some conflicting with others. Students who knew this student could not fully understand and process what they were seeing and, in some cases, believed the papers and television reports even though some of the facts contradicted what they knew to be true. The sentiment that the students expressed was that if it was the news and the papers, it *had* to be true and they were more likely to believe these sources even though at times they were not consistent with one another or themselves (Martha Arendt, personal communication, January 28, 2008). So much trust is invested in media sources that these junior high-aged students struggled with what they were presented with on the news and in the papers and wrestled with the reconciliation between reported "facts" and what they themselves knew firsthand.

We aren't just talking about the rhetoric of war among academics and undergraduate and advanced high school students. The need for media literacy in the curriculum and in frequent instruction prepares students to understand the increasingly complex, media-saturated world in which they live, consume, and communicate. To neglect this aspect of their education is to do them, and society at large, a grave disservice. These are the people who will soon be forming the decision-making masses and taking on voting responsibilities. One of the best opportunities for "interrupting history" lies in the classrooms – public, private, and pre-service – so that, as these students move into adult, independent lives of their own, they can avoid uncritical media consumption and repetition of violent historical events. The prospect of students questioning for themselves is a preferable image to the Orwellian schoolchildren, violently yelling in the streets because someone has told them to and not because they've been given the tools to interrogate media messages themselves.

REFERENCES

Applebee, A. N. (1989). *A study of book-length works taught in high school English courses. Rept. 1.2.* New York: Center for the Learning and Teaching of Literature.

Banks, J. A. (1993). Multicultural education: Development, dimensions, and challenges. *Phi Delta Kappan, 73*(1), 22–28.

Banks, J. A. (1998). Approaches to multicultural curricular reform. In E. Lee, D. Menkart, & M. Okazawa-Rey (Eds.), *Beyond heroes and holidays: A practical guide to K-12 antiracist, multicultural education and staff development.* Washington, DC: Network of Educators on the Americas.

Baudrillard, J. (1988). Simulacra and simulations. In M. Poster (Ed.), *Jean Baudrillard: Selected writings* (pp. 166–184). Stanford: Stanford University Press.

Baudrillard, J. (1995). *The Gulf War did not take place.* Bloomington, IN: Indiana University Press.

Bourdieu, P. (2001). Television. *European Review, 9*(3), 245–256.

Chomsky, N. (1987). *Propaganda: American style.* Retrieved August 24, 2002, from http://www.zpub.com/un/chomsky.html

Chui, S. S. (1997). Reorienting the English classroom: Asian American writers in the canon. *English Journal, 86*(8), 30–33.

Craige, B. J. (1989). Curriculum battles and global politics: Conflict of paradigms. *Phi Kappa Phi, 69*(3), 30–31.

Cumming-McCann, A. (2003). Multicultural education: Connecting theory to practice. *Focus on Basics: Connecting Research and Practice, 6*(B), 9–12.

Derrida, J., & Stiegler, B. (2002). *Echographies of television* (J. Bajorek, Trans.). Cambridge: Polity.

Doll, W. (1993). *A post-modern perspective on curriculum.* New York: Teachers College Press.

Esslin, M. (1982). *The age of television.* San Francisco: W.H. Freeman and Co.

Fox-Genovese, E. (1989). The feminist challenge to the canon. *Phi Kappa Phi, 69*(3), 32–34.

Garcia, J. (1993). The changing image of ethnic groups in textbooks. *Phi Delta Kappan, 75*(1), 29–35.

Gilliam, F. D., Valentino, N., & Beckmann, M. (2002, December). Where you live and what you watch: The impact of racial proximity and local television news on attitudes about race and crime. *Political Research Quarterly, 55*(4), 755–780.

Giroux, H. (2002). Democracy, freedom, and justice after September 11th: Rethinking the role of educators and the politics of schooling. *Teachers College Record, 104*(6), 1138–1162.

Hutchins, R. M. (1953). Preface to "The Tradition of the West". In *The great conversation, Vol. 1, Great books of the western world.* New York: Encyclopedia Britannica.

Huxley, A. (1998). *Brave new world.* New York: First Perennial Classics.

Israel, E. (1997). What can contemporary authors teach us? *English Journal, 86*(8), 21–23.

Lippman, W. (1922). *Public opinion.* New York: Harcourt Brace.

Lipschutz, R. D. (1995). On security. In R. D. Lipschutz (Ed.), *On security* (pp. 1–23). New York: Columbia University Press.

McCarthy, C. (1998a). *The uses of culture: Education and the limits of ethnic affiliation.* New York: Routledge.

McCarthy, C. (1998b). The uses of culture: Canon formation, postcolonial literature, and the multicultural project. In W. Pinar (Ed.), *Curriculum: Toward new identities* (pp. 253–262). New York: Garland.

Moore, M. (Director) & Czarnecki, J. (Producer). (2004). *Fahrenheit 9/11*. [Film]. (Available from Lion's Gate Films).

Morris, J. S. (2005). The Fox News factor. *The Harvard International Journal of Press/Politics, 10*(3), 56–79.

Murphy, J. S. (1991). Some thoughts about class, caste, and the canon. *Teachers College Record, 93*(2), 265–279.

O'Brien, T. (1998). *The things they carried*. New York: First Broadway Books.

Orwell, G. (1983). *1984*. New York: Plume.

Said, E. (1983). *The world, the text, and the critic*. Cambridge, MA: Harvard University Press.

Skretta, J. (1997). Beavis and Butt-head: Two more white males for the canon. *English Journal, 86*(8), 24–28.

Smith, R. T. (1989). Canon fodder, the cultural hustle, and the minotaur deep in the maze. *Phi Kappa Phi, 69*(3), 25–29.

SECTION III
CRITICAL LITERACIES IN PRACTICE

JAMES PAUL GEE

CHAPTER 9

"Basic Information Structure" and "Academic Language": An Approach to Discourse Analysis

This chapter has two purposes. One purpose is to introduce a tool for analyzing some aspects of discourse. This tool is based on what I will call "Basic Information Structure" ("BIS" for short). The second purpose is to apply this tool to a specific example so that I can both make the use of the tool clearly and speak to an issue I wish to address.

The issue I want to address deals with "academic language" (Gee, 2004; Schleppegrell, 2004). Academic language is a general name for many different varieties of language associated with academic disciplines or with academic content in schools; for example, the styles of language and other symbol systems associated with chemistry or social science.

Academic language is technical or specialist language. Of course, there are non-academic varieties of technical or specialist language. Domains such as video games, carpentry, or auto mechanics have their own specialist styles of language, as do professions like law, medicine, engineering, handicapping horse races, or fashion design, and so forth (some such professions, broadly speaking, could be counted as "academic", but not all).

The issue germane to academic language I want to address is this; some people have argued that academic varieties of language are functional in the sense that they have evolved in history to do certain intellectual and interactional tasks necessary for an academic domain to make progress (Halliday and Martin, 1993). They cannot simply be replaced with less specialized versions of language, any more than a tool purpose-built for a specific job can simply be replaced, without loss, by a more generalized tool.

Others have argued that such academic varieties of language are forms of "jargon" and complexity invented to exclude, confuse and frustrate outsiders (non-academics and people outside a given field) and to hide or evade political, cultural, institutional and social issues in the name of "reason" or "logic". In this sense, such forms of language are "ideological" (I am using the word loosely here, see Wiley, 1996 for a more explicit discussion).

This issue, whether academic varieties of language are functional or ideological (in the informal senses I have given these terms here), has played a role in education. Some educators argue that children need to be introduced in school (for example, in science classrooms) to academic varieties of language early on, because mastery of these representational systems is crucial for true understanding

K. Cooper and R. E. White (eds.), Critical Literacies in Action: Social Perspectives and Teaching Practices, 145–158.

and real participation in areas of science, for instance (Halliday and Martin, 1993). Others have argued that academic varieties of language simply serve to make the "rich" kids look smarter than the "poor" ones—because they have had more home-based preparation for such varieties (Lee, 2002). Such academic varieties of language are barriers to understanding and participation, on this view, and need to be replaced with more democratic forms of language, interaction, and participation.

The chapter will proceed in three parts. First I will introduce "Basic Information Structure" as a tool for analysis. Second, I will discuss the issue of academic and other specialized forms of language. Third, I will use BIS to analyze a specific case in order to illuminate the issue of academic language being "functional" and/or "ideological" (we will see, in fact, that it can be both at the same time), as well as to show one of the uses to which BIS can be put.

Before I start, let me say that I do not separate "critical discourse analysis" from "discourse analysis" proper. All language use is political in the sense of expressing (tacitly or overtly) messages about things like status and solidarity and other "social goods" in society. Thus, any form of discourse analysis must pay attention to such issues. I have discussed this issue elsewhere (Gee, 2003, 2005). It will be apparent by the end of this paper that the example I discuss is one where "giving information" and "expressing political, ethical, value-laden messages" go hand-in-hand.

THE DESIGN OF DISCOURSE AND "BASIC INFORMATION STRUCTURE"

This section contains the basic grammatical information necessary to understand what I will call "Basic Information Structure" (BIS). We start with the notion of a "basic clause". The "basic clause" is the fundamental unit of both syntax and semantics (Gee, 2005). A basic clause is any predicate (verb, predicate adjective or predicate noun) and its required arguments. Below are some basic clauses:

1a. Mary <u>touched</u> John [verb]

1b. Mary <u>is healthy</u> [predicate adjective]

1c. Mary <u>has a brother</u> [predicate noun]

Basic clauses can be expanded by adding optional arguments:

2a. Mary touched John <u>on the head</u>

2b. Mary touched John <u>with her lips</u>

2c. Mary touched John <u>on the head</u> <u>with her lips</u>

Basic clauses can also be expanded by optional elements that are not arguments but which modify either the predicate or the whole clause in some way:

3a. Mary <u>lightly</u> touched John <u>on the head</u> ["lightly" and "on the head" modify the predicate "touched"]

3b. <u>Yesterday</u>, Mary touched John ["yesterday" modifies the clause "Mary touched John"]

3c.　Mary is <u>pretty</u> healthy <u>for an older woman</u> ["pretty" and "for an older woman" both modify the predicate "healthy"]

3d.　<u>Fortunately</u>, Mary is healthy ["fortunately" modifies the clause "Mary is healthy"]

3e.　Mary has an older brother in college ["older" and "in college" modify the predicate "brother"]

3f.　Mary, <u>fortunately</u>, has a brother ["fortunately" modifies the clause "Mary has a brother"]

Basic clauses, augmented or not by optional arguments or elements, can be combined or integrated in four ways. First is a "loose" way, when two or more clauses are combined by coordination and both clauses are main clauses:

4a.　Mary is healthy, but she touched John on the head with her lips.

4b.　Mary is healthy and she touched John on the head with her lips.

Second, clauses can be combined in a somewhat less loose way, when one or more clauses is juxtaposed, as a subordinate clause, to a main clause:

5a.　<u>While John was not looking</u>, Mary touched him on the head. ["while" introduces subordinate clause]

5b.　Mary touched John on the head <u>because he was causing trouble</u>. ["because" introduces subordinate clause]

Third, two clauses can be tightly integrated by having one clause embedded inside another one:

6a.　John felt Mary touch him on the head [= "Mary touched him on the head" is embedded inside "John felt …"].

6b.　John believed that Mary had touched him on the head [= "Mary touched John on the head" is embedded inside "John believed…"].

6c.　Mary planned to touch John on the head [= "Mary touched John on the head" is embedded inside "Mary planned…"].

Fourth, in the tightest form of integration, a clause can be turned into a phrase, losing its status as a clause (Halliday and Matthiessen, 1999). This can be done by changing a verb into a noun, as when we change "destroy" into "destruction". It can also be done by changing a verb into an adjective, as when we change "abuse" into "abused" (e.g., "an abused spouse"). It can also be done by turning a predicate adjective into a noun, as when we change "happy" into "happiness". In all these cases, we end up with a part of speech (i.e., an adjective or noun) that can be made part of a larger phrase. This phrase, like all phrases, can then be made part of a clause:

7.　Someone abuses children physically → physically abused children → Physically abused children need help [verb ("abuse") → adjective ("abused")]

8. The Romans destroyed the city → the Romans' destruction of the city → The Romans' destruction of the city was uncalled for [verb ("destroy") → noun ("destruction")]

9. John is happy → John's happiness → John's happiness is infectious [adjective ("happy") → noun ("happiness")]

In some cases where a verb is turned into a noun (e.g., "destroy" → "destruction") or an adjective (e.g., "abuse" → "abused"), or when an adjective is turned into a noun ("happy" → "happiness"), the original verb or adjective is more common than the noun, as in the cases above. In other cases, the two are about equally common:

10a. John got angry → John's anger [is impressive]

10b. John loved Mary → John's love for Mary [is touching]

10c. John punched someone → John's punch [missed Bill]

11a. Someone broke the vase → The broken vase [was mine]

11b. I ripped my jeans → Ripped jeans [are cool]

11c. I frightened the child → The frightened child [needed help]

Sometimes the noun version of a verb, in particular, takes on a somewhat different and more specialized meaning than its related verb:

12a. John studied something → John's study [appeared in print] ["study" = research paper]

12b. John works hard → John's work [involves cars]["work" = "job"]

12c. John speaks to a group → John's speech to the group [was well received]["speech" = "lecture"]

So far, in all the cases above, we have been moving from phrases and clauses to more complex combinations of clauses. But in discourse analysis we must usually go the other way round. We have to start with sentences that are composed of two or more (sometimes many more) clauses (combined or integrated in the ways we have just discussed above and others) and unravel these sentences into their basic clauses and whatever optional arguments or other elements those clauses contain. That is, we have to ask what basic clauses (and optional arguments and elements) the sentences are composed of or, to put it yet another way, what basic clauses (and optional arguments and elements) the sentences combine or integrate. So, to give one example, consider the case below:

13. The present study sought to clarify previous work.

The present study =1. someone (= researchers) study something (= topic) in the present sought = 2. (1) seek (3-4) to clarify = 3. someone (= researchers) clarify (4) previous work = 4. someone (= the field) works on something (= topic) previously

Sentence 13 is a statement that starts a published research article that I will discuss below (Pollak, Vardi, Putzer Bechner and Curtin, 2005). I have shortened the sentence. The phrase "the present study" contributes the clause "someone study something in the present". In the phrase "the present study", "study" is a noun related to the verb "to study" (of course, since it is noun, it has no tense — no time marking — and thus we cannot know what tense it would have had, had it been used as a verb).

When this verb is changed to a noun, the subject of the verb does not have to be mentioned, but we can infer that this subject is the researchers who are publishing the paper (thus, "researchers" is placed in parentheses to mark that it is an inference). What the researchers are studying need not be mentioned either, but, again, we can infer that the object of the verb "to study" is the topic of the paper; that is, the topic the researchers did their research on and are reporting on in the paper (thus, "topic" is in parentheses) — we could, of course, fill in more fully what the topic actually is.

"Sought" is the main verb (predicate) of the sentence. Its subject is the information contributed to the sentence by the phrase "the present study". The information this phrase contains is represented in line 1 — so I place (1) in the subject slot of "seek". "Sought" is the sort of verb that allows an infinitive (another verb, one with no tense marking) to be embedded inside or below it — in this case the infinitive "to clarify". "To clarify", then, is the predicate of a clause embedded inside (or "underneath") "sought"; "<u>researchers</u> clarify something". The "something" that is clarified is expressed in line 4 (thus, "4" is in the object slot of "clarify"). The object of "seek"— what is sought — is the information in lines 3 and 4 (and, thus, "3-4" is in the object slot of "seek").

The phrase "previous work" has a noun ("work") in it related to the verb "to work" and so this phrase contributes the clause: "the <u>field</u> works on <u>topic</u> previously". Here, again, we have to infer that something like "the field" is the subject of "works" (or "researchers who have done previous work in the field"). We can infer, as well, that the object of "works" is once again the topic of the paper, a topic that has heretofore been worked on by others in the field. When the verb "to work" is made into the noun "work", the adverb "previously" (which modifies a verb) becomes the adjective "previous" (which modifies a noun).

Thus, the short sentence "The present study sought to clarify previous work" combines, in various ways, four clauses—or, we can say, it combines four clauses worth of information. Once we know what clauses a sentence combines, we can see that there were many other ways these same clauses could have been filled out and combined. Thus, there are many other ways in which the sentence "The present study sought to clarify previous work" could have been said or written (could have been "designed"). A few examples are given below. These sentences either fill out optional arguments and elements in a different way, spell out inferences that were left unspecified, or combine or integrate the same clauses in a different way. Some of these forms below, while grammatical, would hardly ever or never be used for stylistic or pragmatic reasons. Let's assume for now that the topic of the study is "physically abused children":

14a. We studied physically abused children because we sought to clarify previous work in the field.

14b. The present study sought to clarify work that others had done previously.

14c. The present study studies physically abused children. We seek to clarify previous work.

14d. This study we have done in the present seeks to clarify work done previously.

14e. The present study of physically abused children seeks to clarify previous work.

14f. This study was done in the present. It sought something. It sought to clarify something. What it sought to clarify was work others had done previously.

14g. What the present study sought was to clarify previous work.

14h. The present study of physically abused children sought to clarify previous work.

Above we noted that optional arguments or other elements can be added to a clause (or left out). There are also optional elements that can be added to a sentence combining two or more clauses, elements that do not modify any one clause in the sentence, but either modify the sentence as a whole or communicate information about how the sentence connects to other sentences in an oral or written text:

15a. Fortunately, the present study sought to clarify previous work ["fortunately" modifies the whole sentence]

15b. The present study sought, fortunately, to clarify previous work ["fortunately" modifies the whole sentence]

16a. First, the present study sought to clarify previous work ["first" connects this sentence to others in the text, e.g., the next one starting with second"]

16b. The present sought first to clarify previous work ["first" connects this sentence to others in the text]

When we generate a list of alternative ways clauses could have been filled out and combined (as in 14-16), we also generate the key question: Why were the clauses combined and filled out as they were and not some other way? There can be lots of different answers to this question. For instance, some alternatives are ruled out by the type or style of language required by the communicative task or the genre, here a professional publication. Thus, most or all of the alternatives in 14 are not the "right" style for a professional academic publication. The sentence in 14h — which just spells out something that is left to be inferred in "The present study sought to clarify previous work"— might be avoided either because the authors do not want to name their topic directly or they feel it is obvious from other things in the paper (e.g., the title or abstract) or they feel the topic needs to be named or discussed in a more nuanced way than is possible by placing it as a phrase in this sentence.

A representation like that in 13 shows what I will call the "basic information structure" (hereafter BIS) in an oral or written text. So the BIS in the sentence "The present study sought to clarify previous work" is the four clauses below. Here I leave out the information in 13 that shows how the clauses are fit together and which information is left to be specified by inference:

17a. Someone study something

17b. Someone seek something

17c. Someone clarify something

17d. Someone work on something previously

Such basic information is "packaged"—put together into sentences—by: a) combining and integrating the clauses that the information expresses; b) adding optional arguments and elements to the clauses or the sentence as a whole; c) allowing for inferences to be made to specify information that is left out. Each such "move" (a-c) is a choice and one style of discourse analysis is to ask, for each such choice, why it might have been made and what communicative function it might be serving. We can ask, as well, why other alternative choices were not made (sometimes the answer to this question illuminates the question about why a given choice was made and what it communicates).

SOCIAL LANGUAGES AND THE QUESTION OF SPECIALIST LANGUAGE

This section takes up the issue of academic language (and, more generally, specialist or technical varieties of language). Any language comes in many different varieties or styles used for different purposes (Gee, 2004, 2005). There are different varieties of language used for different social identities and activities — for example, different varieties used by lawyers, doctors, gang members, biologists, carpenters, or video gamers. Such varieties are sometimes called "registers". I will refer to them as different "social languages". Social languages are differentiated from each by the use of different words (vocabulary) and sometimes by particular ways of using the morphological, syntactic, and/or discourse resources of the language.

One major distinction we can make (Gee, 2004, 2005) in regard to social languages is between "vernacular social languages" (vernacular styles of language) and "specialist social languages" (specialist styles of language). Vernacular styles are used by people when they are communicating as "everyday" non-specialist people. Vernacular styles differ across different social and cultural groups. Specialist styles are used by people when they are communicating as a specialist of some sort, whether this be a doctor, minister, academic, or gamer. Specialist styles, of course, draw on vernacular resources, but supplement them in a variety of ways through the use of distinctive words, distinctive uses of morphology, and/or distinctive uses of syntactic or discourse resources. For example, the sentence in 18 below is in the vernacular style and the sentence in 19 is in a specialist style associated with an academic discipline (in this case, some form of biology). In each case, I list the basic information that each sentence packages into a single sentence.

18.   Hornworms sure vary a lot in how well they grow

  18a.   Hornworms vary a lot in (18b)

  18b.   Hornworms grow how well

19.   Hornworm growth displays significant variation

  19a.   Hornworms grow

  19b.   (19a) displays (19c-19d)

  19c.   (19a) varies (19d)

  19d.   (19c) is significant

The vernacular differs from the specialist version in several ways. First the basic predicates (in the BIS) used are different in part: "vary" and "grow" in the vernacular and "grow", "display", "vary", and "is significant" in the specialist version. "Display" and "significant" are Latinate words that are typical of more specialist styles. Second, the two predicates that the two versions share — "vary" and "grow"— are in the specialist version turned into nouns ("growth" and "variation") and made arguments of other predicates ("growth" is the subject of "display" and "variation" is the object of "display").

Segment 18a says pretty much the same thing as 19c and 18b says pretty much the same thing as 19a — so these pieces of information are shared by the two varieties. The information in the specialist variety in 19d — "something is significant"— is conveyed in the vernacular by the adverb "a lot" modifying "vary" and the affective marker "sure" which modifies the whole sentence "Hornworms vary a lot in how well they grow". Of course, "sure … a lot" is not only less formal, it expresses the opinion of the speaker, while "significant" in "significant variation" is both more formal and expresses, not just the opinion of the speaker, but a standard held by a social group (a profession, in this case biologists or statisticians).

Note how in the specialist version the entity "hornworms" and the processes of varying and growing disappear. They are replaced by abstract things: hornworm growth, variation, and growth. This is typical of the distinction between vernacular styles and specialist styles of the sort in 19 above (academic styles of language).

In addition to asking why and how a given sentence packages its basic information as it does, we can, thus, too, ask an additional question: Why and how does a given sentence deviate from a vernacular style of language? Thus, we could ask: Why would anyone use a sentence like (19) rather than (20)?

AN EXAMPLE: ACADEMIC LANGUAGE

Now I turn to use BIS to analyze a specific piece of academic language. My goal here is both to exemplify the use of this tool and to speak to the issue of whether and how such academic language is either functional or ideological. The paper I will deal with is "Physically Abused Children's Regulation of Attention in

Response to Hostility" by Seth D. Pollak, Shira Vardi, Anna M. Putzer Bechner, and John J. Curtin, a paper which appeared in the journal *Child Development* (2005).

Before I turn to a small part of this paper, I need to tell you about the paper in general. Already this raises an interesting issue, since part of what I want to study here is how and why things are said (written) in a certain way and whether they can be said (written) in other ways — and why these other ways may have been avoided. So, I give a summary of the paper, well aware that to say it differently is not really to say the same thing.

The paper begins by asserting that the link between children experiencing physical abuse and thereafter demonstrating behavioral problems (e.g., withdrawal and aggression, attributing hostility to others, and displaying inappropriate affect and behavior) has already been well-established in the research literature. However, the authors claim that "precise mechanisms" linking the two is not well understood; so the paper seeks, not to argue for a link between abuse and behavioral problems (which is already known), but to get at the causal "mechanism" linking the two.

The authors propose that "attentional effects" may be the link between abuse and behavior problems. The idea is this: all young children have limited processing capacity and so can pay attention to only a limited number of stimuli at a time. This limited capacity causes the child to privilege and focus on some (salient) aspects of the environment over others. For physically abused children these salient features are things like threat and anger. Physically abused children may learn to overly attend to threatening cues, perhaps at the expense of other contextually relevant information, and may, in turn, have fewer resources available to regulate their emotional reposes to events that seem threatening to them, but, in reality, would not seem so threatening to children who had not been physically abused.

The sample of children studied consisted of 11 four- and five-year-old children who had been physically abused by their parents and 22 non-abused children (as a control group). Parents gave informed consent after receiving information about the study (To me, at least, the notion of "informed consent" for children seems somewhat odd coming from parents who have admitted to abusing their children).

The researchers are experimental physiological psychologists, people who want to precisely measure physical reactions (things like heart rate and skin conductance). For them, emotions (e.g., fear) are signaled by such physical reactions and it is the reactions they measure directly, not the emotions. But, of course, they need to get people to react to stimuli in order to measure their reactions. In this study, they had the children engage with a task on a computer (which the children thought was the task they were there to engage in), while in the background the children heard what they thought was an angry argument between two adults. The researchers wanted to know how the children — abused and non-abused — would react to (pay attention to) this background anger.

The researchers recorded a seven minute scripted conversation by two professional actors. The conversation started with the actors pretending to be two co-workers meeting and engaging in casual conversation. Then the two characters intensely argue. After that, there is a period of "silent unresolved anger during which one character abruptly leaves the room". Finally, there is a resolution in which the two characters apologize to each other. The conversation was presented by means of a compact disc player placed in a room adjacent to where the child was located. An opening in the wall connected the two rooms, so that the children could hear the argument, but not see that it was a recording and not real people. The children were, thus, meant to believe the argument was real, not recorded.

The task the children did on the computer involved pictures of different objects appearing at the center of a computer screen. The child was instructed to press the space bar in response to every picture except for a soccer ball. This task was meant to be a measure of attention, which might be disrupted to various degrees when the argument occurred.

Various physiological measurements where taken of the children's responses to the anger. For example, the children's emotional arousal was measured by electrodes on their skin that indexed their "skin conductance level". Skin conductance level reflects arousal through changes in the relative activity of the "ecrinec sweat glands" (ecrine glands occur in, among other places, the palms of the hands). Increases in skin conductance level indicate increases in emotional arousal. In order to get such measurements, a space heater was placed in the experiment room to facilitate the adequate release of sweat.

AN ANALYSIS: PART 1: BIS

Below I reprint the part of the paper on which I will base my analysis:

The present study sought to clarify and extend previous work suggesting that physically abused children develop perceptual sensitivity to anger. First, we sought to further examine the ways in which physically abused children can regulate attentional processes when confronted with anger or threat. Second, because prior research suggested that physically abused children would be especially sensitive to anger, the anger-related stimuli presented to the children occurred in the background and were irrelevant to the child's purported task and not personally meaningful. This created a relatively conservative test of children's attentional regulation. The present data suggest that once anger was introduced, abused children maintained a state of anticipatory monitoring of the environment. In contrast, non-abused children were initially more aroused by the introduction of anger, but showed better recovery to baseline states once anger was resolved.

I will here just consider two sentences from this paragraph. Below I show the BIS for each. First, consider (20) below. Here I give the BIS only for part of the sentence, the part I have placed in brackets: "physically abused children can regulate attentional processes when confronted with anger or threat":

20.   First, we sought to further examine the ways in which [physically abused children can regulate attentional processes when confronted with anger or threat].

physically abused children =		1. someone (?) abuse children physically
can regulate	=	2. (1) can regulate (3-7):
attentional	=	3. (1) attend to (5-7)
processes	=	4. (1) process (3)
when confronted	=	5. someone (?) confront (1) with (6/7)
with anger	=	6. someone (?) get angry at someone (?)
or threat	=	7. someone (?) threaten someone (?)

"Physically abused children" is a phrase that encapsulates the information in the clause in line 1: "someone abuses their children physically". Who is this someone? This sentence and the passage from which it is taken are systematically ambiguous in a way typical of this type of scientific writing. When the authors say they want to "examine the ways in which physically abused children can..." are they talking about any and all physically abused children or the specific children studied in this research, children who happened to be abused by their parents? Of course, they want to make a claim about any and all abused children based on these specific children and the ambiguity is, thus, functional.

"Can regulate" introduces another predicate "regulate". Its subject is the information in line 1 (which becomes the phrase "physically abused children" in the text); thus, I write (1) in its subject slot to yield "(1) can regulate (3-7)".

The object of "regulate" (what is being regulated) is all the information in lines 3 through 7, thus I write (3-7) in its object slot: "(1) can regulate (3-7)". What is being regulated (by the children), the information given in lines 3 through 7, is quite complicated, indeed: The children are regulating how they mentally process (line 4) when they attend to (line 3) situations where they have been confronted (line 5) with someone getting angry at someone or threatening someone (lines 6 and 7). This is certainly a form of technical writing with a vengeance.

The verb "confronted" in the text is missing both its subject and object. The object must be inferred to be "physically abused children", the information in (1). However, what we should infer the subject to be is less clear. Who confronted the children with anger or threat? We could be talking about what the researchers did in exposing the children to the taped (but thought to be real) anger. Or we could be talking in general terms about any time anyone confronts abused children (these specific children? all abused children?) with anger or threat. Equally, in line 6 and line 7, it is not clear who is getting angry at whom or who is doing the threatening of whom: Is it the actors that made the tape or anyone who might display anger in front of an abused child? Again, the authors want to draw a general conclusion based on what they did to the specific children in the study and so the ambiguity is, in this respect, functional.

Next, consider the sentence is (21) below:

21. The present data suggest that once anger was introduced abused children maintained a state of anticipatory monitoring of the environment

The present data suggest	=	1. the present data suggest (2-7)
that once anger	=	2. someone (= actor) gets angry at someone (= actor)
was introduce	=	3. someone (=r esearchers) introduce (2) to someone (= abused children)
abused children	=	4. someone (= parents) abuse children
maintained a state	=	5. someone (= abused children) maintain a state of (6-7)
of anticipatory	=	6. someone (= abused children) anticipate something (= threat/harm)
monitoring of the	=	7. someone (= abused children) monitor environment

environment by (6)

So here "suggest" has as its object (what is being suggested) all the information in lines 2-7. The noun "anger" is related to the predicate "get angry at" and introduces the information in line 2. Since the authors used the noun and not the predicate, they did not have to overtly mention the subject (who is getting angry) or object (who or what the anger is directed at). However, the reader can infer that the subject and object of "get angry at" are the actors who role-played anger at each other for the tape and who the children thought were real people. I note this inference by placing "actor" in parentheses.

Similarly, we can infer that it was the researchers (the authors of the paper) who introduced the situation of someone getting angry at someone else (line 2) to the abused children. Likewise in line 4 we can infer — from what the paper has told us — that the people who abused the children were their parents.

In lines 5-7, the state that the abused children are said to have maintained (see line 5) is very complicated and technical. The state is this: the abused children monitor the environment (line 7) by (engaging in the process of) anticipating something (line 6). What are they anticipating? This is, for me, the crucial question. Nothing in the text explicitly tells us what they are anticipating. The inference most readers will make, I believe — if they read deep enough into this technical prose — is that the children feel threatened and are anticipating harm or abuse. Of course, that is the hypothesis of the paper — that abused children will look for and anticipate threat where there is none in reality. But, while in reality there was none in this environment, there is no way the abused children could have known this, since they were not aware that the argument was on tape.

AN ANALYSIS: PART 2: CLAIMS BASED ON THE BIS

We have seen several ways in which this specialist prose is functional. And at a general level it is functional in the sense that as physiological psychologists these authors want to study and write about outward bodily behavioral effects (sweating, heart rate), rather than inner feelings or emotions. Their prose and their practices are well suited to do just that.

At the same time, this specialist prose allows and encourages the authors to evade any direct statement about *who did what to whom*. However, at the level of BIS and the inferences readers can make, it is apparent that the authors are evading (being allowed not to have to say directly) the information that *they threatened five year old children who they admit are particularly sensitive to and vulnerable to threats or anger*.

At the same time, this specialist language allows and encourages the authors, as well, to evade any direct statement about what the researchers did to the children *meant to the children*. The children's' emotions, feelings, fears are obscured and ignored in the authors' prose (and in their practices, academic prose and practices go hand in hand, that is what is meant by "functional"). Their prose and practices foreground outer bodily behavioral effects at the expense of a focus on feelings and emotions. But at the level of BIS the reader can infer that *the children feel fear*.

Finally, in the authors' practice and prose, emotion is effaced as a causal mechanism to be replaced by "attentional effects" displayed or signaled by bodily behavioral effects (like sweating and heart rate). This is really a double displacement of emotion: an emotion like fear is seen first in terms of cognitive processing mechanism ("attentional effects") and then these are signaled by or discovered through bodily mechanisms like sweating, which is what the researches pay attention to and write about. However, at the level of BIS these attentional effects amount to *young children anticipating harm and, thus, feeling fear*.

The evasion of what the researchers did to the children — something no one would approve of had it been said directly and in the vernacular as in "We threatened vulnerable five-year-olds"— is ideological (in this case, an attempt to evade a value-laden ethical issue). In this piece of academic writing, the functional and the ideological are "married at the hip". The function of the language is to allow researchers to distance themselves from the inner world so as to do a science based on the outer world of the body's reactions. In this particular case, that also allowed the researchers not to have to directly state what they had done in terms of what it meant to the children. What things mean is the domain of another academic area, namely discourse analysis. In that sense, discourse analysis stands in a "critical" relation to other forms of language. This does not mean, of course, that it is not itself open to critique (by discourse analysis applied to itself).

Nothing I have said in my analysis implies the researchers themselves believe they did anything unethical or immoral. My only claim is that when we move from BIS (which is closer to the vernacular, though not itself vernacular, thanks to technical vocabulary) something is added (namely, the functional ability of these academics to practice their specialist discipline) and something is lost (namely, a direct focus on what makes the research ethically problematic to some others, some of whom are not specialists in the researchers' discipline and, perhaps, some of whom are, though I have tested that).

The authors of the paper I have discussed can, of course, say that I am an "outsider", thus, not competent to comment on their practices or prose. But, in my view, that response is ideological. It is my belief that, morally, all of us academics must account for any situations where we have used our technical prose to evade what, said in the vernacular, is clearly a violation of the "lifeworld" (that is, a violation of what we as everyday people take to be moral). I do not say the authors I have studied have no such account, only that they owe even those outside their field one.

Can I give empirical evidence for this principle that we academics (and others) must, at a moral level, acknowledge our responsibility to give an account for any situations where we have used our technical prose to evade what, said in the vernacular, is clearly a violation of the "lifeworld"? As I have pointed out in earlier work (Gee 1990, 1996), no I cannot. With a such a principle, one that I have argued in earlier work is a basic moral principle of both discourse analysis and human linguistic interaction (Gee 1990, 1996), we reach the limits of our shared "form of life" (Wittgenstein 1958). Outside the principle, that is, denying it, "We don't know what to say" (Austin 1961) and must leave words and resort to actions in our own defense.

REFERENCES

Austin, J. L. (1961). Other minds. In *Philosophical papers* (pp. 44–84). Warnock, Oxford: Clarendon Press.

Gee, J. P. (2005). *An introduction to discourse analysis: Theory and method* (2nd ed.). London: Routledge.

Gee, J. P. (2004). *Situated language and learning: A critique of traditional schooling.* London: Routledge.

Gee, J. P. (2003). Discourse analysis: What makes it critical? In R. Rogers (Ed.), *An introduction to critical discourse analysis in education* (pp. 19–50). Mahwah, NJ: Lawrence Erlbaum,

Gee, J. P. (1996). *Social linguistics and literacies: Ideology in discourses* (2nd ed.). London: Taylor and Francis.

Gee, J. P. (1990). *Social linguistics and literacies: Ideology in discourses.* London: Falmer.

Halliday, M. A. K., & Matthiessen, C. M. I. M. (1999). *Construing experience through meaning: A language-based approach to cognition.* New York: Continuum.

Halliday, M. A. K., & Martin, J. R. (1993). *Writing Science: Literacy and discursive power.* Pittsburgh, PA: University of Pittsburgh Press.

Lee, O. (2002). Science inquiry for elementary students from diverse backgrounds. *Review of Research in Education, 26*(1), 23–69. Washington, DC: American Educational Research Association.

Pollak, S. D., Vardi, S., Putzer Bechner, A. M., & Curtin, J. J. (2005). Physically abused children's regulation of attention in response to hostility. *Child Development, 76*(5), 968–977.

Schleppegrell, M. (2004). *Language of schooling: A functional linguistics perspective.* Mahwah, NJ: Lawrence Erlbaum.

Wittgenstein, L. (1958). *Philosophical investigations.* Oxford: Basil Blackwell.

Wiley, T. G. (1996). *Literacy and language diversity in the United States.* Washington, DC: Center for Applied Linguistics and Delta Systems.

HILARY JANKS

CHAPTER 10

Critical Literacy: Methods, Models and Motivation

When I first thought of the title for this paper, I wanted to call it *Critical Literacy: Methods, Models and Motives.* It sounded right. I liked the balance created by the two three-syllable words followed by the three two-syllable words, and the rhythm created by the alliteration. But the word *motives* bothered me. Murderers have motives. The word "motive" keeps bad company. We think of people as having 'hidden' or "ulterior" motives. We think of motives as being self-interested more often than we think of them as being pure. The word *motivation,* on the other hand has had better press. It is associated with a beneficial psychological force that enables us to do good things. We think of people who are "highly motivated" as achievers, as having positive attitudes. As teachers we all want motivated learners but are likely to distrust students with motives. So, harnessing all the positive connotations of the word "motivation", I made it a count noun, chose the plural form, and changed my title to *Critical Literacy: Methods, Models and Motivations.*

However, being a linguist, I decided to check my intuitions by referring to the British National Corpus (http://sara.natcorp.ox.ac.uk/lookup.html). When you type in a word it gives you the number of occurrences of the word in the corpus and 50 random examples of the word in sentences. I searched for *motive* and *motives* and for *motivation* and *motivations.* I then analyzed the sample for positive and negative connotations. Any data that was not clearly negative or clearly positive, I discounted. Examples of positive, negative and unclear connotations appear in the results of the analysis tabulated in Figure 2.

From examining the corpus, it became clear to me that people often use the word *motivations* as a synonym for *motives.* It is also interesting that the clearest difference in connotation is in the singular. *Motivation,* in the singular, is the word that carries the positive connotations that I intuited and *motive,* in the singular, carries the negative connotations. So I changed my title again, to *Critical Literacy: Methods, Models and Motivation.* Never let it be thought that Critical Literacy is only useful for reading texts. It is also a powerful tool for designing texts. Because I want to talk about Critical Literacy work having a strong social justice agenda, I avoided the tainted word – *motive.*

MOTIVATION

Let me begin then with motivation – with what drives work in Critical Literacy. In South Africa, it was initially the struggle against apartheid, a political system based

K. Cooper and R. E. White (eds.), Critical Literacies in Action: Social Perspectives and Teaching Practices, 159–169.
© *2008 Sense Publishers. All rights reserved.*

Examples from the corpus of the words used with positive connotations
Instead the eyes settled on her, searching out the motive for such a protective gesture.
With no other interest than glory, and no other motive than a sense of vocation.
If jobs were carefully designed ... then high levels of satisfaction and motivation would result.
Aspirations, a sense of how we can realise our potential, give us power and motivation.
Examples from the corpus of the words used with negative connotations
All her appeals to the students to end the demonstrations had an ulterior motive.
Even today suggestions are being made as to Judas' motive.
Managers can motivate staff - motivation is at the control of the individual.
... subject to allegations of political motivation and partiality ...
Examples from the corpus of the words used with unclear or neutral connotations
Let us please seek for more stronger motives.
Motive power is provided by No 40092.
There is the same motivation.
The majority failed to understand the motivation of the same characters.

Figure 1. Examples from the corpus of words

Word	Number in the corpus	Positive connotations	Negative connotations	Connotation: neutral or not clear
Motive	1043	7	28	15
Motives	1028	9	21	20
motivation	1524	29	2	19
motivations	237	13	13	24

Figure 2. Results of the analysis

on ethnic racism. But racism is not the only cause of social injustice. We all need to think about the inequalities in our own backyards. In South Africa there is still much work to be done with regard to poverty, racism, ethnocentrism, sexism, rape, abuse, xenophobia, homophobia, linguistic prejudice, class exclusion, religious intolerance, elitism, consumerism, global capitalism, HIV/AIDS, corruption. The list is not complete.

In Chapter 7 of the Truth and Reconciliation Commission Report (1998) entitled *Causes, Motives and Perspectives of Perpetrators*, the commissioners offer a sophisticated view of the role played by language in the gross and often brutal violations of human rights in my country. The report argues that:

> It is a common place to treat language as mere words, not deeds, therefore language is taken to play a minimal role in understanding violence. The Commission wishes to take a different view here. Language, discourse and rhetoric does things: it constructs social categories, it gives orders, it persuades us, it justifies, explains, gives reasons, excuses. It constructs reality. It moves people against other people. (TRC: 7,124,294).

> Language in its many and varied forms, is the central element in ideology as power. ... In the South African context it is important to understand how multiple discourses combined, intersected and intertwined to create climates of violence. In this respect the ideologies of racism, patriarchy, religions, capitalism, apartheid and militarism all intertwined to "manufacture" people capable of violence. (TRC: 7,131, 296).

> Put most simply, people do not act only due to personal or individual attributes. We also act in terms of the norms, values, and standards of groups that provide us with social identities (racial, national, ethnic, gendered). (TRC: 7,101, 287).

It is clear from this analysis that language is a form of social action and that the discourses we inhabit play a crucial role in constructing our multiple identities. In examining the language of the State, the security apparatus and the liberation movement, the commissioners conclude that 'a spiral of discourses increasingly dehumanised the "other", creating the conditions for violence' (TRC: 7,125, 295). What this suggests is that one needs to look at how competing discourses affect and infect one another. It is not enough to look at the language of the oppressor in isolation. Both sides in the struggle used language to support their positions. For Foucault, discourse is the power to be seized (1970). It is this that motivates Critical Literacy.

METHODS

Because Critical Literacy is concerned with the relationship between language and power it always needs to be embedded in specific social contexts. The examples that I will give are taken from the South African context. They illustrate possible classroom activities that are designed to give readers ideas of how to construct their own classroom activities.

The first activity works with language policy and is designed to help students to think about how languages, which have been afforded the same legal status by the South African Constitution, are nevertheless not equally valued in all social domains of use. One of the ways of getting students to think about how languages in a multilingual country are stratified is to do a language map of the class. All the languages spoken by students are listed on the board and then, in groups, students are asked to rank these languages from high to low status. They also have to work out the criteria they will use to do so. This activity includes other languages spoken in South Africa such as heritage languages, for example, Guajarati, Greek and Portuguese spoken by established communities, religious languages such as Arabic and Hebrew, and foreign languages spoken by new immigrants. Increasingly this includes foreign African languages. The discussion requires students to think of the different domains in which all these languages are used and to consider the prestige attached to these domains. The ranking usually results in bands, as students often elect to give equal status to some of the languages. This task helps students to understand the difference between a language's legal status and its social status and it also makes them aware of their own, often intolerant and prejudiced, attitudes to other languages.

Students are then asked to think about how this hierarchy of languages is maintained in the society and what they can do to change it. The constitution gives South Africans the right to use their own languages in all dealings with the State, yet few people claim these rights. Few people realize the extent to which the use of English has been naturalized and can be contested.

Educational institutions will have to formulate defensible language policies and teachers, who have not already done so, will have to think about how to institute multilingual practices in their classrooms. Teachers, and I include myself, have to weigh up the benefits and disadvantages of code-switching in English medium classes and even in teaching subject English. In the urban areas many of our students speak five to seven languages so we have to work out how to use the linguistic and cultural diversity in our classrooms as a resource.

We have also had to wrestle with what we have come to call the 'access paradox' (Granville et al, 1998; Janks, 1995; Lodge, 1997). This paradox points to an essential contradiction: if you provide more people with access to the dominant language, you contribute to maintaining the language's dominance. If on the other hand you deny students access you ghettoize them and perpetuate their marginalization in a society in which this language is powerful. If we provide access without valuing linguistic diversity, we fail to encourage our students to develop their full linguistic repertoire. It is not enough simply to celebrate diversity, we have to find ways of making it a productive resource in our classrooms. The access paradox applies equally to the teaching of other dominant forms: genres, language varieties, norms of interaction, systems of representation.

Of course languages and language varieties are tied to whole ways of being in the world. I use *Joe's Beat* a regular column in *Pace* magazine to work with multilingualism as a resource, code-switching as a means of encoding meanings that are not possible in a linguistically 'pure' text, and language varieties as engines of linguistic dynamism. *Joe's Beat*, March 1997, is an example of the kind of multilingual text students need to engage with in English classrooms. In order to work productively with this text, students need to:

– Understand the language. For this they have to rely on those students who understand township slang;
– Understand the cultural practices that this language signifies – the way of life encoded by the language: ways of greeting grannies, types of music, food and what counts as a delicacy, stokvels, ancestor worship. They need access to the combinations of saying-(writing)-doing-being-believing-valuing that informs this text, the combinations that Gee calls Discourses;
– Defend a position on whether or not this text, published in an English language magazine, can be considered to be an *English* text in the South African context.

Students can be asked to rewrite this text in standard South African English to see what is lost and what is gained by this conservative transformation of the text. This method can be used with any text written in a subordinated language variety. I have seen South African teachers use this method successfully with African American literature.

In the discussion so far I have touched on three key concepts that underpin a critical approach to language education. They are dominance, diversity and access (Janks, 2000). In order to illustrate their interdependence, I will discuss the teaching of *Tea-time*, a children's poem written by Michael Rosen (1988), from a Critical Literacy perspective. In this poem, the family is sitting at the table for 'tea. The father asks his child to fetch the milk. No sooner has the child sat down than the father asks the child to fetch the butter, which the child dutifully does. When the father then asks the child to get a teaspoon the mother intervenes. She says to the father: "Once you get that bum of yours stuck in a chair you never get it off again, do you?"

A critical approach to language and literacy education is fundamentally concerned with the relationship between language and power: both in the ways language is used to maintain and reproduce existing relations of power and the ways in which it is used to contest the existing social order. This poem is fundamentally about power relations in a family: between parents and children (the father expects the child to do his bidding and the adult poet now teases the father); between the parents (the mother challenges the father's treatment of the child and asserts herself against her husband). Rosen's poem subverts the hierarchy in the family. His use of taboo language – "bum" – defies social norms and is simultaneously humorous. If the poem is itself a critical reading of social conventions how might we teach it using a critical approach?

The following questions, which reveal the conditions of possibility of this poem, work effectively with South African students.
– Describe meal times in your family.
– Could your mother talk to your father like this? Explain.
– Do you think the child is a boy or a girl? How do you know?
– Have you ever wanted an adult to side with you like this? Give examples.

The first three questions quickly allow the cultural diversity in the class to surface. In South Africa, many students live in extended families – this poem suggests a nuclear family. Families who live in small four-roomed houses, referred to as "matchboxes" in Soweto, do not always have space indoors for sit-down meals. In addition, many parents work long hours and are not at home for meals. Tea-time, where it exists at all in South Africa, is not a meal – it is a cup of tea, sometimes with a cookie. Many traditional and rural African communities are patriarchal: the men do not eat with the women and children, and are served their meals by their wives and daughters; respect for the male head of the family is inviolate. In Tshivenda there is a saying which translated literally is "the child is the oil to be sent". This shows the expectation that children have a duty to run errands for adults. Wives are not permitted to challenge the authority or rights of the head of the house. As a result of all these cultural and material differences, many of my students are shocked by Rosen's poem.

The last question provides a space for the students' fantasies. The desire of the underdog to see the oppressor punished; the wish to triumph over the father; the dream of seeing the tables turned. Fantasy is not culture-bound; poems are not reality. Literature helps us to imagine other possible worlds. Seen from this perspective, it becomes possible for students to engage with the poem across their differences.

Critical Literacy requires that we engage with and distance ourselves from texts, also described as reading with a text and reading against a text. Here, students who are alienated from this poem because it is so "rude", start from a position of estrangement. They have their own cultural knowledge as a basis for deconstructing and resisting the text. They see that the father has been undermined and they side with him. Those students who are feminists, on the other hand, are more likely to engage with the text – to accept the power of the mother and to relish her put-down of the father. They are less likely to notice the ways in which specific cultural values and context-dependent assumptions are privileged by the poem. In heterogeneous classes it is possible to use students' different reading positions to generate both perspectives. Some students produce "ideal" readings, others produce oppositional readings. Critical Literacy requires both. Each on its own is a form of entrapment.

> Engagement without estrangement is a form of submission to the power of the text regardless of the reader's own positions. Estrangement without engagement is a refusal to leave the confines of one's own subjectivity, a refusal to allow otherness to enter. Without the entry of the other, can we be said to have read the text at all? What then might we be resisting? (Janks, 1995, 133)

The published version of the poem is accompanied by an illustration in which the father is reclining in an armchair and the child, a boy, is fanning him with an oversized leaf. I read this illustration as an ironic reflection on the father's last statement that he "can't get a moment's peace around here". It also provides an inter-textual reference to earlier representations of colonial masters being fanned by their colonial subjects, or of pharaohs and emperors being pampered by their slaves. The picture anchors the child in the poem as a boy, and pre-empts discussion of whether fathers expect only their daughters to do household chores.

Critical Literacy teachers have found that an excellent way of denaturalizing a text is to provide a similar text as an alternative reference point. Morgan (1992) refers to this as rubbing texts against one another. A method that works well is *to get students to produce these alternative texts.* Here, students could be asked to illustrate the poem. Only once they have done so, should they be given the published illustration. They can then be asked to compare all the illustrations in order to work out how their different designs position the characters in and the readers of the poem differently. For example, students could be expected to analyze the different representations of bodies, facial expressions and clothing as well as the relative size of the different figures. It also possible to give students the published illustration and ask them to redesign it.

To read multi-modal texts critically, it is essential that we understand how what is selected works to construct the reader from the overall design of a visual text to the angle of vision or the choice of gesture. Selection operates at every level: from which language a multilingual person chooses to use, down to the minutia of whether to select "a" or "the", "motive" or "motivation".

One of the ways of helping students to notice what was selected, and to think about its effects, is to substitute an alternative – a different selection, with different effects. With regard to the mother's comment in this poem, students could be asked to think about the difference in effect if the poet had chosen 'mother' instead of 'mum' or used indirect speech instead of direct speech. They could consider how the omission of the tag question ("do you?") would have changed the mother's comment. They could think of if, and how, the word 'bum' translates into their other languages and whether or not the word is taboo or could be used.

"Selection" suggests that writers and speakers make conscious linguistic choices as I did when I made a decision to use *motivation* rather than *motive* in the title of this paper. In fact, many of the "choices" we make are social choices that are learnt and are often unconscious. Every society has conventions, which govern people's behaviour, including their language behaviour. Hymes (1974) argued that there are "rules of use without which the rules of grammar would be useless" (15). These unwritten rules of use govern what a speech community considers appropriate language behaviour. According to Gee:

> At any moment that we are using language, we must say or write the right thing in the right way while playing the right social role and (appearing) to hold the right values, beliefs and attitudes. What is important is ... saying (writing)-doing-being-valuing-believing combinations. These combinations I will call Discourses (1990:142).

Gee would say that we all learn the ways of making meaning of the different discourse communities to which we belong.

Appropriateness, a key concept for communicative language teaching, is often a reflection of dominant social norms (Fairclough, 1992). From a Critical Literacy perspective, it is important to understand whose interests are served by maintaining these norms. They usually reflect the values of the people or groups in society who have power. Furthermore, where different discourse communities have different rules for interaction, whose rules prevail in situations where speakers come from these different communities? Should students who are taught not to make eye contact at home when speaking to an elder, have to make eye contact at school when talking to a teacher? Here, we have to weigh the value of diversity, against the importance of access to mainstream discourses and to recognize that differences get ranked, with some practices being more highly valued than others.

One of the ways of helping students to 'see' the invisible rules is for them to observe them in practice. In *Language and Identity* (1993a), I set up the following investigation. I used the idea of a 'visitor from another planet' to enable students to see what to them was natural, through the eyes of a stranger.

Research project
You should work on this project in pairs or small groups.

Write down
for a visitor from another planet,
all the rules for
talking or not talking in your school.

These rules should be based on careful observation
of the different aspects of school life:
different lessons, school assembly, speech days, sports events, meetings and so on.

Figure 3. Research project

Once students had completed this research and the class had discussed the findings of the different groups, students were given the following four questions and tasks.

1. It is worth discussing how these rules help to form our social identities? You can do this in pairs or with the whole class.
2. BREAKING THE RULES FOR SPEAKING
   a. Now write down all the ways in which people break these rules.
   b. Write down reasons why people break the rules.
   c. Write down some of the consequences of breaking these rules.
   d. Do you think that breaking rules can lead to changing rules?
3. If rules help to form our social identities what does breaking rules do to our identities? What difference does it make to our identities if we break rules on our own or in a group? What difference does it make if we break rules by mistake or on purpose?
4. A man named Garfinkel conducted an experiment in which his students deliberately broke some of these rules to study people's reactions. For example they might answer the phone and say 'who's speaking' instead of 'hello'. You might like to try this to see what happens. Be careful not to break rules that get you into trouble. Have fun garfinkeling!

These four questions were designed to reintroduce agency into what is otherwise a very deterministic view of language. Without this view we construct language users as subject to rules of both accuracy and appropriacy without providing space for either contestation or creativity.

Earlier work in Critical Literacy focused on power as negative. Power was conceived as power over others, a form of domination or oppression. The focus was on the power of discourse to construct subjects, the power of texts to position readers, to hail them into subject positions. How texts construct readers is well-illustrated by a short exercise from *Language and Position* (Janks, 1993b, 9). In relation to the text which follows (Figure 4), teachers should ask students to consider

– How the writer constructs the reader in the first paragraph;
– How the writer constructs him./herself in the second paragraph;
– How the writer constructs its relationship with the reader in the third paragraph:
– And finally how the writer constructs the reader in the last paragraph.

Greetings Earthling ...

I am from another planet.

I have transformed myself

into this page and I am presently

making love to your fingers.

I know that you are enjoying it as I can see you smiling....

Figure 4. Greetings from another planet

However, it is also possible to focus on the way in which human subjects can use multiple systems of representation creatively to re-construct their worlds. The word subject is usefully ambiguous. The grammatical subject is the agent or actor, the 'doer', not the one who is 'done to'. Critical Literacy operates with both a *constructed* and *constructive* view of the subject. It recognizes the constitutive power of social practices in general, and of discourse in particular, while at the same time emphasizing the importance of transformative production and re-construction. For example, Adegoke (1999), a Nigerian student studying in South Africa, did a detailed analysis of the ways in which African countries outside of South Africa and their nationals are portrayed in the South African press. She used this work to argue for the inclusion of xenophobia in a Critical Literacy curriculum in order to assist students to construct alternative, more positive representations of Africa and Africans. Students in schools can be assisted to do similar work. They can look at the construction of young people in advertising, unemployed youth in newspapers, academically weak students in their school, or whatever interests them, in order to re-write them, to 'write back'. This term taken from post-colonial studies captures the idea of people at the margins refusing the constructions made of them by the centre, and reclaiming their right to 'write' themselves.

It is important that classroom work on Critical Literacy works with the construction and re-construction of texts and not just the deconstruction of texts. I have suggested ways of doing this in practice.

- I designed and redesigned the title of this paper;
- I asked students to consider how they can change their own language practices to changes in the way languages are used and valued in the society;
- I invited students to redraw the illustration for *Tea-time*;
- I allowed students to play with what it means to break rules that regulate their talking and not talking in schools;
- I gave you the example of how Adegoke analyzed xenophobic discourse. In the process she was able her to re-write herself, as a foreign African, in the South African context.

In the latter parts of this section on methods, I have added the concepts of design and redesign, taken from the work of the New London Group (1996) on multi-literacies, to the concepts of domination, diversity and access. I see design as textual production, which includes production across a range of signifying systems in different modalities for a range of media. I see redesign as providing agency within a theory of the discursive construction of subjectivity.

There is of course no guarantee that students' redesigns will be transformative. I have argued elsewhere (Janks, 2000; Shariff and Janks, 2001) that they are often conservative. Sometimes they are even more conservative than the original text that the students are reconstructing. Critical Literacy strives for transformative change, it cannot ensure it.

AN INTERDEPENDENT MODEL OF CRITICAL LITERACY EDUCATION

Elsewhere I have developed a model that synthesises the work done in Critical Literacy education. There I argue that the different orientations in the field cohere around the concepts of domination, diversity, access and design. The literature in the field tends to emphasize one or other of these orientations, but I believe that in addition to each orientation being important in its own right, they are also crucially interdependent. Critical Literacy has to take seriously the way in which meaning systems are implicated in reproducing domination and it has to provide access to dominant languages, literacies and genres while simultaneously using diversity as a productive resource for redesigning social futures and for changing the horizon of possibility (Simon, 1992). This includes both changing dominant discourses as well as changing which discourses are dominant. Any one of domination, diversity, access or design without the others creates a problematic imbalance. Teaching the dominant forms of language without creativity or redesign runs the risk of reifying these forms; deconstruction without reconstruction reduces human agency; diversity without access ghettoizes students. Domination without difference and diversity loses the ruptures that produce contestation and change. Reconstruction needs deconstruction in order to understand the "manifold relationships of force that take shape and come into play in the machinery of production" (Foucault, 1978, 94).

I have tried to show how we can use these concepts to construct lively classroom activities. We need to find ways of holding the different elements in productive tension to achieve what is a shared goal of all Critical Literacy work: equity and social justice. At the same time we have to make space for pleasure and play so that students can examine the issues of their time, in both local and global contexts, with both humour and delight.

REFERENCES

Adegoke, R. (1999). *Media discourse on foreign Africans and the implications for education.* Unpublished Masters research report, University of the Witwatersrand.

Author. (n/d). *British National Corpus.* Retrieved from http://sara.natcorp.ox.ac.uk/lookup.html

Fairclough, N. (1992). The appropriacy of appropriateness. In N. Fairclough (Ed.), *Critical language awareness.* London: Longman.

Foucault, M. (1978). *The history of sexuality* (Vol. 1., R. Hurley, Trans.). London: Penguin.

Foucault, M. (1970). The order of discourse. Inaugural lecture at the College de France. In M. Shapiro (Ed.), *Language and politics* (1984). Oxford: Basil and Blackwell.

Gee, J. P. (1990). *Sociolinguistics and literacies. Ideology in discourse.* London: Falmer Press.

Granville, S., Janks, H., Joseph, M., Mphahlele, M., Ramani, E., Reed, Y., et al. (1998). English with or without g(u)ilt: A position paper on language in education policy for South Africa. *Language and Education, 12*(4), 254–272.

Hymes, D. (1974). On communicative competence. In C. J. Brumfit & K. Johnson (Eds.), *The communicative approach to language teaching* (1979). Oxford: Oxford University Press.

Janks, H. (2000). Domination, diversity, access and design: A synthesis for critical literacy education. *Educational Review, 52*(2), 175–186.

Janks, H. (1995). *The research and development of critical language awareness materials for use in South African secondary schools.* Unpublished doctoral thesis, Lancaster University.

Janks, H. (1993a). *Language identity and power. Critical language awareness series.* Johannesburg: Hodder and Stoughton and Wits University Press.

Janks, H. (1993b). *Language and position. Critical language awareness series.* Johannesburg: Hodder and Stoughton and Wits University Press.

Lodge, H. (1997). *Providing access to academic literacy in the arts foundation programme at the University of the Witwatersrand in 1996 – the theory behind the practice.* Unpublished Masters Research Report, University of the Witwatersrand.

Morgan, W. (1992). *A post-structuralist classroom: The example of Ned Kelly.* Victorian Association for the Teaching of English, Carlton.

New London Group. (1996). A pedagogy of multiliteracies: Designing social futures. *Harvard Educational Review, 66*(1), 60–92.

Rosen, M. (1988). *The Hypnotiser.* London: Harper Collins.

Shariff, P., & Janks, H. (2001). Redesigning romance: The making and analysis of a critical literacy comic in South Africa. *English in Australia, 131*, 5–17.

Simon, R. (1992). *Teaching against the grain: Texts for a pedagogy of possibility.* Toronto: OISE Press.

Truth and Reconciliation Commission. (1998). *Truth and reconciliation commission of South Africa report.* Cape Town: Juta and Co.

JACKIE MARSH

CHAPTER 11

"Am I a Couch Potato?" Blog: Blogging as a Critical Literacy Practice

There is not a well-established tradition of Critical Literacy work in English primary classrooms, as is the case in other countries such as Australia. The reasons for this are various, but must include the fact that English schools have had to adhere to a national curriculum since 1988, which has inevitably narrowed both curriculum and pedagogy. Whilst a range of work has been undertaken in classrooms which adheres to some of the principles of Critical Literacy (Evans, 2004; Marsh and Millard, 2005), there is no single body of research on Critical Literacy in primary schools that can be identified within the English context. We look, then, to our international colleagues in order to determine some of the guiding principles for Critical Literacy practice. In particular, the work of Comber (2001) and Freebody and Luke (1990) in Australia has been important in establishing conceptual frameworks for research on Critical Literacy. In this chapter, I outline a study which draws from the "core dynamic principles and repertoires of practices" underpinning Critical Literacy work identified by Comber (2001). She suggested that Critical Literacy practices should be characterized by the following pedagogical moves that include teachers and students:
– Engaging with local realities;
– Researching and analyzing language-power relationships, practices and effects;
– Mobilizing students' knowledges and practices;
– (Re)designing texts with political and social intent and real-world use;
– Subverting taken for granted "school" texts;
– Focusing on students' use of cultural texts, and
– Examining how power is exercised and by whom (Comber, 2001, 276).

This is a powerful model as it starts with the premise that Critical Literacy should begin with students' own experiences and contexts. Whilst the notion of 'empowerment' is contestable because of the misguided concepts of transfer of power it sets up (Ellsworth, 1989), this process must involve a transformation of local knowledges.

The process of recontextualization of knowledge is key to Critical Literacy practices. In her work on young children's engagement with media texts in the writing curriculum, Dyson (2002) illustrates how children revise their understanding about their worlds through the process of juxtaposing out-of-school and in-school texts. In Dyson's studies (1997; 2002), this process is very much led by the children. They are the ones who challenge normative educational discourses when they bring out-of-school interests in popular culture and media into the classroom,

K. Cooper and R. E. White (eds.), Critical Literacies in Action: Social Perspectives and Teaching Practices, 171–183.

although of course this can only happen when teachers offer pedagogical spaces for the texts of homes and communities to filter through into school life. Nevertheless, it is possible for this recontextualization process to occur when teachers introduce popular cultural texts into the curriculum, if this occurs in ways respectful of children's cultural practices, acknowledging the pleasures these texts bring (Alvermann, Moon and Hagood, 1999; Larson and Marsh, 2005; Marsh and Millard, 2005).

The project outlined in this chapter was conducted with a class of Year 5 children aged nine and ten in Monteney Primary School in Sheffield, England. The teacher involved in the project, Peter Winter, was keen to engage the children in work which involved the undertaking of critical analyses of texts that related to their own lives. I worked alongside Peter in order to trace the processes and outcomes of the project. We decided that a key feature of the project should be that it involved the children directly in gathering data that could then be analyzed within the parameters of the project design. As Cooper and White suggest, "A key to fostering Critical Literacy in educational institutions is the democratization of research and knowledge producing practices" (2006, 2).

Guided by the principles outlined by Comber (2001) above, we acknowledged that the starting point for the project should centre on local knowledges. The focus of the study was to be the children's own media worlds. Both Peter and I were concerned about a proliferation of negative reports in the media regarding children and young people's use of media and new technologies and we therefore felt that a project which engaged children in examining these discourses would be timely.

CHILDREN AND TECHNOLOGY IN THE MEDIA

The study featured in this chapter engaged pupils in a review of their own media use alongside analysis of popular myths regarding this use. Moral panics regarding children and young people's use of technologies are a recurrent feature of media coverage in the UK. For example, in January 2008, media reports of a spate of teenage suicides in a town in Wales led to headlines such as 'Police fear Internet cult inspires teen suicides' (Britten and Savill, 2008), as many of the teenagers involved had used the social networking site *Bebo*. Police subsequently denied that they had identified the Internet as a key common component across the suicides, but this did not prevent extensive media coverage that suggested this was the case. This example is not isolated; children's engagement with media has been linked to obesity, linguistic deficiency and asocial behaviour, amongst other problems. Moral panics have always occurred in relation to the cultures of children and young people, as Springhall (1999) outlines, but the intensity with which recent media reports have dealt with this matter indicates that there has been a material shift in the moral panic discourse. Luke and Luke (2001) suggested that the reactions against children and young people's engagement with new technologies could be traced to the growing gap between the communicative practices of adults and youth, with the former based on traditional print-based practices and the latter moving increasingly to on-screen reading and writing.

In more recent work, Lankshear and Knobel (2006) have used the concept of "mindsets" to describe this disjuncture. Conversely, the term "insider mindsets" characterizes learners who recognize the changes to communication that technologies have brought and thus transform practices accordingly and the phrase "outsider mindsets" indicates individuals who have a propensity to continue to treat the world in much the same way as before, with digital technologies failing to promote fundamental changes to practices. The juxtaposition of these mindsets, in conjunction with epistemological and ontological anxieties about the sea-change occurring in the communication landscape (Kress, 2003), may be at the root of the recurrent moral panics. To some it may seem as if, based on an analysis of current social and cultural transformations, we are in a 'runaway world' (Leach, 1968).

In order to ensure that the analysis of this moral panic discourse was manageable for the pupils, it was decided to draw on one particular example. The focus for this study was the case of the murder of 14-year-old Stefan Pakeerah, who was stabbed to death with a claw hammer by his friend, Warren Leblanc, aged 17, in a park in Leicester in 2004. Stefan's parents alleged that the murder was based on a computer game, 'Manhunt'. This is a game that has attracted much negative attention because of its violent content, and although it was classified as containing adult-only content, these under-18-year-olds had played it together. The reference to the game by Stefan's parents was a theme quickly adopted by the popular press and it led to headlines such as that emblazoned on the *Daily Mail* on 29th July, 2004: "Murder by PlayStation".

In fact, police later rejected these claims and stated that the motive for the murder was robbery, as Leblanc used drugs. The reporting of this, case, therefore, offered an opportunity for pupils to reflect on debates relating to the alleged negative effects of media use.

It is pertinent to note here that the conservative agenda with regard to children and technologies identified in the press can also be traced in matters relating to the literacy curriculum. Despite widespread evidence that children are engaged with a wide range of new technologies outside of school and are becoming increasingly competent in their use (Demos, 2007; Livingstone and Bober, 2005; Marsh et al., 2005), the school curriculum remains locked into a print-focused milieu. Whilst there have been recent moves to recognize the impact of technological changes in the literacy curriculum in England, with the latest revision of the curriculum including multimodal texts, the policy context remains resistant to more radical revision. Indeed, in the same year that the curriculum opened the door to the analysis and production of multimodal texts, the Rose Review of early reading took place (DfES, 2006), with its revisionist agenda regarding the teaching and learning of phonics. This is a clear example of the policy phenomenon Luke and Luke (2001) note, which is:

A rhetorical displacement of the emergent problems raised by new communications technologies, cultures and economies for print based educational systems onto a new emphasis on early inoculation models of basic skills in print literacy (Luke and Luke, 2001, 95).

It is important, therefore, to continue to challenge the conservative rhetoric with case studies of innovative practice in order to demonstrate to policy-makers and others that some teachers are forging ahead with a forward-looking curriculum in the absence of encouragement from governments and educational establishments.

This is certainly the case in relation to the teaching and learning of literacy in England, which has been subject to a range of competing and conflicting discourses. Part of the difficulty lies in the fact that distinctions are still being made between 'traditional' literacy, focused on print on paper and the alphabetical principle, and 'new' or "digital literacies", which incorporate a range of modes and include a variety of media. A more fruitful way forward would be to focus instead on the notion of communication (Street, 1997) and refer to communicative texts, practices and events as they are instantiated across modes and media. In this conceptual framework, "literacy" would signify engagement with lettered represent-ation (Kress, 2003) on paper, screen and the wider environment and the interaction between literacy and other modes such as sound, image and gesture would be accepted as normal practice. The production and analysis of multimodal, multimedia texts would be embedded within curricula frameworks and emphasis placed on developing learners' skills, understanding and knowledge with regard to communication across all modes and media. In this model, there would be little need then to maintain the distinction between 'traditional' and 'new' literacies. Whether or not this takes place within a subject titled 'English' is a moot point, but there is a need to challenge the current policy fixation with literacy as the defining term for this subject, a "literacy fetishism" (Green, 2006, 17) driven by neo-liberal concerns, which means that those engaged in literacy education constantly struggle with terminology in order to make this meaningful in a digital era.

The work conducted in this chapter did involve children in the production and analysis of digital texts, which involved reading and writing activities on screen and paper. In particular, the project focused on the production of multimodal, multimedia texts in the practice of blogging, the creation of weblogs/blogs. Blogging has become an increasingly popular practice in schools, partly because:

> New blog technologies provide new affordances which can be at once both simple and complex; simple because they share some of the characteristics of paper-based texts (such as typographical conventions, spelling, paragraph, layout and so on) and complex because of the capabilities offered by hypertext (Davies and Merchant, 2007, 168).

Pupils can develop multimodal blogs and draw on still and moving image texts in addition to inserting links to external sites. However, the primary appeal of blogging for teachers and pupils alike may be that it enables writing to occur for authentic purposes and for 'real' audiences. Readers of blogs can comment on individual posts and this promotes interactivity and writing as a collaborative process.

Blogging is typical of the contemporary literacy practices that characterize social networking, practices which many children and young people engage in outside of school (Dowdall, in press; National Schools Board of America (NBSA), 2007). These practices have been identified as promoting the role of "produsers"

(Bruns, 2006), that is, actors becoming involved in both the consumption and production of media content. Lankshear and Knobel (2006) outline how the 're-mix' or 'mash-up' process involved in this practice, in which individuals re-use web content for new productions, is creating new kinds of texts. However, Dyson (2002) outlined the 'writing development remix' process in her *Brothers and Sisters Learn to Write* study and drew on musical genres and processes such as rap, sampling and remixing to describe how children created texts:

> Analogous to rap artists, the children appropriated and adapted thematic content, textual features, technological conventions, actual lines, and whole practices themselves as they constructed their unofficial and playful practices...No single multimedia production, and no written text, could be understood in isolation from the constellation of communicative practices that comprised the children's worlds (Dyson, 2002,173).

What is "new" in relation to contemporary practices, then, may be the ease with which children can create a bricolage of multimodal, multimedia texts because of the plethora of hardware, software and Web 2.0 products and services that are now available. This is certainly promoting a "D-I-Y" media culture outside of schools (Sharp, 2006), which will inevitably impact upon the school curriculum as educational establishments begin to respond, however slowly, to the 'digital capital' (Merchant, 2007) pupils bring with them to school.

THE STUDY

The study was carried out with a class of Year 5 pupils, aged nine and ten. The school they attend serves a largely white, working-class community that has well-established roots. Peter Winter is an ICT teacher in the school and works with all classes on the ICT curriculum. I had worked with Peter and the children in this class for two years, as the pupils had started blogging when they were in Year 4, aged eight and nine (see Marsh, 2007). In this project, the children constructed blogs focused on their analysis of their own media use and of the common discourses surrounding children and young people's media use. The main blog was titled, rather provocatively, 'Are You a Couch Potato?'

The children began the project by keeping media diaries, in which they documented their media use over a four-week period. Children were given digital cameras, which they took home in order to take photographs of the media they used. They were then interviewed in school about this media use. Pupils placed extracts from their media diaries on a blog linked to the main project blog. The children also devised their own questionnaire to find out about each other's media use. They completed the questionnaires and posted the outcomes on a third blog.

At one point during the project, the pupils focused on the use of computers and so they developed a blog in which they reflected on the question, "Are computers good for you?" Towards the end of the project, they were invited to post their conclusions about issues relating to media, technology and childhood on another blog entitled "Conclusions". On completion of the project, the children reflected on what they had learned about blogging during the project on a final blog, entitled "Blogbrains". Throughout the project I interviewed children, made field notes recording my observations of teaching sessions when they worked on their blogs and recorded children's talk as they worked on aspects of their blog. These data are drawn upon in the rest of the chapter in order to identify how the pupils responded to the project. The children created their own pseudonyms to use whilst they were online and those pseudonyms are used throughout the chapter.

The children in this class were avid users of a range of media in their homes. They all lived in households with at least one television, DVD player and mobile phone and many households had more than one of these items. The majority of the children had televisions in their bedrooms, along with other equipment such as CD-Rom players and console games. Twenty of the twenty-four children who completed the media questionnaires had internet access at home. They engaged in a wide range of online activities, as outlined in Table 1.

Table 1. Pupils' out-of-school Digital Literacy Practices

20 out of 24 had Internet access
12 downloaded music from the web
10 sent emails
10 shopped on the Internet
9 used instant messaging
8 used video sites (You Tube; Google video)
5 used chat rooms
5 maintained blogs
4 used social network sites (MySpace; Bebo)
1 played on a MMOG (World of Warcraft)

These pupils could be characterized as a generation of learners for whom technology was well embedded in their daily lives and who would therefore typify the vision of childhood at the heart of many media moral panics about 'digital natives'. This made the project even more pertinent to the class. In the rest of the chapter, I outline some of the work undertaken in the project and identify the ways in which the children constructed images of themselves and others in the light of media discourses.

"I AM NOT A COUCH POTATO"

During the project, the children collected a wealth of data regarding their use of technologies and media. They used this to inform their judgments about levels of media use in the class. Pupils generally held clear views about what they considered to be excessive engagement with media. For example, Los the Lollipop and Dan considered what they wanted to include in their blog post about the conclusions they had drawn from the project. The transcript of their conversation as they were developing this blog post indicates that they felt that their classmates watched too much television and played too many computer games.

[Los the Lollipop writes on the blog post: 'People watch too much TV and video games']

Los the Lollipop:	We can put people watch up to three to two hours.
Dan:	Yeah, but Jacob Skywalker said five hours. No - one of them said seven hours.
Los the Lollipop:	Seven hours…so thirty minutes to seven hours then, because Ads only watches it for thirty minutes a day.
Dan:	The least amount of television is 30 minutes and the most amount is seven hours.
Los the Lollipop:	[with distaste] Seven hours is longer than the school day!
Dan:	I know.
Los the Lollipop	[writing] Seven hours in ONE – we'll do "one" in capitals – day.

However, the responses on their own questionnaire posts reveal that Los the Lolliop recorded watching television for "3 – 4 – 5 hours" and Dan for "four hours a day", hardly a light timetable by their own standards. This was not uncommon. Banana and El, for example, concluded that television viewing and computer game playing could be beneficial if it was selective and distanced themselves from those who lay on sofas eating whilst they watched television.

Nevertheless, Banana's media diary revealed that she identified that she watched television for four hours a day. A similar pattern can be detected in Dumplin's post. Dumplin felt that only someone who engaged with one type of media to the exclusion of others could be a couch potato and that as he played half the day on his Playstation3 and in the other half watched television, he could not be categorized as an excessive user of media.

A constraint refrain throughout the 'Conclusions' blog was that, whilst children could recognize over-use of media in others, they themselves were not couch potatoes. This pattern is not exclusive to this project. In research on children and television, Buckingham (1996) found that children frequently made judgements about what they considered to be uncool or immature practices wih regard to television viewing, but were quick to distance themselves from these practices.

It was not possible to determine children's actual media use from the questionnaires, as children may have incorrectly estimated this use. For example, Benebenbow did report watching what one might consider to be an excessive amount of television (seven hours per day), but in an interview with him, it was clear that he engaged in a wide variety of activities, including sport and playing with friends outside of school, and so how accurate his estimate was remains unclear. Indeed, the interview data did indicate that children generally led socially varied lives outisde of school in which media played a central part, but not exclusively so. This was also the case in a study focusing on the media habits of 1,852 0-6 year-olds (Marsh et al, 2005), in which it was identified that the young children moved across a wide range of technologically-mediated and non-technologically mediated activities in a typical day. Nevertheless, the accuracy of the data was not of paramount interest in this study. It could be argued that the act of data collection itself prompted critical reflection on the issues by children, which enabled them to draw on tacit knowledge of media practices in their analysis of popular media discourse.

BALANCED REPORTING

Many of the pupils attempted to offer a balanced view of the benefits and drawbacks of media and new technologies. In the introduction to the topic, Peter had emphasised the need to consider all aspects of a particular question before drawing conclusions. Some of the children had appeared to take this on board, stating that their use of media could be considered both excessive and balanced. Indeed, in the comments made on each other's posts, one of the criteria for success appeared to be how far children looked at both sides of the story. So, on Sptato's post, a peer commented, "brill, i like the way you have done a bit of both".

The pupils were developing their skills in reviewing evidence they found in internet searches throughout the project and this enabled them to take a critical stance in relation to negative media discourses surrounding technology and childhood. This is important, given that some studies indicate the lack of criticality that is sometimes demonstrated towards material located on the internet (Buckingham, 2006; Livingstone and Bober, 2005). However, in many cases, judgements were based not on material they had identified from research, but on their own personal experiences. From these experiences, they developed tacit knowledge about how media had a negative impact on behavior. For example, Los the Lollipop and Dan reviewed the copy of the *Daily Mail* story mentioned previously, which reported on the death of Stefan. They were skeptical of the claims that PlayStation games could promote copy-cat behaviour and began to add a section on their blog post about this:

Los the Lollipop: I think they're exaggerating.

Dan: Because if, say, like, I was playing on a race car game, I wouldn't just go out and buy a race car and just ride off in it...if you were playing a race car game, you couldn't just, like, get in a car and run somebody over.

Los the Lollipop: And like an army game where you have a gun, you wouldn't just like get a gun and shoot your best mate...

Dan:	…No, would we, [name]?
Los the Lollipop:	[reading what she had written] He killed his friend by going on a PlayStation.
Dan:	And his mate were only 14 years old!
Los the Lollipop:	[writing] By going on the PlayStation game… have I spelt PlayStation right? Apparently, a newspaper…
Dan:	…Apparently, allegations in a newspaper, he killed his friend by going on a PlayStation game and watching all the violence.
Los the Lollipop:	And thinking that…
Dan:	…he was the PlayStation game. [Name], it says on here with a claw hammer and knife.
Los the Lollipop:	Just a minute, just a minute…
Dan:	I think it is exaggerated because most people use their common sense.
Los the Lollipop:	And at the end we can say because people use their common sense and would not go out and really do stuff to their friends.

The children demonstrate their skepticism of this story with the use of language such as "apparently" and "allegations" and their contention that the report was exaggerated. The rationale they offer is based on the notion that simply because one role-plays an activity, it does not mean that this activity would then be undertaken in the 'real' world. Indeed, they appear to understand implicitly that the relationship between violence as depicted in games and 'real' life is not straightforward, as Buckingham points out:

> …the "violence" that so preoccupies adult critics of computer games is often so ritualised and dream-like that players themselves do not perceive it to have any significant analogy with real-life behaviour (Buckingham, 2006, 22).

The next stage in the development of the pupils' critical analysis would be to ask Los the Lollipop and Dan to analyze the evidence drawn upon by the journalists in the construction of their newspaper report in order to trace the circumstantial nature of it, at the same time as examining the evidence collected about the class's engagement with media in order to reflect upon how far this experience had impacted upon their own propensity for anti-social behaviour. But this example offers an instance of an important initial stage in this work, which is the identification of fallacies in arguments presented about media use and the use of personal experience to inform judgments made. As Dyson suggests, "At any age, Critical Literacy is always a personal as well as a political (power-related) matter because it entails reconsidering one's own experience" (Dyson, 2001, 5).

Overall, the children concluded that the media reports about the negative impact of new technologies on children's lifestyles were exaggerated and that the media brought both benefits and disadvantages, depending upon what was used and how it was used. Importantly, this aspect of the project enabled them to engage in reflection on a key aspect of their own lives and thus offered a productive pedagogical practice in which the "connectedness" of the school curriculum to the outside world was paramount (Lingard et al, 2001).

CRITICAL PRACTICES

Whilst the project itself was intended to develop pupils' Critical Literacy skills, it became clear as the project progressed that the process of blogging itself enabled Critical Literacy practices to take place. For example, the use of the commenting facility enabled some critique of others' posts, as in the example above. However, the act of commenting was also linked to the performance of friendship, as peers used the commenting facility to leave comments on the posts of best friends or friends they wished to impress (Marsh, in press).

Nevertheless, the process of blogging could be viewed as a Critical Literacy practice because it required children to make informed judgments about the texts they would draw on as they developed their posts. They discounted certain images if they were felt to portray feelings about children's use of media that they did not want to promote, such as children slouching on settees, eyes glued to the box. Images chosen to feature on the blogs were generally neutral portrayals of hardware, although some adorned their posts with images related to their favourite media topics. This was a common practice, as blog posts were used to perform identities (Marsh, in press) in a manner similar to that of adults' construction of blogs (Carrington, 2006; Davies and Merchant, 2007). Blogging thus required the children to engage in textual bricolage and this process of remixing, or "mash-up", is inevitably a critical act (Dyson, 2002; Lankshear and Knobel, 2006).

CONCLUSION

This project enabled children to engage critically with the "toxic childhood" (Palmer, 2006) discourse and to review the claims made about children's engagement with media in the light of their own experiences. From their internet searches, they identified reports which outlined purported negative effects of media, such as damaging eyesight, but in the main the blog posts indicated that the children recognized the educational benefits of media and the need to develop a balanced use of new technologies. This could, of course, be simply an indication that children felt they should adopt a particular viewpoint in order to demonstrate criticality rather than offering firm evidence of the move towards an informed position. Nevertheless, the project did provide an opportunity for children to engage in a debate in which they themselves are centrally placed and in which they rarely have a voice.

Critical Literacy is always a social practice and I would suggest that blogging offers the potential to facilitate Critical Literacy because of the affordances of the tool. The features of blogging which promoted Critical Literacy practices can be identified as the following:

- The ability to create posts which include multimedia, multimodal texts, produced in ways that involve critical engagement in the design process and the execution of critical judgments about sources of material.
- The ability that bloggers have to embed links to relevant websites in their posts, which can extend their intellectual project and offer counterpoints to arguments made.
- The facility for children to leave comments on each other's posts, which can promote critical engagement with ideas.
- Blogs enable critical engagement with internet safety practices in ways which draw on out-of-school experiences, thus offering 'authentic' contexts for Critical Literacy practices that involve making judgments about the provenance of texts and the identity/reliability/authority of others.

Inevitably, blogging can be used in non-critical ways, therefore the key aspect of any project that involves critical use of blogging is the pedagogical approach adopted by the teacher. In this project, the development of the blogs was led by the children's interests. They decided what they wanted to post and decided how the different blogs would emerge and relate to each other. This encapsulated a pedagogy based on the principles outlined by Comber (2001), detailed at the beginning of this chapter, in which teachers mobilize students' knowledges and practices and facilitate the (re)design of texts with political and social intent and real-world use.

As we move ever more firmly into the digital age and pupils engage with an increasing number of texts outside of the classroom, projects such as this can contribute to the development of the kinds of skills, knowledge and understanding needed in order to make sense of the digital landscape. In particular, the project's insistence on the social construction of knowledge reflects a desire to ensure that pupils are able to operate effectively in networks of collaborative learners, a skill which is becoming increasingly essential in an era in which young people's use of social networking sites is growing (Lenhart. Madden, Macgill and Smith, 2007). Unless Critical Literacy practices are embedded in classroom approaches to the use of media and Web 2.0 applications, we may simply be offering pupils a set of reference points for the new communication landscape without allowing them to develop the skills, knowledge and understanding necessary to develop a map of the territory for themselves.

REFERENCES

Alvermann, D., Moon, J. S., & Hagood, M. C. (1999). *Popular culture in the classroom: Teaching and researching critical media literacy.* Newark, Delaware: IRA/NRC.
Britten, B., & Savill, R. (2008, January 24). Police fear internet cult inspires teen suicides. *Daily Telegraph.* Retrieved January 25, from http://www.telegraph.co.uk/news/main.jhtml?xml=/news/2008/01/23/nsuicide123.xml

Bruns, A. (2006). Towards produsage: Futures for user-led content production. In F. Sudweeks, H. Hrachovec, & C. Ess (Eds.), *Proceedings: Cultural attitudes towards communication and technology 2006* (pp. 275–284). Perth: Murdoch University. Retrieved August 22, 2007, from http://snurb.info/files/12132812018_towards_produsage_0.pdf

Buckingham, D. (2006). *The media literacy of children and young people*. London: Ofcom. Retrieved January, 2008, from http://www.ofcom.org.uk/advice/media_literacy/medlitpub/medlitpubrss/ml_children.pdf

Buckingham, D. (1996). *Moving images: Understanding children's emotional responses to television*. Manchester: Manchester University Press.

Carrington, V. (2006). *Texts, fugue, digital technologies*. Paper presented at Daiwa Foundation supported UKLA/University of Nara Seminar, May, 2006.

Comber, B. (2001). Critical literacies and local action: Teacher knowledge and a "new" research agenda. In B. Comber & A. Simpson (Eds.), *Negotiating critical literacies in classrooms*. Mahwah, NJ: Lawrence Erlbaum.

Cooper, K., & White, R. E. (2006). Introduction to Part I: Critical literacy for a democratic education. In K. Cooper & R. E. White (Eds.), *The practical critical educator: Critical inquiry and educational practice* (pp. 1–2). Dordrecht, The Netherlands: Springer.

Davies, J., & Merchant, G. (2007). Looking from the inside out: Academic blogging as new literacy. In M. Knobel and C. Lankshear (Eds.), *A new literacies sampler* (pp. 167–197). New York: Peter Lang.

DfES. (2006). *Rose review of the teaching of early reading: Final report*. London: HMSO.

Dowdall, C. (in press). The texts of me and the texts of us: Improvisation and polished performance in social networking sites. In M. Robinson, R. Willett, & J. Marsh (Eds.), *Play, creativities and digital cultures*. New York: Routledge.

Dyson, A. H. (2002). *Brothers and sisters learn to write: Popular literacies in childhood and school cultures*. New York: Teachers College Press.

Dyson, A. H. (2001). Relational sense and textual sense in a US Urban classroom: The contested case of Emily, girl friend of a ninja. In B. Comber & A. Simpson (Eds.), *Negotiating critical literacies in classrooms* (pp. 3–18). Mahwah, NJ: Lawrence Erlbaum.

Dyson, A. H. (1997). *Writing superheroes: Contemporary childhood, popular culture, and classroom literacy*. New York: Teachers College Press.

Ellsworth, E. (1989). Why doesn't this feel empowering? Working through the repressive myths of critical pedagogy. *Harvard Educational Review, 59*(3), 297–324.

Evans, J. (2004). Introduction: The changing nature of literacy in the twenty-first century. In J. Evans (Ed.), *Literacy moves on: Using popular culture, new technologies and critical literacy in the primary classroom* (pp. 6–14). London: David Fulton/New York: Heinemann.

Freebody, P., & Luke, A. (1990). Literacies programs: Debates and demands in cultural context. *Prospect: Australian Journal of TESOL, 5*(7), 7–16.

Green, B. (2006). English, literacy, rhetoric: Changing the project? *English in Education, 40*(1), 7–19.

Green, H., & Hannon, C. (2007). *Their space – Education for a digital generation. Demos*. Retrieved August 20, 2007, from http://www.demos.co.uk/files/Their%20space%20-%20web.pdf

Kress, G. (2003). *Literacy in a new media age*. London: Routledge.

Lankshear, C., & Knobel, M. (2006). *New literacies: Everyday practices and classroom learning* (2nd ed.). Maidenhead, Berkshire: Open University Press.

Larson, J., & Marsh, J. (2005). *Making literacy real: Theories and practices for teaching and learning*. London, New Delhi, Thousand Oaks, CA: Sage.

Leach, E. (1968). *A runaway world: The 1967 Reith lectures*. Oxford: Oxford University Press.

Lenhart. A., Madden, M., Macgill, A. R., & Smith, A. (2007). *Teens and social media*. Pew Internet and American Life Project. Retrieved January, 2008, Retrieved from http://www.pewinternet.org/pdfs/PIP_Teens_Social_Media_Final.pdf

Lingard, B., Ladwig, J., Mills, M., et al. (2001). *The Queensland school reform longitudinal study* (Vols. 1 and 2). Brisbane: Education Queensland.

Livingstone, S., & Bober, M. (2005). *UK children go online: Final report of key project findings.* London: London School of Economics and Political Science.

Luke, A., & Luke, C. (2001). Adolescence lost/childhood regained: On early intervention and the emergence of the techno-subject. *Journal of Early Childhood Literacy, 1*(1), 91–120.

Marsh, J. (in press). Productive pedagogies: Play, creativity and digital cultures in the classroom. In M. Robinson, R. Willett, & J. Marsh (Eds.), *Play, creativity and digital cultures.* London: Routledge.

Marsh, J. (2007). New literacies and old pedagogies: Recontextualizing rules and practices. *International Journal of Inclusive Education, 11*(3), 267–281.

Marsh, J., Brooks, G., Hughes, J., Ritchie, L., & Roberts, S. (2005). *Digital beginnings: Young children's use of popular culture, media and new technologies.* Sheffield, UK: University of Sheffield. Retrieved June 11, 2006, from http://www.digitalbeginings.shef.ac.uk/

Marsh, J., & Millard, E. (Eds.). (2005). *Popular literacies, Childhood and schooling.* London: Routledge.

Merchant, G. (2007). Mind the gap: Discourses and discontinuity in digital literacies. *E-Learning, 4*(3), 241–255.

NSBA. (2007). *Creating and connecting: Research and guidelines on social – and educational – networking.* Retrieved August 20, 2007, from http://www.nsba.org/site/docs/41400/41340.pdf

Palmer, S. (2006). *Toxic childhood: How the modern world is damaging our children and what we can do about it.* London: Orion Press.

Sharp, D. (2006). Participatory culture production and the DIY Internet: From theory to practice and back again. *Media International Australia Incorporating Culture and Policy,* Issue 118, 16–24.

Springhall, S. (1999). *Youth, popular culture and moral panics: Penny Gaffs to Gangsta-Rap, 1830–1996.* New York: St. Martin's.

Street, B. (1997). The implications of the new literacy studies for education. *English in Education, 31*(3), 45–59

CHAPTER 12

The Difference of Critical Literacy: A Diverse Discourse Dialogue on "Taken-for-Granted Practices" in English Education

A vision of community is at the root of the educational problematic. Its dimensions actively construct the cultural basis of our philosophical lineage as teaching and steadfastly determine the pedagogical exigencies of what it means to think, to teach, to learn, to know. It grounds the ambitions of our theory via practice within the classroom by defining the parameters of who we are as subjects according to a desire for a self-affirming celebration of sameness, an idea of togetherness, unity and cohesion that fortifies the walls of community against the threats of difference and otherness. I will juxtapose this traditional conception of a "community of knowledge" against the vision of a "community of the question," some of the characteristics of which, I will develop and use as a focal point for the teaching of reading, writing, and literature in the multiliteracy English Education classroom.

A CURRICULAR HISTORY

In this piece, I highlight the value of utilizing a 'critical' approach in literacy research. I do so by looking at a methodological quandary in my own research that gave me cause to reflect upon, and eventually change, the way I conducted research into the history and theory of English Education.

In 2005, I started a Social Sciences and Humanities Research Council of Canada (SSHRC) funded project in Canada's Atlantic region. This project, amongst other things, involved carrying out a curricular history of subject English in Newfoundland and Labrador, the easternmost province in Canada and the easternmost point in all of North America. Newfoundland and Labrador is an island in the North Atlantic Ocean with a total population of just over a half million people. Conducting research in this place was intriguing for several reasons. First, Newfoundland and Labrador has a five hundred-year history, which includes the first documented North American school in 1727. I was interested in how conceptions of the literate student, and literacy generally, might have developed and shifted over such a long period of time. Second, part of the intrigue with conducting this type of research on Newfoundland and Labrador relates to fact that it is Britain's oldest colony, a long-time American military stronghold, and Canada's newest province. Thus, it is a unique place to study English education and the evolution of literacy – an island in the North Atlantic that has been impacted by three substantial world currents, namely British, American, and

K. Cooper and R. E. White (eds.), Critical Literacies in Action: Social Perspectives and Teaching Practices, 185–205.

Canadian. I wondered how these 'currents of influence' might have shaped the philosophy of English manifested in the curricula of different periods. I was also curious about the status of the Newfoundland and Labrador 'voice' in this history and how indigenous approaches might have been perceived in the midst of such overarching influences from the outside. Such a project is consistent with international research elsewhere concerned with raising new questions about neocolonial cultural practices and the selective use of narrative fictions within state schooling. And, thirdly, Newfoundland and Labrador has recently experienced a massive change to the English curriculum in the schools of the province. What constitutes subject English in this region of the country has been radically redefined under the terms of the Atlantic Provinces Educational Foundations (APEF). Everything from the conception of the text to the very definition of literacy has been overhauled beyond recognition.

ON THE RIGHT TO TEACH

Above all, I am a teacher: I think and live as a teacher within the spaces of questions that arise concerning the propriety, trajectory and hope of my actions. And I tell myself what I have often related to my students and them in their own way to me: *Teaching is not a natural right, it is a responsibility that is well-earned and sanctions one with the power to affect the life of another, in principle and practice, presumably for the benefit of the individual and society.* The act of teaching therefore bestows upon us a consummate obligation that we must honour with respect to ourselves and to the community-at-large, essentially by acknowledging the debt of the responsibility we owe to those others around us for allowing us this gift that enables us to know who we *are* or *could be* as teachers. This obligation more often than not goes unquestioned. We know it and so we simply take it for granted. It is forgotten. We seldom have to think, talk, or write about it. The seriousness of our vocation has always been a vital part of the cultural heritage of the West and underlies the ethical core of our being, our debt and duty as educators. And yet, what would it mean to question the nature of our pedagogical responsibility by reflecting upon the ground of our obligation to the community-at-large? How would we have to rethink not only the bounds and boundaries of our own roles as teachers, but also to re-conceptualize the grounds of our obligation to and for a community that would not also be the same as before?

In preparing critical educators and thinkers of the future, I have tried to ask these questions of myself and of the pre-service teachers and graduate students that I have taught. And these questions envelop the praxis of teaching as the ideo-performative formations of a reflective pedagogy informing the conception of literacy writ large, multiplied, and complicated by the ever proliferating changes in what it means to read, to write, to know. The vision of what I have called a "community of the question" after Jacques Derrida (1974) is part of an on-going search for answers to the problems of teacher responsibility and obligation that I have posed above in relation to the multiple sites of what is a *Critical Literacy in action*. Its characteristics manifest themselves as the purposes and products, goals, ambitions, or outcomes of teaching practice resulting from the application of reflective pedagogical principles to the classroom. The theory behind this vision is thus grounded within the methodological context of my own experience of fourteen years as teacher of English, E.S.L., and Language Arts or English Education. In short, a "community of the question" is what I have striven to create in the English Education classroom and its ethical sensibilities that are aimed toward nurturing a reflective practice are what I attempt to apply to my teaching of pre-service teachers and graduate students.

MY INITIAL APPROACH

In 2005, I went to St. John's, the capital city of Newfoundland and Labrador, to complete several months of research. Because Newfoundland formally joined Canada in 1949, I decided to look at English education in pre- and post-confederation Newfoundland and Labrador and, generally, restricted myself to the years between 1940 and 2003. I wanted to read everything that had been written about education and English in the history of the region. I went to the Center for Newfoundland Studies, as well as the Curriculum Materials Center at Memorial University. There I found no shortage of writings about Newfoundland and Labrador. Many of these documents contained chapters or whole sections on education. From all of this readily available information, I began to piece together a picture of the different episodes within Newfoundland and Labrador's English curricula. I read everything vaguely related to the subject, from exhaustive histories to annual school reports, ministry releases on subject English to the specific texts in each curriculum. My goal was to leave no stone unturned. I would write a comprehensive history of the province's English evolution.

When I began researching English education in the 1940's, I was struck by the considerable continuity of the reports and texts written upon the subject. The general consensus of many historical accounts is that this is a period of "considerable continuity" for the discipline (Medway, 1990, 3). My immediate reaction was that the task of putting together a curricular history of subject English in Newfoundland and Labrador was a surprisingly uncomplicated process. Surely, it took great time to synthesize the plethora of official reports and historical documents that I was reading. But, that said, I was quickly painting a picture of how things used to be in Newfoundland and Labrador classrooms. Less than three months into the task, I had almost completed my whole section on the English program of the 1940's. It was a neat and tidy portrayal of a foundational, conservative approach to the subject. There were very few absences or discontinuities at all.

At this point, I became interested in how English had developed in the rest of the country. I decided to take a quick glance at the English curricular history of another region of the country to compare it to my own research in Atlantic Canada. A basic search produced some information on a 'radical' curriculum document put out by the Ontario Ministry of Education. Interested in how a document came to attain such a status, I endeavored to look into the matter.

DEFINING MULTIPLE LITERACIES

I define multiple literacies, neither in relation to the technical competence required to decode the signs of a form of expression and thus unlock its meaning or content, nor in the means of production that might bring together forms in what I call *a cross-medial synthesis* of modes of representation: for example, multi-platform media such as CDs, hypertext or digital writing, the picture book, film and video. That is, multiple forms of literacy that contain both lexical and visual, oral and auditory, even tactile or syn-aesthetic, components which engage the faculties of the subject. I define multiple literacies in terms of how the subject is always already implicated in questions of ethics, responsibility, and social justice by way of language when it comes to decoding and interpreting texts. Any sign or image, be it lexical, pictorial, sensory, or imaginary calls openly—self-consciously—for an interpretation of itself. It is a moment of interpretative completion that demands the responsibility of a response and, in turn, the response produced must be responsible to others by explaining itself and the conceptual ground of its logic. An interpretation therefore must do justice to the call of the text for a response in accordance with the open responsibility we have to put forward a response, an argument, an interpretation, to justify the difference of ourselves to the difference of another. Responding means a responsibility to respond responsibly. That is, to justify a response and yet to remain open to and welcome the possibility to the challenge of different responses so as to pave the way for a dialogue with another. In this sense, the ethical sites for literacy in a community of the question as I have defined them are open, unpredictable, and multiple. They demand that the teacher and the student develop capacities for:

- Moving beyond discursive norms,
- Crossing the borders of textual propriety,
- De-centring authority for an ethic of collaborative meaning constructions, and
- Reinventing self and community, which demands sustained reflection on difference.

THE ONTARIO HANDBOOK

In the 1980's, the Ontario Ministry of Education claimed that a handbook issued to guide teachers in setting their own school leaving exams represented a "radical" approach. It was considered 'radical' because it enabled teachers, and not the Ministry, to make up the final examinations. Yet, when I went and assessed the Handbook in question, I saw that it went on to painstakingly detail all the forms of question-asking, test design, and marking schemes that teachers could utilize so that they might "adapt their current practices to ministry standards" (Handbook for Designing and Marking, 1986). While the advent of the Handbook, and the overall shift in policy generally, clearly made less work for Ministry committees and personnel, it never really relinquished its grip on how the final exam would be constituted.

The term 'radical' here seems to be narrowly defined as not actually providing the exam questions, whilst still keeping teachers on a short enough leash by defining the boundaries and nature of the questions to be created. Short of putting in the words, the ministry situated every other parameter, including asking schools to keep all past examinations on file for ministry inspection.

My inquiry into the Ontario Handbook was an important eye-opener for me. Looking a little deeper at this document, I saw first hand how liberties could be taken with terms to create a desired impression or effect in a given historical period. Such is the case with the use of the word 'radical' in this context.

My experience with the Ontario document also left some residual questions for me. If a conventional history of Ontario educational policy or practice were to be written about this period, might the term 'radical' resurface again as a descriptor attached to these particular educational policies? And is it possible that the term 'radical' might simply reappear in any generalized histories of the region, government budget statements, school reports, or newspaper 'year-in-review' articles? In "English and Englishness", Brian Doyle (1989) writes about such uses of history through English committees that "purport simply to offer an objective historical narrative" (51). Sweeping across broad periods, such histories have to cut details and make assumptions. After all, it is not really possible to include everything in a totalizing history or an overview of a period. And was I doing the same thing with the curricular history that I was writing for Newfoundland and Labrador? Was it indeed such a conservative, uncomplicated educational milieu in Newfoundland and Labrador in the 1940's? If not, how could I carry out a history that was not wholly predicated on the 'official stance' or based solely on what I read about education in the region? Realizing that original depictions or labels, such as 'radical' in the Ontario case, often come to stand as the taken-for-granted or accepted definition, I would have to find another way to read the current history in Newfoundland and Labrador. My literacy research would have to become altogether more 'critical'. This meant abandoning my approach to date and looking for another way. Merely surveying different episodes in Newfoundland and Labrador's English curricula would no longer do. I wanted my research to offer an original, theoretically informed means of intervening into current English studies, casting new light on many of its taken for granted practices. How could I tease out the complicated set of factors that gave rise to a distinct brand of subject English on the island? This led me to adopt a more 'critical' historical methodology and a more 'critical' perspective towards reading and researching historical curricular texts generally.

MOVING BEYOND DISCURSIVE NORMS

To move beyond the maintenance of discursive norms within the classroom is to acknowledge the complex ambiguities of multiple heterogeneous forms of communication that students of diverse cultural backgrounds bring to the scene of teaching. Rather than simply acknowledging the relational character of language as a meaning-making system, it is necessary to recognize that the signs and symbols of discourse (spoken text) are imbued with valences (pivotal points of inter-pretative direction) relating to a conceptual framework coded and driven by specific valuations and exclusions that have been conceived across the cultural vicissitudes of space and time. Language is not so much a facet of culture as it is the expression of culture. When we speak as teachers from the perspective of truth, we carry the burden of a responsibility to recognize, value, and include the realities of others within the immediate scope of our discursive milieu. The acquisition of language requires the social and cognitive construction of mind and knowledge. To draw students into an exchanging of perspectives is to broaden the hermeneutical horizons between self and other, not to supplant the truth of subjective experience with our own expert claims to a single, dominant form of literacy, but to supplement the knowledge we all have to share with well-lived perspectives other than our own. Recognizing multiple literacies entails the responsibility to address the form and content of difference and multiple perspectives in relation to what we already accept as true. It is in the production of interpretative differences that meaning lies.

To create an awareness of the presence of multiple literacies in the English classroom is to acknowledge the importance of traditions of oral language or spoken text as a distinct and legitimate marker of experiential similarities and differences among cultures. It is necessary for teachers and students to engage in active forms of research into the narrative structures and codic frameworks of cultural texts that have roots in storytelling. For example, fables or tales about common sense and wisdom, appearances and deception can be found in the oral tradition of many cultures: "Truth and Falsehood" (Greece), "Getting Common Sense" (Jamaica), "Rich Man, Poor Man" First Nations, Asian, African, eastern European, and so on. By comparing the transformations in plot, character, fabula, stock elements, and rhetorical elements of style or diction among these tales, it is possible to analyze the distinctive aspects and techniques of storying that give rise to diverse interpretative frameworks. The stories are representative of the culture that produced them as a whole, but also ways of understanding that enlighten us to different conceptions of the human condition and similarities that exist between them. The fact that these stories are produced across cultures shows us both the commonality of experiences as well as the arbitrary nature of the explanations within these stories given rise to by questions about the nature of reality and existence in the world. The point of this exercise is *to take into account* and *to try to account for* the similarities and differences between narrative forms of corresponding typology — those that relate to valuations and exclusions expressed thematically through the discursive structures of the texts chosen. The comparative aspect of this method in effect critically contextualizes the questioning of normative discourse structures and the codic patterns they exhibit by placing within the practical purview of the students an ethical concern for realizing the linguistic ground of cross- and inter-cultural awareness through the study of the similarity and diversity in oral traditions of storying and storytelling. It is through the process of sustained and active reflection upon the inter- and trans-cultural dimensions of the narrative elements of story-telling that our understandings of the similarities and differences of the human condition can be embellished and re-grounded anew.

FOUCAULT, NIETZSCHE AND GENEALOGY: CRITICAL AND EFFECTIVE
HISTORICAL METHODOLOGY

*My sense of a critical and effective historical approach is owing to Michel
Foucault's historical methodology. For this reason, it is useful to delineate my
approach through an analysis of Foucault on this matter. And because Foucault's
thoughts are certainly owing to Frederic Nietzsche in this area, it is probably best
to assess the connection between the two through their sense of genealogy and the
critical, effective nature of the historical.*

*Foucault's methodology and vision of the role of the historical emanated from
his sense of Nietzsche's work on history, primarily as it was explicated in "The
Genealogy of Morals" (1989) and Nietzsche's second "Untimely Meditation". In
"Nietzsche, Genealogy, and History" (1977), Foucault attempted to derive from
Nietzsche a vision of genealogy as a historical methodology. In fact, Foucault
began the essay with a definition of genealogy that affirmed its historical nature:*

> *Genealogy is gray, meticulous, and patiently documentary. It operates on a
> field of entangled and confused parchments, on documents that have been
> scratched over and recopied many times... Genealogy does not oppose itself
> to history as the lofty and profound gaze of the philosopher might compare to
> the mole like perspective of the scholar; on the contrary, it rejects the meta-
> history deployment of the ideal significations and indefinite teleologies (139).*

*To Foucault, the genealogist had to firstly be the good historian in the archives.
For the genealogist is "not concerned with the comparing of masses of scientific
data, but with an intense appreciation of the small revealing details; the tattered
and coffee stained texts of human understanding" (Kosalka, 2000, 11). The
genealogist does not seek in historical documents "some pure model of reason and
human community, but rather should seek the origins in the muddy, disparate and
arbitrary wreckage of history" (Ibid.). He certainly did not seek to use documents
to reconstruct some supposed historical reality that lies behind and beyond them.
For Foucault, historical methodology should not aim at a global synthesis.
Foucault asserted, in Nietzsche's vision, "if the genealogist listens closely to
history, he finds that there is something altogether different behind things. It is the
dissention of other things. It is disparity" (Foucault, 1977, 142). It was this myth
breaking potential of history that intrigued Foucault.*

*Foucault saw in genealogy the potential to liberate the human individual from
historical determinism. He contrasts this with more traditional narrative models of
history. He, like Nietzsche before him, was particularly critical of overly
generalized, evolutionary historical visions, with their distinctively Hegelian bent.
In "Untimely Meditation" (1874), Nietzsche argued that there was no more
dangerous vacillation or crisis of culture in the Nineteenth century than that
perpetuated by the confident, evolutionary historical vision. Nietzsche argued that
the "enormous and still continuing influence of this Hegelian philosophy or point
of view has accustomed the Germans to talk of a 'world-process' to justify their
own age as the necessary result of this 'world-process'" (Nietzsche, 1874, 104).
This is, in fact, a trend that Nietzsche found dangerous. For the person "who has*

learned to bend his back and bow his head before the power of history at last nods... to every power, whether it be government or public opinion or a numerical majority... at the precise rhythm at which any power pulls the strings" (Nietzsche, 1874, 105). Like Nietzsche, Foucault thought history had to serve some other function, which also had to be useful to life. To stand over history to see that nothing comes of it but more history was simply wrong for both Nietzsche and Foucault. From this vision of genealogy, Foucault developed his vision of an effective and critical history.

Mitchell Dean (1994) says that we can call our historical method "effective" to the extent that it upsets the colonization of historical knowledge from any transcendental model or approach to history, and is "critical" in proportion to its capacity to engage in the tireless interrogation of what is held to be given, necessary, natural, or neutral (Dean, 1994, 20). An effective history, then, is an essential methodology in illuminating the problems of division and difference within history, as well as in preventing overly generalized understandings of the past that seek to make the present a simplified resultant of a necessarily continuous chain of events. Foucault (1972) often called himself a historian of the present in this regard. This is because he turned his attention to a history that could address problems. Foucault wanted a 'history of the present' that could address these problems for the sake of life and action. Foucault believed that history could be employed as a means of understanding and releasing present issues and deployed for the improvement of life over and above the sole attainment of knowledge.

Foucault did not believe that society required a total history so as to look down on the insignificance of human achievements. He questioned those histories that are subordinate to supra-historical perspectives. He was suspect of the imposition of transcendent perspectives on history that tell of the progress of reason, the rise and decline of civilization, and the emancipation of humanity's true being in a completed development over time. An effective and critical history "historicizes that which is thought to be trans-historical, grasps rather than effaces the singularity of events and processes, and defines levels of analysis that are proper to its objects" (Dean, 1994, 18). For Foucault (1972), we need a history with which to interact, to understand and improve the condition of one's life. The goal was not to "make the subject disappear through the zooming out to the greater forces and trends of history, but to engage it through a zooming in on the historically particular" (Kosalka, 2000, 14). Foucault turned his attention toward specified discursive practices and isolated threads in history, movements of ideas and institutions. It is a corrective to the conventional historiography that seeks to abandon concepts in the quest for an exhaustive reconstruction of the past, for telling it like it was (Dean, 1994, 21). Foucault found this "effective" or "critical" history as an essential aspect in the attempt to live freely and allow for a free construction and care of the self. It is a method that does not get bogged down in meta-narratives of progress, reason or emancipation nor yield to universalistic concepts of rationality or subjectivity. Such a methodology refuses to use history to merely confirm some pre-established notion of our identity or the necessity of the present. It problematizes the imposition of a global, inclusive, and encompassing theory of history.

A critical and effective historical study offers a methodology with a "profound impact and appeal" and has become a "current orientation" in research that cuts across both disciplines and major schools worldwide, including even the strongest school of history in France, the Annales (Dosse, 1994, 46). Comprehending Foucault's work in our current educational climate is itself a "necessary condition of doing social-scientific work by state of the art standards" (Bauman as cited in Dean, 1994, 214). In large part owing to this, there has been an "explosion of new methodologies and approaches to inquiry in contemporary educational research...with an emphasis on lively, accessible, and theoretically sound exploration of the issues" (Peters and Burbules, 2004, 11). To this end, an effective and critical history is "capable of wresting historical thought from its complacency and from its typical moves, of inducing the effects necessary to examine our own purposes in historical study" (Dean, 1994, 19). It is a "way of analyzing multiple, open-ended, heterogeneous trajectories of discourses" (35). It permits one to "know how and to what extent it might be possible to think differently, instead of legitimating what is already known" (Foucault, 1989, 9).

CROSSING THE BORDERS OF TEXTUAL PROPRIETY

I have long pondered the question of what it is proper to teach. It is a question, I believe, that all of us, as teachers, are engaged with to some extent day-to-day. I encourage my teacher education students to take up and to consider the question very seriously indeed, because the answers we invent or discover determine the curricular ground of our successes and failures within the classroom. In some instances, we have no choice but to resign ourselves to using a pre-selected text or utilizing pre-scribed teaching material mandated by some higher institutional authority or general rule of statutory law. In others, we are at the mercy of our own judgment to pick and choose between a myriad of possible texts that could enable us to fulfill the pragmatic aims of our pedagogical goals and objectives.

With respect to the choice of literature to be used in an English classroom, whether it be a poem, a short story, a novel, or a play, it is the question of representation that comes to occupy the foreground of the rationale for selecting a text to read with students. The propriety of the text in this instance is not only a matter of weighing the case of content, its appropriateness of topic to the task at hand, but of gauging the way content is presented stylistically and treated thematically by the writer through the formal elements of fictional enplotment as conceived via the workings-out of the literary imagination.

For example, a point that has been made regarding an anti-racist pedagogy of the text is that Canadian Literature in English has not been produced by a homogeneous group of first language speakers that are colour-less and colour-blind. It includes immigrants, native peoples, visible minorities, and ethnic groups that have had something important to say about the uniqueness of their lived-experiences in making the foreign-ness of the Canadian landscape a home dwelling and have set it down in the form of a writing that reflects the interpretative multiplicity of experience. Here I am defining multiple literacies as an autobiographical type of reading and writing of the self and the other that takes shape via language and allows us to storify the experience of existence by giving the complexity of both visual and verbal articulation to perspective. To break through the barriers of racial and ethnic prejudice, students and teachers must explore the breadth of their own responses to short stories, poems, essays and images circulating within and without the classroom. Multicultural English texts de-center the mono-dimensional subject of the English family album as Robert Morgan (2000) has put it, by illuminating a plethora of contradictory and conflicting viewpoints regarding self, place, and otherness. To interpret a text, it is necessary to possess the critical tools of analysis that allow for reflection upon the nature of our own interpretations. Literary theory is useful when we apply principles of criticism toward an open discussion and self-conscious questioning of the motivational ground of our reactions to images and texts in order to assess the cognitive and affective sources of responsivity. Students and teachers must be aware of the different lenses that can be applied to an analysis of lexical and visual, oral and auditory texts. For example, a reader response method yields certain habits and forms of reading while a new historicism encourages others. Students and teachers need to acknowledge the specificities that each critical method of reading produces. But that does not mean limiting the range of interpretative responses in the classroom. The opposite is true. Armed with a rudimentary knowledge of the principles of criticism via literary theory, any reader becomes more self-conscious of how meaning is made by the subject in relation to a text. While teaching through the principles of literary criticism, we still have to proceed via the premise of remaining open to a critical questioning of the subjective differences of interpretation. To honour the grounds of each critical perspective is to call into question the grounds of one's own certainty as well as those of others. The demands of this strategy require a great deal of listening to others speak and a patient questioning of critical conclusions while reserving moral judgment in relation to the pre-occupations of the insights presented, for it is too easy to stigmatize and therefore marginalize a response by rejecting its logic without a rigorous questioning of the ground of its responsibility to the self and to the other. That does not mean, of course, that all interpretations are valid or equal. Their value is determined neither by their completeness of vision nor by the ideological or political acceptability of their points of view, but by the open responsibility of the reader to justify the rational grounds of the response in relation to the difference of the other. If we ask, "Is an interpretation or reading good or bad?" what we are really asking is, "Does the interpretation or reading do justice to the text?" But how can we answer this question if we cannot know the correct interpretation of a text or its authorial intention because language is not a transparent medium. Its levels of narrative production are complex and multiple, demanding both intentional and ex-tensional acts of decoding and meaning-making. So, the problem of doing interpretative justice to a text invokes the ethical necessity of having to justify the ground of a response, to take responsibility for the reason of its difference, face-to-face with the alterity of another. Only by exposing the rational ground of a reading or interpretation to the internalized contradictions of argument that undo the force of its logic can we come to subjective conclusions about its value and validity. Teaching and learning can then take place on the basis of what we may have learned about the difference of another or could teach others about the difference of ourselves and the sources of our responses from this interchange of reflections. For it is only by questioning the responsibility of our responses and subjecting them to the ethical legitimacy of having to openly justify to another that textual representations of human subjects and actions that reduce the dignity of an individual or group through stereotyping or tokenism that we can hope to overcome the virulent ignorance of bigotry and the crime of hate. Multiple literacies relates in this way to looking again at how we learn to divide the world.

A 'SYMPTOMATIC' APPROACH TO READING AND RESEARCHING HISTORICAL TEXTS

Sparked by a recent wholesale policy and paradigm shift in English Language Arts in the province of Newfoundland and Labrador, and equipped with this new critical approach to my research, I began to approach reading historical curricular texts in a different manner. Instead of trying to read everything, and to simply organize a mass of information into some coherent form, I began to 'symptomatically' read curriculum through defining moments from subject English's past in the province. This method of analysis calls for a close reading of pertinent historical and curricular texts to recognize the presence of more than one discourse in a text, to separate them out and discover how and where they intersect (Althusser and Balibar, 1970). These different discourses, or voices, housed within a text are thought to interact to produce multiple layers of meaning that can complement, suppress, and displace one another at various points (Althusser, 1996). Because the philosophy under-girding the teaching of English as a school subject was also experiencing a radical expansion of its usual boundaries internationally in this period, a close or symptomatic reading of the English curricula in the different periods was almost a necessity for my research. In fact, Stephen Ball et al (1990) argue that at least four different versions of the discipline could be located throughout the 1960's and 1970's, some of which forged an identity for the first time. Generally speaking the great literary tradition of Leavisite English was forced to share space with those who challenged, through Critical Literacy, the state's long entrenched conceptions regarding the subject. A more individual and student centered progressive approach, as well as a manifestation of the subject more deeply committed to equipping the student with the necessary life and workplace 'skills', both made their way onto the agenda of the day as well. Ball et al (1990) argues that in each version of English, the "root paradigm of meanings within and about English differs and conflicts" (80). This is certainly the case in my own research, where an active analysis of key terms like 'critical judgment' and 'literacy' revealed significant shifts in meaning between texts and, even, within the same text at times (English Handbook to the Course of Study, 1940; Secondary

School English Curriculum Guide, 1970). Oftentimes, these shifts were not acknowledged, or possibly even recognized by the authors, and the lack of consistency sometimes called the internal coherence of the document into question.

Locating different discourses through closely reading sections of the 'text' of curricula documents is also facilitated by creating an awareness around how epistemological conceptions have been 'contested' and how these sites of past struggle have come to inform the creation of curricula in given periods. To this end, Ball et al (1990) contends that "each version of English contains and informs a particular epistemology" (80). As a result, my theoretical entry point for this type of reading and my particular critical and effective historical approach involves a problematized notion of knowledge. Reading history documents in this way, through competing conceptions of epistemology evident in the text, ensures an active and overarching critical perspective toward text, which, in my case, is also informed in large part by Foucault's (1977) conception of historical methodology. Historical documents as texts are "always apprehended through the sedimented layers of previous interpretations and through the reading habits and categories developed by previous and current interpretive discourses" (Jenkins, 1995, 11).

DE-CENTERING AUTHORITY FOR AN ETHIC OF COLLABORATIVE MEANING CONSTRUCTIONS

What does it mean to renegotiate the ground of one's authority as a teacher? This problem is at the heart of debates about collaborative learning and pedagogical methods that mitigate the instrumentality of the role of the teacher as "disciplined instructor" or "corrective agent" in the educational process. Within the context of the multi-literate, multicultural classroom, the question is of great significance because traditionally teacher authority is directly related to the legitimating of master narratives that work through the repressive power of teacher-talk to categorize and mark student performance or achievement relative to ideal standards of success determined by a dominant or ruling culture. Indeed the linking of power with knowledge in this case is obvious as the teacher here generally enforces the hegemonic criteria of a narrow code of discourse and its cultural capital by being the arbiter of truth. That is, one who closes off the space for interpretative freedom or inter-subjective negotiation with resolute distinctions of what is right and what is wrong rather than allowing teaching and learning to take place within the dialogy of open discussion and free-thinking.

It is difficult for teachers however to consciously downplay or subvert the cultural logic of their own authority or social status by renegotiating the privileged ground of their power to speak for others. Speaking for others who are silenced and cannot speak for themselves can sometimes implicate the speaker in the production of dangerous and erroneous representations. It is, I believe, better to engage in a "speaking and listening to others." Whereby, the responsibility to respond and to be open to dialogue and the possibility of a productive resistance to discursive norms in the name of social justice and social reconstruction is neither given-up nor missed. De-centering the teacher voice would diminish the presumption of authenticity that gives the teacher's interpretation of a text more intellectual and ethical weight than a student's. For a subjugation of voice denies the production of new discourses or counter-narratives, stills the birth of multi-literate forms of representation that could move forward our ethics and our knowledge. How could one do this? In one sense, I have already answered the question. And yet, within the classroom, we often forget to personalize the register of our speech as we address a whole group, talking over the heads of those seated below us to no one subject in particular, by leading discussions centered around themes or topics concerned with the conceptual sustenance of an image of a general culture, a faceless, sexless, classless type-casting of humanity. A pedagogy of possibility that recognizes the authenticity of multiple sources of literacy — and respects the difference of infinite rendering of subjective interpretations — goes beyond the surface tensions of requiring a patronizing and tolerant discourse to give it a reason for being. It demands the truly collaborative endeavour of wanting to share the reason of its methods and responses within a public space of meaning negotiations such as the classroom so as to enhance the opportunity for inter-cultural communication and to thereby improve the psychic and semantic fields of our mutual self-understanding. In my own classes, its features are produced by the dialogical exchange of subject positions that results from the relating of personal histories to the scene of teaching. The complex localities of these multiple interfaces of subjective identity are the stuff of lived experience that is carried over to the act and mission of our teaching selves contained in the auto-bio-graphical contents of the reflective logs, teaching journals or literary diaries. In an effort to bring the discussion from the private sphere of personal response into the public sphere of responses relating to the creation of a community of the question, I have extended discussion in my courses on blogs to facilitate the public exchange of information. This allows students to be publicly accountable for their response to questions of reading and pedagogical method and theory that are posed by myself and the class as well as giving them a way to access, use, and create multiple forms of literacy that are produced in and via the virtual spaces and medium of technology.

THE VALUE OF A RENEWED CRITICAL SPIRIT

Informed by Foucault's (1977) sense of historical investigation, I began to take the basic tenors of a critical and historical approach to an analysis of subject English in Newfoundland and Labrador. A massive policy shift in subject English in the province provided the impetus for an investigation of the ways in which curriculum comes to be construed and often justified around the nature of knowledge. Through strong interpretive readings of the patterns and import of carefully selected episodes within Newfoundland and Labrador English studies, based on a "symptomatic reading approach" which seeks to locate and unlayer the multiple discourse or voices housed in a text, I am producing a 'critical' and 'effective' curricular history of subject English in the province. I am currently in the process of writing up the results of this study. Suffice it to say that I am writing a very different story of English and literacy in this region than I previously could have.

I have learned a lot by struggling with the accepted texts and definitions and perceptions of English in each period. What we sometimes take as givens when delivering curriculum as English teachers today are often sites of past struggles and competing conceptions deposited by history. For this reason, there is a substantial need for a critical re-take of our lived curricular history, for framing the unconscious or taken-for-granted in our past practices and discovering the multiplicity of the discourses that interact in the texts of a period. Otherwise, an original depiction or an official stance, such as labelling a document 'radical', could come to stand as the taken-for-granted or accepted definition. I suspect that the colonization of historical knowledge often happens in this way and may be intentional or completely unintentional on the part of the author. Things sometimes get overlooked because of the need for efficiency or, worse yet, because terms such as 'radical' come to operate as givens several removes from the original context. Regardless of why it happens, there is a strong need to move back through the removes, avoid the hurdles that come via assumptions, and re-examine what is held to be given, necessary, natural, or neutral. It requires that we be 'critically literate' in our research and reading practices; that we read texts 'closely' or 'symptomatically', thereby recognizing the presence of more than one discourse in a text. And this need not be seen as discarding traditional research approaches either. In this instance, there is very much a place for conventional, in-house, and genetic histories as well. If anything, we want the form that informs, even if the meaning can only ever be provisional. By necessity, we need to hold a period together long enough to look at it. But, that said, we best then look at it differently, holding it up to the light through a lens that allows for another level of interpretive displacement in the already stated discourses or covered terrain; a 'shift' in the ground of the analysis, so to speak. There is great value in "re-visiting, re-reading, and seeking to add to the archive by encouraging and engaging in careful, informed, critical inquiry" (Green, 2003, 138).

A LIMITLESS RESPONSIBILITY TO THE OTHER REQUIRES AN AFFIRMATIVE OBLIGATION

The question of ethical and moral objectivity is more or less a moot point for a "community of the question" because the relational or interactive nature of knowledge as collaborative meaning construction demands the suspension of a teleological notion of truth that would exclude values of response based on the extent of their adherence to a predetermined notion of right and wrong, good and bad, and so on. The emphasis would be on the engagement and openness of the subject to an analysis of the ideological pre-dispositions, claims to morality or correctness governing attitudes and standards of behaviour. Edward Said (2003), in his book *Orientalism*, for example, has contested the image of "the Orient" reproduced and perpetuated through generations of Western scholarship and literature. He shows how the moral foundation of Occidental reasoning secures the ethnocentric underpinnings of its mythological and racist representation of an "oriental laziness" of demeanour thoroughly permeated by an Eastern guile of exotic irrationalism. To combat the ruses of this contemptible metaphor is to expose the contradictions of argument that underlie the logic of such a subject position. The challenge situates itself on the rhetorical ground of such spurious claims to objectivity and hence an illusion of truth achieved through a frightened mask of prejudice and racism. Without an openness to the possibility of otherness and difference there can be no vision or testimony to a reality that calls out for a reciprocal affirmation of another beyond the horizons of the Self that enables us to see ourselves as the difference of another. Such a stance requires the subject as moral agent to challenge accepted ethical standards or the teleology of a principle of reason so as to problematize and to think through the cultural ground of the logic of rationality guiding the bias of our responses. To relate this notion of an affirmative ethics to the English Education classroom, we could ask the following question, one that I have asked of my students recently: How should a Western reader attempt to read multicultural literature? Without a doubt, the question implies the necessity of meeting the pedagogical imperative of teaching a mode of reflective reading, or at least engaging in a specific form of reading preparation or schema building. From my own point of view reading is both identification and resistance; it is a filling in of the gaps of subjectivity where the irreconcilable differences of one's own sources of knowledge, desire, and experience are exposed and supplemented through an engagement of the Self with the text itself. The semantic nuances of a textual ideolect strike us by enframing the vision of a possible world that calls for a response. When there is a level of comprehensible input that allows us to produce readable psychic images (an interpretant) from the arbitrary codings of textuality, then the contextual immanence of our cognitive schemata becomes adducible, it gathers energy as the affectivity of associations build and enable us to go beyond the simple act of decoding and thus we begin to make meaning. If this is absent at some level, then the gaps of knowledge are magnified and we are at a loss to make meaning of the responses initiated by the reading experience. It would seem imperative and yet not so obvious then, that for a text to be understood at some basic level of its lexical production, it needs to be framed within a cadre of other texts that magnify and multiply its readability through cognitive and affective acts and associations that can help our attempts at meaning-making. And so inter-textuality feeds schema, building beyond the parameters of our readerly competence to bolster the ground of understanding for the purpose of making meaning.

When I was a Postdoctoral Fellow, in the Department of Language and Literacy Education at the University of British Columbia, I taught a series of Language Arts courses. In these classes my students worked on the creation of resource-based integrated units that also had an instructional technology component to them. The assignment gave students the opportunity to co-operatively plan a series of lessons in collaboration with a teacher-librarian and myself. The purpose of the exercise was to focus the lessons of the unit on the meeting of critical challenges conceived in relation to the intended or prescribed learning outcomes set out by the B. C.

Ministry of Education guidelines in the K-7 Language Arts Instructional Resource Package while putting into practice some concepts of lesson planning and curriculum development studied in the course. Working from a resource-based perspective, the pre-service teachers concentrated on planning lessons that would enable their students to hone critical thinking skills and work on problem solving techniques at the same time. An unexpected obstacle for some students was the challenge of choosing resources to build their units on. In particular, a group of First Nations students who chose to work on a revisionist history of their band, the Nis'Ga, discovered that the text books, picture books, short stories, novels, and other resources they found were largely inaccurate or presented a culturally insensitive portrait of their own people as lacking any distinguishable sophistication of identity. They told me that they could not read these texts that represented the history of their people in this erroneous and insulting way, let alone use these resources as a pedagogical foundation to base the content of their units on. So, the task is to put forward a critical method for actualizing a resistive reading of the ethnocentric representations of the Nis'Ga that eventually became the pedagogical focus of their assignment. Their aim was to develop a set of interpretative tools that students could use to read and view texts about people of the First Nations which would challenge students to take responsibility for their responses. This critical tact would also allow them to articulate the subjective sources of resistive reading at a very personal level. The point was to teach students to deconstruct the Euro-centric bias of the history of their people by relating these stereotypical images in texts depicting First Nations to the historical sources of such culturally insensitive and racist depictions. They wanted to show how stereotypes, prejudice and discrimination are linked, in that the formation of stereotypes leads to the objectification of peoples and the development of prejudices. Prejudices in turn create the attitudinal framework and value formations from which discrimination arises. Stereotypes and prejudices are the attitudinal component whereas discrimination is the action component of racism. Their point was to show the moral dilemma of the responsibility we have to carefully scrutinize a response to reading and writing that claims to represent the truth of another, that purports to speak for another in the name of truth by squelching the democratic right of voice and self-expression, when it is more appropriate and infinitely more just, to listen to, or to speak with another.

CONCLUSION

Being critically literate involves adopting an active, challenging approach to reading and textual practices. For me, it meant carrying out a different type of historical inquiry into changes in English and the shifting definition of literacy over time. Rather than merely surveying different episodes within Newfoundland and Labrador English curricula, it required that I symptomatically read them within competing conceptions of knowledge. This critical approach to reading research texts helps reveal how earlier versions of the subject still speak to us in a way that a generalized, empirical reading of a body of texts never could. In utilizing curriculum texts as data in this way, there is no attempt to reconstruct what the past was "really like" (Kendall, 2001, 26). In fact, "such texts are of importance to qualitative research because the information provided may differ" (Hodder, 2000, 704).

In my initial approach, I tried to produce a frozen snapshot of bygone eras in Newfoundland and Labrador's history. I proceeded from the assumption that the curricular history 'evolved' and that I could readily paint a tidy picture of how things came to be as they are in Newfoundland and Labrador English classrooms today. At the outset of such an enormous task, simply synthesizing all the available data can sometimes overpower one's tendency to approach each and every research text critically. But without the latter practice, I ran the risk of producing an overly generalized history of English in the region; a history that did not raise new questions about colonial schooling practices. In short, I ran the risk of producing something of merely local or antiquarian interest, as opposed to something that possibly illuminates deep currents elsewhere in the field. A 'critical' approach, (owing to Foucault, Althusser, and the others I have mentioned), was the important corrective.

And a critical perspective always changes the tenor of the questions. What can such an analysis of the curricula of these periods tell us about what counted as significant literature and language forms in Newfoundland and Labrador? How has the nature of knowledge been implied, defined, or constructed throughout this curricular history? How did this conception of knowledge affect schooling or curriculum? What counts as truth for a particular past period in subject English? Was this stable or conflicted? What can the discourse tell us about what counted as a knowing student? What did it imply about what it meant to be a literate, cultured and contributing member of society? What defined an English expert or a teacher? Were multiple discourses reflected in the curricular texts of each period? If so, how did they interact, inform, or contradict one another? What were students and teachers of English invited to become and how might this have changed over time with relation to the English curricular history? And, most importantly, how can such an exploration of this curricular past be used to invest present curricular practices with meaning? The possibilities are different now.

Prying open the official curricula from different periods in English's past in this light, open and aware of competing conceptions of epistemology in the field, also matches Foucault's own aims, which involve problematizing taken-for-granted categories to show how they may help shape discourse in the period. Vick (1998) argues that this critical approach allows for multiplicity, openness, and new ways of thinking around the way we read texts and conduct research. It calls us to actively analyze that which has been archived and accepted. And it requires that we "call up for scrutiny, whether through embodied action or discourse practice, the rules of exchange within a social field" (Luke, 2004, 26). For a text is always more than the words on the page. It is always more than the sum total of its dominant reading too. It is also defined, in equal measure, by its underlying messages and the words that are left out. This realization led me to fundamentally change the way I carry out my research. It led me to be critically literate in my research practices.

REINVENTING SELF AND COMMUNITY, WHICH DEMANDS SUSTAINED
REFLECTION ON DIFFERENCE

Forms of knowledge produced at the margins of a dominant culture (such as world literatures and North American minority literatures), as Henry Giroux (1992) notes "can be used to redefine the complex, multiple, heterogeneous realities that constitute those relations of difference that make up the experiences of students who find it impossible to define their identities through the cultural and political codes that characterize the dominant culture." The suggestion is "to engage students in cultural re-mapping as a form of resistance" by allowing them to analyze how the dominant culture constructs the borders of difference to exclude and silence its Others. And so, within the English Education classroom, the heterogeneous representations of subjectivity and lived-experience that multicultural literature conceived as multiple literacy provides, can help students and teachers to break down essentialist notions of self and identity. The diversity of representation furnishes the opportunity for a questioning of a monocultural vision of every day life that is normalized as the way things are or should be. And it assists students and teachers to examine how the prevailing images of a dominant culture that have affected the way they have come to see themselves and others by learning to divide the world.

The research I have been conducting over the past year deals with these problems of reading and writing the other that we eventually come face-to-face with in the English Education classroom. I have made use of the various conceptions of subjectivity and identity developed by the discourse and practice of feminist pedagogies, critical pedagogies, anti-racist or postcolonial pedagogies and sexuality-based (gay and lesbian) pedagogies (Sears, 1992) to rethink the conceptual ground of difference.

I will elaborate. The idea of difference has provided the conceptual groundwork for educational theorists of diverse ideological perspectives working toward the ethical purpose of actualizing equitable curricular contexts for teaching and learning that are responsive to individuals and groups within a society or culture regardless of race, class, gender, or sexuality. Yet this altruistic desire for securing equitable educational environments and opportunities is also the practical juncture at which feminist pedagogies, critical pedagogies, anti-racist or post-colonial pedagogies, and gay and lesbian pedagogies begin to part company with respect to the concept of difference. Difference therefore becomes an intrinsic point of theoretical validation, as I have stated, for asserting the legitimacy of such pedagogical discourses and their practice by justifying the ethics of the methods each puts forward for the creation of equitable educational environments.

For example, virtually all feminist pedagogies have validated the need to analyze the construction of sexual difference as a means for overcoming the bias of gender-role stereotyping. Some critical pedagogies have validated the importance of examining the socio-political ground for differences of subjectivity to illuminate the ideological subtext of human interactions (Freire 1970; McLaren 1986, 1997; Simon 1992), while others have concentrated on the economic distinction of class differences to address the bounds of social injustice and exploitation (Apple 1993;

Aronowitz and Giroux 1991). Anti-racist or postcolonial pedagogies have generally validated the necessity of acknowledging the uniqueness of racial differences as a heterogeneous marker of identity that gives a powerful voice to ethnic specificity in the face of discrimination against minorities and the rule of cultural hegemonies (Bhabha, 1994; hooks, 1994; McCarthy and Critchlow, 1993; Spivak, 1993). Gay and lesbian pedagogies have tended to validate the significance of recognizing differences of sexuality or sexual orientation to situate the essence of subjectivity at the psychic and somatic core of human desire (Britzman 1991; Pinar 1994).

Indeed, some aspect of difference has informed the attempts of these pedagogical movements to break down and reconceptualize the normative basis of subjectivity that has been operationalized in strictly ethical terms by the Western conventions of schooling systems as a manifest curricular goal or outcome. Here I would contend that the history and spirit of curricular reconceptualization and progressive education that originally began with the social reconstructionist movement of the 1920s has continued to the present day in the form of these, more or less, revolutionary pedagogies (Pinar, Reynolds, Slattery and Taubman, 1995; Stanley 1992). The focus of educational reform for achieving democracy and social justice has necessarily been re-translated over time, after John Dewey and his contemporaries, to include the recognition of the values of difference as a legitimate and integral feature of a modern civil society. But a question arises, and its significance is paramount to the future of democratic educational reform, the effects of which we only can see in our classrooms: To what extent can the idea of difference help us to redefine or rethink the principle of educational equity?

How could we most properly adjudicate between the values of difference we are presented with to gauge both their argumentative and ethical validity? It would not be possible to arbitrarily choose among differences of race, class, gender, or sexuality to privilege some forms or aspects of difference while marginalizing or rejecting others and still adhere to the democratic spirit of the principle of educational equity. The concept of difference cannot be analyzed unproblematically and this is especially so when it is couched in the politically and ethically regressive terms of a desire for competing validation. As Henry Giroux (1992) suggests:

> organizing schools and pedagogy around a sense of purpose and meaning that makes difference central to a critical notion of citizenship and democratic public life . . . [is] the basis for extending the struggle for equality and justice to the broader spheres of everyday life (174).

If so, then we need to have some way of synthesizing the unifying threads of the divergent notions of difference I have detailed above. The cultural work of education, in theory and in practice, must move, I believe, toward a re-awakening of an egalitarian consciousness that bridges the (negative) values of difference while recognizing their uniqueness or particularity. To reduce the numbing sense of divisiveness permeating the public sphere of our lives and classrooms requires the solidarity of a community of difference borne of affirmation and respect for others rather than a simple celebration of a community of differences where subjects are perceived to exist, more or less, independently of each other as the multiple sites of isolated or marginalized selves. This is crucial if we wish to enrich our knowledge of the border crossings of teaching and learning so as to adapt educational practices and institutional structures in a truly democratic way to the needs of all students regardless of race, class, gender, or sexuality, thereby ensuring the equitability of the principle of educational equity.

It is within the affirmative ethics of a "community of the question" and the multiple sites of literacy that arise from within it that a synthesis of the negative values of difference as a foundational concept of democratic education can occur, thereby providing a philosophical and methodological means through which to rethink the grounds of the principle of educational equity beyond the competing distinctions of either/or categories that separate us into male vs. female, white vs. non-white, heterosexual vs. homosexual, rich vs. poor, and so on.

REFERENCES

Althusser, L. (1996). Freud and Lacan. In O. Corpet & F. Matheron (Eds.), *Writings on psychoanalysis* (pp. 7–32). New York: Colombia University Press.

Althusser, L., & Balibar, E. (1970). *Reading capital.* London: NLB.

Apple, M. (1993). *Official knowledge: Democratic education in a conservative age.* New York/London: Routledge.

Aronowitz, S., & Giroux, H. (Eds.). (1991). *Postmodern education: Politics, culture, and social criticism.* Minneapolis, MN: University of Minnesota Press.

Ball, S., Kenny, A., & Gardiner, D. (1990). Literacy, politics, and the teaching of English. In I. Goodson & P. Medway (Eds.), *Bringing English to order: The history and politics of a school subject* (pp. 47–86). London: Falmer Press.

Bhabha, H. K. (1994). *The location of culture.* New York/London: Routledge.

Britzman, D. (1991). *Practice makes practice: A critical study of learning to teach.* Albany, NY: State University of New York Press.

Dean, M. (1994). *Critical and effective histories: Foucault's methods and historical sociology.* London: Routledge.

Derrida, J. (1998). *Of grammatology* (G. C. Spivak, Trans.). Baltimore: Johns Hopkins University Press.

Dosse, F. (1994). *New history in France: The triumph of the annales* (P. Conroy, Trans.). Urbana, IL: University of Illinois Press.

Doyle, B. (1989). *English and Englishness.* London: Routledge.

Foucault, M. (1977). Nietzsche, genealogy, history. In D. Bouchard (Ed.), *Language, counter-memory, practice: Selected essays and interviews* (pp. 140–164). New York: Cornell University Press.

Foucault, M. (1972). *Archaeology of knowledge and the discourse on language* (A. M. Sheridan Smith, Trans.). London: Tavistock Books.

Foucault, M. (1989). On literature. In *Foucault live.* New York: Semiotext(e).

Freire, P. (1970). *Pedagogy of the oppressed.* New York: The Seabury Press.

Giroux, H. (1992). *Border crossings: Cultural workers and the politics of education.* New York/London: Routledge.

Government of Newfoundland and Labrador. (1940). *Department of Education: English handbook to the course of study.*

Government of Newfoundland and Labrador. (1970). *Department of Education: Secondary School English curriculum guide.*

Green, W. (2003). Curriculum inquiry in Australia: Towards a local genealogy of the curriculum field. In W. Pinar (Ed.), *International handbook of curriculum research* (pp. 123–142). Mahwah, NJ: Lawrence Erlbaum Associates.

Hodder, I. (2000). The interpretation of material culture. In N. Denzin & Y. S. Lincoln (Eds.), *Handbook of qualitative research* (2nd ed., pp. 155–175). Thousand Oaks, CA: Sage Publications.

Hooks, b. (1994). *Teaching to transgress: Education as the practice of freedom*. New York/London: Routledge.

Jenkins, K. (1995). *On what is history: From Carr and Elton to Rorty and White*. London: Routledge.

Kendall, G. (2001). Normality and meaningfulness: Detailing the child in eighteenth-century England. *History of Education Review, 30*(2), 26–36.

Kosalka, D. (2000). Foucault's Nietzschean historiography. *Historian Underground*.

Luke, A. (2004). Two takes on the critical. In B. Norten & K. Toohey (Eds.), *Critical pedagogies and language learning* (pp. 21–29). Cambridge, UK: Cambridge University Press.

McCarthy, C., & Crichlow, W. (Eds.). (1993). *Race, identity, and representation in education*. New York/London: Routledge.

McLaren, P. (1986). *Schooling as a ritual performance: Towards a political economy of educational signs and gestures*. Boston: Routledge and Kegan Paul.

Medway, P. (1990). Into the sixties: English and English society at a time of change. In I. Goodson & P. Medway (Eds.), *Bringing English to order* (pp. n/a). London: Falmer Press.

Morgan, R. (2000). Uncertain relations: English and cultural studies. In B. Barrell & R. Hammett (Eds.), *Advocating change: Contemporary issues in subject English* (pp. n/a). Toronto: Irwin.

Nietzsche, F. (1989). *Genealogy of morals* (W. Kaufmann & R. J. Hollingdale, Trans.). New York: Random House.

Nietzsche, F. (1874/1997). *Untimely meditation: On the use and abuse of history for life*. Cambridge, UK: Cambridge University Press.

Ontario Ministry of Education. (1986, March). *Handbook for designing and marking the O.A.C. 1: Written Examination in English*.

Peters, M., & Burbules, N. (2004). *Poststructuralism and educational research*. Lanham, MD: Rowman and Littlefield.

Pinar, W. F. (1994). *Autobiography, politics, and sexuality: Essays in curriculum theory, 1972–1992*. New York: Peter Lang.

Pinar, W. F., Reynolds, W. M., Slattery, P., & Taubman, P. M. (1995). *Understanding curriculum: An introduction to the study of historical and contemporary curriculum discourses*. New York: Peter Lang.

Sears, J. (Ed.). (1992). *Sexuality and the curriculum*. New York and London: Routledge.

Simon, R. (1992). *Teaching against the grain*. South Hadley, MA: Bergin and Garvey.

Spivak, G. C. (1993). *Outside in the teaching machine*. New York/London: Routledge.

Stanley, W. B. (1992). *Curriculum for Utopia: Social reconstruction and critical pedagogy in the postmodern era*. Albany, NY: SUNY Press.

Said, E. W. (2003). *Orientalism*. London: Penguin Books.

Vick, M. (1998). Narrative history: Truly writing the past. *History of Education Review, 27*(2), (pp n/a).

ABOUT THE CONTRIBUTORS

Jonathan Arendt is in his third-year of the PhD program at OISE/UT after earning degrees in both Education and Literature at Louisiana State University. He was an award-winning high school English teacher for five years in Houston, Texas. Jonathan's primary research interests in this Postmodern Era are Cultural Studies, Media Literacy, Critical Pedagogy, and Educational Equity in terms of Race and Class.

Karyn Cooper is Associate Professor at the Ontario Institute for Studies in Education. Dr. Cooper's research and teaching focuses on the sociocultural dimensions of literacy, teacher education and qualitative research. Publications include *Burning Issues: Foundations of Education* (2004) and *The Practical Critical Educator* (2006). She is currently working on two books that explore the nature of qualitative research in education to be published later this year.

Kelly Freebody lectures in the Faculty of Education and Social Work at The University of Sydney. She has taught English and Drama in high schools in Australia, Hong Kong, London, and Taipei, and has conducted classroom and online research in Australia and Singapore. She currently teaches and publishes in the areas of English and Drama Education, classroom organization, and the use digital online learning materials.

Peter Freebody is Research Professor in the Faculty of Education and Social Work at The University of Sydney. His research interests are in literacy education, educational disadvantage, and methodology. He has contributed numerous invited entries to international handbooks and encyclopedias on literacy, Critical Literacy, digital technologies, and research methodology. He has served on numerous advisory groups for state and national governments in the areas of assessment and literacy education.

James Paul Gee is the Tashia Morgridge Professor of Reading at the University of Wisconsin-Madison. He received his PhD in linguistics in 1975 from Stanford University and has published widely in linguistics and education. His new book, *Why Video Games are Good for Your Soul*, shows how good video games marry pleasure and learning and have the capacity to empower people.

Hilary Janks is a professor in Applied English Language Studies at the University of the Witwatersrand, Johannesburg, South Africa. Her research is in the area of Critical Literacy and she is best known for the *Critical Language Awareness Series*, a collection of classroom materials for teaching students about the relationship between language and power, which she edited.

Carolyn McKinney joined the discipline of Applied English Language Studies as a Lecturer in 2004. Prior to this she has worked in research and teaching positions at the Human Sciences Research Council, the Open University, UK and the Universities of Stellenbosch and the Western Cape. Dr McKinney has published in the areas of research methods in language and literacy, Critical Literacy, identity/subjectivity and learning as well as critical pedagogy.

Jackie Marsh is Reader in Education at the University of Sheffield, UK. She directs the Ed.D. Programme and is an editor of the *Journal of Early Childhood Literacy*. Jackie is involved in research that examines the role and nature of popular culture, media and new technologies in early childhood literacy, both in- and out-of-school contexts. Her most recent work was the Digital Beginnings project, funded by BBC Worldwide and the Esmée Fairbairn Foundation.

Kate Pahl is a Senior Lecturer in Education at the School of Education, University of Sheffield. She has written books with Jennifer Rowsell on the New Literacy Studies, multi-literacies and multimodality. She is currently working on a research project funded by the Arts and Humanities Research Council in the UK on artifacts and narratives of migration in the homes of the Pakistani/Kashmiri community in Rotherham, Yorkshire, UK.

Wendy M. Pullin is Professor of Psychology at Concordia University College of Alberta, Canada. Research interests include literacy and youth, qualitative research and issues in clinical psychology. Dr. Pullin is currently a department head and divides her time between research, teaching and administrative duties.

Jennifer Rowsell is an Assistant Professor of Literacy Education at Rutgers Graduate School of Education. She has co-written books and articles in the areas of multimodality, multiliteracies, and New Literacy Studies. She currently conducts research in early years, adolescent learners, and teacher education through a multimodal, New Literacy Studies lens in New Jersey, USA.

Peter Trifonas is Associate Professor at the Ontario Institute for Studies in Education. His areas of interest and scholarly accomplishments extend to ethics, philosophy of education, literacy, media, technology, and curriculum. Professor Trifonas' most recent published works include: *The Ethics of Writing: Derrida, Deconstruction, and Pedagogy; Ethics, Institutions, and the Right to Philosophy* (with Jacques Derrida); and *Pedagogies of Difference* (edited).

Sarah Vander Zanden is a doctoral student and instructor in the Language Education Department of the School of Education at Indiana University, Bloomington. Her research interests are in Critical Literacy and working with English Language Learners. Prior to studying at IU she was a public school teacher in Falls Church, Virginia. Sarah has presented at local and national venues including NCTE and WLU.

Vivian Vasquez is an Associate Professor at American University in Washington DC. Critical Literacy is the overarching framework from which she engages in Research, Teaching, and Scholarship. In summer 2006, she began Podcasting and currently hosts the Critical Literacy in Practice Podcast, which is an on-demand Internet broadcast on Critical Literacy as it is talked about and practiced in different spaces and places.

Robert E. White is an Associate Professor in the Faculty of Education at St. Francis Xavier University. Professor White is Chair of the Department of Curriculum and Leadership at StFX. Research interests include Critical Pedagogy, Leadership, Social Justice Issues, Globalization and corporate investment in educational institutions. He is currently working on two books, *Diversity and Its Discontents* and *Principles in Succession,* both to be published later this year.

John Willinsky is currently on the faculty of the Stanford University School of Education. Until 2007 he was Pacific Press Professor of Literacy and Technology and Distinguished University Scholar in the Department of Language and Literacy Education at the University of British Columbia. He is the author of *If Only We Knew: Increasing the Public Value of Social Science Research* and *The Access Principle: The Case for Open Access to Research and Scholarship.*